I0816037

BISON
BOOKS

BUMMERLAND

Ruin and Restoration in Trump's New America

Randolph Lewis

University of Nebraska Press Lincoln

Manufactured in the United States of America

The University of Nebraska Press is part of a land-grant institution with campuses and programs on the past, present, and future homelands of the Pawnee, Ponca, Otoe-Missouria, Omaha, Dakota, Lakota, Kaw, Cheyenne, and Arapaho Peoples, as well as those of the relocated Ho-Chunk, Sac and Fox, and Iowa Peoples.

Publication of this volume was assisted by research support from the College of Liberal Arts at the University of Texas at Austin.

For customers in the EU with safety/
GPSR concerns, contact:
gpsr@mare-nostrum.co.uk
Mare Nostrum Group BV
Mauritskade 21D
1091 GC Amsterdam
The Netherlands

Library of Congress Control Number: 2025020251

Designed and set in Adobe Text Pro by L. Welch.

For my brother Erik, a good-hearted progressive
stationed deep behind the Pine Curtain (aka East Texas)

What do you do when you have lost faith
in the place you call home?

—Eddie Glaude

Since March 2020, when sh*t met fan, Americans' happiness levels have plummeted while their depression and anxiety have soared. By April, call volume to the Disaster Distress Helpline had spiked 891 percent from the same time the year before. By November, calls were still up from the normal baseline by 128 percent. Then came winter.

—*Cosmopolitan*, January 2021

Learn how to turn customers into fanatics.
Employees into ambassadors.
Products into obsessions.
And brands into religions.

—Qualtrics software advertisement

CONTENTS

BUMMERLAND

Introduction

American life took a weird turn in June 2015, when an aging reality star descended a golden escalator in a Manhattan high rise to announce his improbable bid for the White House. From that moment forward, it felt like the country began to slip into an endless fever dream churning with chaos, uncertainty, and fear. Wanting to capture something about how things went sideways in a hurry, I drove all over the Sunbelt trying to understand what was happening. I went on sojourns to an apocalyptic slab of the Mojave Desert, the paradoxical land around Colorado Springs, the seductively deranged city known as Las Vegas, the expat communities of Central Mexico, the racial hot spots of the Deep South, and even the fjords of Norway, from which, surreally, I watched the unfolding news of the school shooting in Uvalde, Texas, and decided I would head there. Other people would cover the major stories of Trump and Biden's America for years to come, but as an American studies professor for almost three decades, I wanted to write in a different register, one that was darkly comic, mournful, meditative, and personal. Hoping to offer a different kind of portrait of American life in the 2020s, I tracked a complex trajectory of cultural burnout mixed with a profound yearning for something better than a Neo-Gilded Age of fear, hustle, and hype.

What emerged is a book about Apple Inc., apocalypse culture, the American West, backwoods murder, the musician Bill Callahan, civil rights tourism, consumerism, depression, Elon Musk, expat life, fascism, *Idiocracy*, infertility, January 6, jewel thieves in my backyard,

Joy Division, Las Vegas, the Lone Star state, lowered expectations, postmodernism, sex robot brothels, suburban blues, surrealist comedy, tent cities of the homeless, toxic masculinity, the Trump family, and trauma. All these angles allow me to sketch out something important about the era when America lurched uncertainly into the 2020s with its democratic norms barely intact and its systems straining. In his recent book on James Baldwin, the scholar Eddie S. Glaude followed the extraordinary writer's footsteps to France, looked back over his shoulder, and thought about his own life at home as a Black man in the Trump years. He then expressed something that I think many people have felt in recent years: "For me the daily grind consumes. I cannot escape the news. I am drowning in it, and in all the nastiness of a country that seems, or feels, like it's going underwater." Or as *The Economist* put it during the pandemic, "The shared world is increasingly intolerable." Or to quote a *Slate* headline from election night 2024: "Americans Just Voted to Burn It All to the Ground."[1]

It's not all grim. Early in the pandemic, the novelist Marilynne Robinson wrote a powerful essay describing how the crisis had revealed the flimsiness of a system that had long seemed rock-solid. It contains this oddly hopeful passage: "Over the decades we have consented, passively for the most part, to a kind of change that has made this country a disappointment to itself, an imaginary prison with real prisoners in it. Now those imaginary walls have fallen if we choose to notice. We can consider what kind of habitation, what kind of home we want this country to be." Even if she penned these words well before the Supreme Court stripped away long-cherished rights, long before *The Guardian* opined in 2023 that "serial liar George Santos is the politician Americans deserve," and long before venture capitalist fauxbilly J. D. Vance served up nasty propaganda about Haitian immigrants eating puppies in the final weeks before the 2024 election, I remain hopeful that we might find some kind of salvation in recognizing our systemic failures and rethinking our national identity. Perhaps *everything is terrible*, as one snarky website puts it, but even more reason to imagine that something sweeter is possible. We deserve better than what we've endured in the chaotic wake of the forty-fifth/forty-seventh president, who has taken the worst elements of American capitalism, nationalism, and celebrity worship and elevated them into a rancorous political ideology of hate and neglect.

Bummerland explores how things are curdling under the surface and why the country often feels more like a woodchipper for the soul than a safe place to call home. This is the subject of essays that range mostly across the U.S. West, with a special emphasis on the mysteries of the Lone Star state, where I have lived much of my life, watching this strange red giant called Texas from the relative safety of its funky blue capital of Austin. On and off since the mid-1980s, this super-hyped Sunbelt metropolis has been my home base for exploring an unsettling new world of dead ends: young people who will never afford a home, never pay off their student loans, never have job security. Forty-somethings who will never have a pension and worry about "memory care" insurance policies in case they suffer dementia in their final years. Older people who can never retire (the average American retired with less than $90,000 in savings in 2024 while estimating that they would need $1.46 million to "retire comfortably"; even worse, 25 percent of them hit sixty-five without any savings at all).[2] Health care that is so costly and heartless that the internet explodes with laughter when a CEO is assassinated on the streets of Manhattan. Social media and streaming platforms that often leave us disconnected while providing the illusion of connection. Cities that are designed for cars instead of community, making them "easy to get to, but not worth arriving at."[3]

Frankly, it sucks. Like a lot of people, I am often wiped out from the stress, uncertainty, and despair of living in such chaotic times. Suffering from a raft of health problems that I describe in an essay called "Healing Inc.," I barely squeaked through lockdown life under Trump and its muddled aftermath, not to mention his disheartening political resurrection in 2024—and yet I still carry a utopian spark that these years haven't extinguished. I know things could be different if we could reimagine the cruel structures—national, economic, social, ideological—in which we are stuck. What I'm suggesting is not so different from the love-beaded message of the great surfer, poet, and beatnik publisher Lawrence Ferlinghetti, who wrote a Cold War anthem called "I Am Waiting" in 1958:

> I am waiting
> for the American Eagle
> to really spread its wings
> and straighten up and fly right
> and I am waiting
> for the Age of Anxiety
> to drop dead
> and I am waiting
> for the war to be fought
> which will make the world safe
> for anarchy
> and I am waiting
> for the final withering away
> of all governments
> and I am perpetually awaiting
> a rebirth of wonder.

Almost sixty years later, our national waiting has turned into something like Xanax-laced despondence, even in places where hope and idealism should be flourishing—like the state university where I work.

Even though I've been doing it a long time and am lucky enough to have a post at the big public university in Austin, I'm not a typical academic. Back in the 1970s and 1980s, I grew up in a working-class home on the Jersey Shore and never met anyone who went to college other than my schoolteachers. With the exception of a wiry little scholar who lived near the funeral parlor at the end of our dogleg street, we were a modest row of car mechanics, bartenders, maids, factory workers, stock car drivers, car salesmen, and HVAC guys like my dad (Mom was a secretary and then a nanny well into her sixties). In 1985 I became a first-generation college kid who could attend the University of Texas only because we bought a rickety mobile home near the Louisiana border, which translated into cheap in-state tuition for me. This was the peak of state support for higher education, and Austin was still a low-budget dream. A decade later, my first jobs out of grad school were not as a postdoc or tenure-track professor; instead, I was a part-time UAW organizer in California higher education and a nighttime bank janitor with a dead-serious boss, who told me, "You can keep anything you find in the trash!" Given this not-so-prestigious background and the intensity of the class filtration system in the United States, it amazes me that, at least for now, I'm a professor who can write about what's happening in the anxious world around me. More than you might realize if you met me in my current incarnation as a Prius-driving "soy boy" (a right-wing slur for men who don't act like Ted Nugent at a gun range), I still look at the world through blue-collar eyes—and that includes how I look at the Lone Star state, my ever-vexing home.

If you want to understand how things went awry in the past decade, it makes sense to start in Texas, which along with Las Vegas, has always been the steroidal overdrive version of the USA—*it's XXL America*. With its outsized political and economic influence, Texas is at the heart of the new America, which means you probably can't grasp our national paradoxes if you don't understand it as something more than a red state stereotype.[4] Yes, it's the kind of place where armed men in pickups try to run the Biden campaign bus off the interstate in the middle of the afternoon, and yes, the suit-and-tie equivalent of those guys are running the political show at the state level, but it's more than its worst attributes. Millions of kind, compassionate people are trapped inside the astonishingly cruel structures here—literally in the case of migrant kids at the border, nonviolent criminals in cells without air-conditioning, or blue-collar workers who are injured, unpaid, and unable to unionize within the corporate juggernauts that dominate Texas life.[5] The transphobic gadfly billionaire Elon Musk may have donned a black Stetson and moved his high-tech empire to Texas, along with hundreds of thousands of tech workers and other job seekers, but the rah-rah rhetoric of economic boom conceals the deeper reality of living in a state where schools are underfunded, violence is unchecked, "right to work" jobs are precarious, and elections are gerrymandered into submission. Some of the economic statistics about Texas (or the United States generally) might sound promising, but as we were once warned by the clock-sporting rapper Flavor Flav, *Don't believe the hype!*[6] When it comes to housing, health, education, environment, labor, infrastructure, or anything else that should matter to a sane civilization, Texas is starting to look like a libertarian bait-and-switch that promises freedom and opportunity while building a *Hee Haw* police state that controls everything from abortion access to campus protests to the shelves of the local libraries, not to mention a winner-take-all economy that immiserates more people than it benefits. In a terrific recent book, Russell Cobb shows how the neighboring state of Oklahoma engages in a similar kind of "swindle" against historical honesty and economic decency.[7]

Of course, it's not just Texas and Oklahoma. If living in this country for a half-century and teaching about it for almost thirty years has taught me anything, it's that actual American life has generally been about limits, control, violence, conformity, toil, and uncertainty, with a nice subplot of progress, fairness, and decency. It's a hard path with few options for anyone who didn't grow up in a gated suburb with an Escalade parked in the circular drive and who might wonder, perhaps at this very moment, what in tarnation I'm talking about. I think the rest of us, aka the 99 percent, know what it's like to live in this increasingly bad trip of a nation, in this gooey quagmire of the national soul that I'm calling "Bummerland," where a newly invigorated politics of cruelty is quashing our hopes for a healthier, fairer, more forgiving society. Too often, decent folks seem overwhelmed and uncertain, while the mean and ignorant flock to an antidemocratic strongman who promises a mythic restoration of purpose if they're willing to embrace his dogma of cruel intensity and dark comic barbarism. And sadly, Trumpism will probably outlive its namesake. With his Yale pedigree and emo eyeliner, J. D. Vance adds a slick new energy to the dark machinery of his spray-tanned boss that seems hellbent on dismantling institutional competence, hawking nationalist fables to low-information voters, and vilifying anyone to the left of Stephen Miller with a sadistic passion that would have made Nixon blush.

Even in the 1980s, the situation wasn't so dire. Without a shred of nostalgia for the Reagan administration or the lousy sitcoms and hair metal of that era, I can tell you that I miss the vision of possibilities ahead that I had as a seventeen-year-old in 1984. Things weren't great then: trickle-down economics, atomic anxieties, feathered hair, polyester "action suits," *The Cosby Show*, the Ford Tempo. People in small towns were just starting to worry about something called AIDS, which had been devastating San Francisco and New York for a while. But eventually, the Berlin Wall came down, the Soviet Union crumbled, HIV treatments were developed, and *The Cosby Show* reruns went off the air around the same time that its namesake went to jail. Anything seemed possible if we just hung on for a few more years.

Who feels that way now? In an era of climate change, post-pandemic anxiety, income stratification, political animosity, and civic atrophy, the vision of a bright road ahead seems like something from a children's book, an antiquated notion that we have no right to possess in the jaded and exhausted 2020s. The college students I teach nowadays are just as freaked out as their elders—Gen Z's psychological struggles are well documented—and they often share with me a level of frustration, overwhelm, and despair that is unlike anything I've seen in thirty years of teaching. My middle-aged peers are pretty much the same: depressed, scared, and looking for the exit. I don't know a huge number of octogenarians, but the ones in my orbit are raging and scared of things that don't even affect them, especially after they get their daily dose of Fox News, which is pretty much hydrochloric acid for the political soul.

So, what is Bummerland? Well . . . it's a world of sick systems and faded dreams. It's a way of living that creates more depression than it cures—as the English filmmaker Adam Curtis once quipped, "The reason you feel bad is that you live in a shitty society." Like the shabby characters who ransom dogs and rob card games in Andrew Dominic's brilliant 2012 film *Killing Them Softly*, pretty much everyone knows our national trajectory is going nowhere good, but no one knows how to change course. The late, great English theorist Mark Fisher described a similar phenomenon he labeled *capitalist realism*, a kind of learned helplessness in which we know we are trapped but can't imagine a way out. Instead of planning for something better, we struggle for the best spot in the human centipede of oligarchic capitalism (pro tip: it's not in the rear). No doubt, this metaphorical insect traps some bodies more than others for what the scholars call "intersectional" reasons having to do with race, class, gender, and other factors mixing together, but ultimately, we're all stuck in its digestive tract praying for the best.

This book is not an argument about root causes or specific reforms. Instead, it explores what it's like to live inside some of the cruel structures that govern our lives and wonders if we appreciate the full toll that they're taking on our bodies and minds. I think the systems in which we live are better at creating social distinctions, transferring assets to the 1 percent, and perpetuating intergenerational wealth than bringing pleasure, security, health, joy, and meaning to ordinary Americans. Almost none of them ground us in the sublime pleasures of art, nature, spirit, love, and communion. Almost none of them offer a sense of being swept up in something vital, hopeful, and meaningful. Almost none of them are imbued with a vision of the future that excites and inspires. Which begs the question: *Why do we put up with them?* Why have resource-draining mega-systems for finance, politics, health care, housing, transportation, education, and national defense if they don't serve our day-to-day well-being? It's a question that politicians rarely ask. Instead, they "sanewash" batshit policies. They pantomime empathy while scheming to preserve their sinecures. Only Trump, in his reckless perversity, would admit as much. "I don't care about you," he told a crowd of sweltering supporters in Las Vegas in June 2024. "I just care about your vote."

My hope is that by paying close attention to the infrastructure of despair, the subtle and not-so-subtle ways in which alienation, emptiness, and fear are imposed on us, we can focus our rage, laugh at our oppressors, and renew our sense of the possible. If you wonder how sketches of sick systems and cultural delusions can represent anything other than nihilism, I will say this: If it takes some kind of neo-beatnik dispatch with dark comic shadings, I've got you covered.

I'm committed to the idea that we need a gentler path forward; that we need a more sustainable rapport with nature, animals, and one another; and that ultimately, we need a soft revolution of purpose and practice that moves us toward minimal waste and maximum solidarity. Our collective burnout might be an invitation to homegrown fascism, but it's also an opening for deep regeneration.

Do I have the plan mapped out and available for download on some billion-dollar Bummer App? Not at all. I'm too skeptical of any self-proclaimed architect of the future or media-anointed "visionary" (one of the worst rhymes with *Freon Tusk*). But what I can offer is a particularly dank diagnosis as well as a general prescription of *smaller sweeter slower lighter*. Often implicitly, through slightly gonzo stories of loss and disenchantment, this book suggests that we must create networks of neighborliness and compassion on a smaller scale, invest in sustainability and creativity, and embrace new forms of empathetic citizenship and economic humility. Our national dreams, ambitions, and rhetoric must be shrunk to human scale because the proverbial "big talk" about big empires and big corporations and Big Data and big profits is as damaging to the planet as our individual well-being. There's a reason American Caligula's favorite word is *big*. It's what dullards confuse with greatness.

Passionate critique and utopian longing for something beyond the anxious new world we inhabit in 2020s America—that's what you'll find in the pages ahead. Although I pop up a lot in ways both comic and tragic, this book isn't about me—I'm just a crash test dummy thrown into the various cultural collisions that these pieces seek to illuminate. Think of them as (true) short stories with attitude or secular sermons of loss and love or an angry punk rock prayer for our sharply divided nation or simply sketches of where we've ended up right now, why it feels so wrong, and how we might find our way out of Bummerland.

1 The Super-Hyped, Ultra-Rich Technopolis of Despair

Security just told me *No photos* of the sleek Apple campus in Austin, Texas. No images of the pristine white hallways. No images of the sterile landscaping between the glass and concrete buildings. No images of the brightly lit cafeteria where I'm waiting for my wife to return from the medical facility for Apple employees. Although she only works part-time in the Apple store in the mall, she gets better benefits than what I receive as a tenured professor—but I'm not bitter. By the inedible standards of campus dining, I'm in a Michelin-starred restaurant, and they have fancy everything, even gelato, at subsidized prices for lucky Apple insiders.

There is only one exception to their prohibition against image making: we are permitted to take selfies. Which seems weird but fitting. The corporation that has made untold and allegedly untaxed billions from the selfie craze that has turned a nation of supposedly rugged individualists into a bunch of filler-injecting, self-promoting narcissists is making sure I don't point my iPhone at its makers and marketers. I'm not even sure how they noticed me taking a quick pic, but I apologize to the guard who gives me the "no second chances" look and disappears into some hidden door like Houdini. Wearing a difficult-to-get visitors badge, I'm not eager to get booted out because this might be my only chance to see inside the kingdom that Mac made. It's fascinating here, even if it makes me feel a little bit like a medieval heretic, dirty and bearded, who has snuck over the walls of Vatican City to gawk at the papal riches and priestly rituals. And make no mistake about it: Apple is the Catholic Church of the new millennium—infinitely rich, aesthetically seductive, insidiously influential, and absolutely sacred to the culture it both serves and devours.

Other aspects of the North Austin campus, one of only two in the United States, feel more like the sci-fi version of the twenty-third century. Surfaces are as white and perfect as a new set of dentures, and everything feels precisely engineered in a way that is overpowering (it's beautiful but intimidating). When I was there just before the pandemic, it was already a million square feet of real estate, but a billion-dollar expansion of the Austin campus was soon in the works. Even for a big corporation, a billion dollars might seem like a vast sum, but in June 2020, in the midst of the global pandemic, Apple became the most valuable publicly traded company in the world, with a market cap approaching two trillion dollars.[1] It's very hard to imagine the enormity of a billion, let alone a trillion, dollars, so I won't even try to provide an analogy of its *almighty Mother of God* bigness. On second thought, I'll give it a shot. To a company that is worth as much as the entire GDP of Russia, that has kept an astonishing two hundred billion dollars in cash on hand for several years running, a billion dollars is like a hundred dollars to a middle-class person: you will miss it but not that much.

But down the road is something else, a place where a missing one hundred dollars would be devastating, a place that wouldn't even exist if someone dropped a spare billion on it: it's the other side of our modern pseudo-abundance. I'm talking about the explosion of little tent cities for Austin's homeless—some just a few scattered urban campsites, others with dozens or more—that have sprung up along the major roads in one of the most prosperous and fastest-growing cities in the United States. Inside the tents are the forgotten casualties of neoliberalism, the winner-take-all ideology that exalts the individual at the expense of any kind of social accountability or state intervention. Neoliberalism is like a rich man who tells his poor cousins to work harder and stop bellyaching. Writ large, it is a mindset of profound political cynicism in which social safety nets are sliced into disrepair and then mocked for their own deficiency: *I told you government pro-*

grams don't work! If that sounds familiar, it's because it's deep in the withered heart and soul of modern Republicanism.

The whole thing works beautifully for the few and terribly for the many, but nowadays radical disparity is accepted as the cost of doing business even in cities with progressive reputations. Income inequality, already severe in a nation inclined to worship wealth while ignoring poverty, became even worse during the pandemic, resulting in a COVID recession that struck with disproportionate fury at the least among us. Much of that suffering landed on people of color, which is not surprising given that 37 percent of Black families have zero or negative wealth, meaning that bankruptcy or homelessness are never too far away.[2] Living like this is bad for everyone, not just for the poor: social psychologists have shown that inequality elevates fear and anxiety among the rich and poor alike, although for different reasons. The poor sense they are falling further behind in unequal societies, while the rich see how far they might fall into precarity if their wealth were threatened.

But Americans have always been people of paradox: we are a nation that celebrates individualism and bootstrapping but practices conformism and nepotism, that enshrines the separation of church and state but allows the U.S. Senate to hire an official chaplain (all Christians so far!), that maintains "Anyone can grow up to be president" even though the presidential portraits almost all bear a striking resemblance to one another in terms of race, gender, and religious background. Which is to say, I'm not naive about our capacity for self-delusion, and I am aware that cultural contradiction is as American as wearing a greasy mullet to the state fair for some deep-fried butter sticks. But when the gap between ideology and reality reaches a level that sends the contradiction Geiger counter into click spasms, I wonder if we are gearing up for the revolutions that we saw in 1917 or if we are just becoming permanently stratified like Brazil or Russia.

Several thousand homeless people live on the humid streets of Austin, which has long had a not-so-great reputation for its unhoused population (one reliable estimate claims forty-five hundred, though the city likes to say around twenty-five hundred).[3] I've heard stories that smaller cities in Texas cynically hand out bus tickets to Austin, almost as punishment for its liberal reputation: *Let the bleeding heart liberals take care of this*. Except we don't, not really, and homelessness in Austin remains unsolved, half-addressed, and controversial. When I arrived, in 1985, the unenlightened discourse was about "drag worms" bumming spare change and hassling people on the street around the UT campus. Runaways hung out on sidewalks next to people who had been pushed out of mental institutions in the Reagan years. Today our vocabulary has improved but not the conditions on the pavement, even though every new mayor claims that it's near the top of their agenda.

For a couple of years, at the start of the 2020s, the unhoused in Austin had a kind of hypervisibility, with colorful tents filling the flat space underneath freeway ramps and overpasses, creating temporary neighborhoods of the dispossessed within a rapidly gentrifying city. Because Austin relaxed its ban on public camping in 2019, people stopped hiding from police citations in the dark alleys and built somewhat safer and certainly more stable communities in plain sight alongside the access roads of major freeways. For a few years we could see what was hidden before: hunger, thirst, trauma, grief, pain, loneliness, mental illness, addiction. These makeshift settlements of large nylon tents, surrounded by broken bikes, trash bags, and plastic coolers, were the floating campground of neoliberal shame.

What does it mean? It's not that complicated really. Such profound disparity of experience, from the glorious summit of techno-capitalist opulence to the dirty off-ramps (literally) of despair and precarity, all within a small radius, even on the same exact road, is a sign of barbarism plain and simple.

But how can that happen in the allegedly progressive mecca of Austin? After all, the city has been mocked as "the People's Republic of Austin" since the 1970s, when it was an overgrown college town that the rest of the state loved to hate for its serape-wearing guitarists and angry feminists (or was it angry guitarists and serape-wearing feminists?). Back then it was an escape hatch for 80 percent of the free spirits south of the Red River, a chill place where you could hide out, feel safe, and build a good life when small-town Texas was too constrained (although the *you* in that sentence never applied to people of color as much as white Austin progressives assumed). Before the great overbuild of the twenty-first century, when Austin got as steroidally "swoll" as Lance Armstrong's thighs, it was a pleasant city with affordable tree-lined neighborhoods and more discount fun than you could shake a stick at. Back then the city nurtured something genuinely bohemian and wild: the first psychedelic rock band, the 13th Floor Elevators, started here in 1965; the outlaw country scene of Jerry Jeff and Willie took shape here in the 1970s; the punk and blues rock scene of the 1980s was equally influential. It was a place where you could see an underground musician like Daniel Johnston singing on the main drag for free and then disappear into an ocean of stoned hippies celebrating the birthday of a minor Winnie the Pooh character (sorry Eeyore!) with an annual orgy of bongo banging and hacky sacking. Despite the challenges of being landlocked in a gigantic red state, late-twentieth-century Austin was something like the San Francisco of the Southwest, or at least that's how it felt whenever I drove back to town from anywhere else.

A lot of thoughtful, creative, talented people still live here and are still trying to "Keep Austin Weird" in accordance with the local bumper stickers, but in many ways it's too late: the city has already been reborn as something very different over the past twenty years. Now Austin is home to super bros like Elon Musk, Joe Rogan, and innumerable California transplants who have turned ramshackle hippie cottages into multimillion-dollar acquisitions. (The notorious Alex Jones would be on the list, but he's been in Austin since the 1980s, slowly morphing from an access TV novelty act into a supplement-hawking, Sandy Hook–denying, Trump-boosting media machine on steroids.) Half of Austin renters in 2024 were living in housing they couldn't afford.[4] Although it's still quirky and fun in certain pockets if you know where to look, this formerly laid-back city is busy morphing into a pretentious clone of Houston, Dallas, Los Angeles, or any other Sunbelt mess clogged with extreme traffic, economic inequality, and aesthetic chaos. Many of the main arteries are ugly in a way that boggles the urban imagination, and during the six or seven months when its dangerously hot outside, confused newcomers might wonder, "What are people supposed to do here other than slurping down overpriced drinks in noisy bars filled with twenty-somethings?" Don't get me wrong—it's a great place to invest your crypto cash in short-term rentals for the bachelorette party scene or to party with some rump-paddling frat daddies on a bender, but good luck finding something "weird" in an increasingly cold, corporate city that risks becoming another one of Mike Davis's "evil paradises," where "bright archipelagos of utopian luxury" are layered on top of everyday immiseration.[5] Long timers will protest that the weirdness is still here if you look hard enough, and of course that's true, but I suspect the cumulative weirdness adds up to much less than Houston has to offer (and they do a better job with the unhoused).

Put it this way: it's a far cry from the sweetly stoned goofballs who populated Richard Linklater's *Slacker* in Austin three decades ago, a time and place that I knew and loved and joyfully inhabited, where cheap tuition and low rent enabled a proletarian renaissance of counterculture brilliance with which even Governor Ann Richards seemed pretty cool. Thirty years later the preternaturally uncool governor would rather lock up or kick out anyone who disagrees with his ideological narrowcasting. After several decades of trying to wriggle free and forge an independent identity that was more Willie Nelson than Ted Cruz, more Butthole Surfers than John Cornyn, Austin has mostly been brought to heel by its red state masters and corporate overlords, who stick the prefix *giga-* in front of every giga-thing under the stars and call it progress. The result is a place that is weirdly indifferent to the importance of public transportation, affordable housing, serious museums, world-class architecture, or a downtown that offers more than barhopping, hotels, and condos. Boosters can point to the migration numbers and ask me why sixty thousand people are moving here each year if the city is so lame. I'll address that situation later, but for now let me say: if this is Sunbelt success, *uh-oh*. As the Austin band Timbuk 3 ironically sang in their hit song in the late 1980s, "The future's so bright I gotta wear shades."

One day I went half-ass birding in a field in west Austin where the new tech money is concentrated. It's definitely not the weird Austin of yore, filled with sweaty slackers queuing up for an eighty-cent Shiner Bock in cafés where the communal CD player was gloriously befouled by Jesus Lizard albums. No, this is a slick new Austin of Elon-wannabee bazillionaires and aspiring tech bros zipping their Teslas through the twisty roads of West Austin, commuting from a nondescript modernist home to a nondescript modernist office at some start-up designed to solve a problem you didn't know you had. These are the people for whom the nearby Lamborghini dealership exists—ten years ago we wondered; now we know. These are the people for whom the local restaurant scene has gone goofy with pretension. Instead of the joyously greasy slop of the old hippie joints or the starch mania of the long-gone Spaghetti Warehouse, we now have glass-walled restaurants that proffer steaming piles of molecular gastronomy to the expense account crowd that you associate with New York or San Francisco. Most of the old punk clubs have long since retired to that big mosh pit in the sky, having been demoed to make room for sleek condos and cafés in areas with ominous nicknames like "Little Dallas," an adjunct to the anti-gentrification bumper sticker that pleads, so far with exactly zero success, "Don't Dallas My Austin!" The precise spot where I saw the punk legends Hüsker Dü in a warehouse in the late 1980s now has a swank retail district with a chocolatier that sells eight-dollar bonbons next to a café that only sold fifteen-dollar salads, nothing else, until it went out of business. But nearby there is a bronze statue of Willie Nelson that was unveiled a few years back on the groovy date of 4/20 (a weed allusion in a state that will be the last to legalize it), so I guess we're still *keeping Austin weird* in accordance with our official slogan of institutionalized eccentricity. Nowadays, the phrase signifies a steaming pile of nothing—at best it's a wistful reminder to locals that something beautiful has disappeared; at worst it's a tie-dyed T-shirt sold to tourists who think *weirdness* is a guy who plays banjo in the park or a young server with her blue hair shaved on the sides.

The allure of Austin is simple: we've got the sunshine and progressive sheen of California but allegedly without the steeper taxes (I say "allegedly" because the truth is more complex: elite earners are better off here, but the real tax burden may be worse in Texas despite its lack of a state income tax).[6] Although we don't have access to mountains, beaches, or a charming downtown, we have some spots of real scenic beauty—a gorgeous natural spring, a pretty river, a few so-so lakes, a lively nightlife for young people, and some massive music festivals—and that's often what draws the celebrities. By 2020 the city had become a place where Elon Musk and his then-girlfriend, the avant-pop star Grimes, would buy a house in which to raise their child, whose unpronounceable legal name is X Æ A-12, which for all I know might be the secret formula for Dr. Pepper. If you want to get a house in the new Austin, you may not have to compete with Musk, but you'll certainly have to compete with multiple offers that are well above the asking price (nowhere in the United States in 2021 were houses going for so much above list price).[7] Young people, in particular, are hopelessly priced out, while older folks on fixed incomes just wince and wonder how to survive the suddenly high cost of everything and the increasing hardness of the city. In 2024 a company announced its plans for a $1.3 billion artificial lake "surf park" that would be the biggest in the world. Housing the unhoused? Nah . . . But the best fake ocean this side of Dubai? *Hook 'em Horns!*

San Francisco went through this metamorphosis a decade or two before Austin. In one of the great books of the past decade, a scathing, insightful look at life inside the digital economy called *Uncanny Valley*, Anna Wiener writes about how San Francisco changed around 2010. As "homeless encampments sprouted in the shadows of luxury developments," she explains, "people slept and shat and shot up in the train stations, lying beneath advertisements for fast fashion and productivity apps, as waves of commuters stepped delicately around them."[8] Even as a worldly New Yorker, she admits, "This concentration of public pain was new to me, unsettling."

Anyhow, that is the paradox of Austin now: Elon and Willie and McConaughey and McMansions and hippie bungalows and Apple and homeless encampments, all rolled into one city with the libertarian podcaster Joe Rogan chattering in the background, embracing Trump

Fig. 1. The view from Austin's new downtown library: an urban landscape of interchangeable condos, ugly infrastructure, and a city-sponsored scat sculpture, January 2025. Photo by author.

in the 2024 election even though he'd called him "an existential threat to democracy" two years earlier. It's the kind of place that makes you dream of being here and dream of leaving at the exact same time, even though almost everyone says they like it, at least for the first year or two. Of course, it takes a bold person to go against the casual hegemony of the *all right all right all right* vibe, which may even propel McConaughey to the governor's office, despite a profound political vagueness that leaves Texans wondering if he's a Republican, a Democrat, or just a guy who likes the sound of his own mellifluous voice.

But what does it mean to say you like living in Austin, the ultimate super-hyped American city of the new millennium, the shining star of the new American West? Does it mean that you prefer California but could no longer afford it? Or that you're simply relieved not to be stuck in Waco or Amarillo? Or that it feels *nice* to think about the funky hippies and cosmic cowboys who danced and smoked weed here back in the day, even though almost the last of the old music joints, the very spot where Janis Joplin learned the blues, closed during COVID, and Texas won't legalize recreational marijuana and mushrooms for another thousand years? Or maybe it simply means that you appreciate how there's a certain self-satisfied mythology to the place that's easy to buy into and even incorporate into your own personal brand of laid-back feel-good, so that you can feel vaguely progressive without confronting anything in the deep substratum of historic ills that formed this deeply segregated city (and it'll be increasingly hard to learn that story in a state that banned the teaching of critical race theory in 2023).[9]

Such lip service progressivism is what we got when locals asked what should be done about the several thousand homeless men, women, and children forming encampments along the highways in the country's most economically segregated city.[10] Sadly, despite the heroic efforts of some local nonprofits, the larger answer is *Not much*. The city is adept at commissioning new studies of a decades-old problem while the rest of us keep moving forward, windows up, eyes straight ahead because too many of us have learned the art of not feeling, not connecting, not quite believing that anything can really change in the new Gilded Age of radical disparity.[11] We've all learned this skill to some degree, but as the city has transformed into a playground for the rich, too many Austinites learned to tune out the suffering under their noses. As the anthropologist Katie Stewart says, *The unthinkable thing is happening all the time now, and we do all sorts of perceptual tricks just to make life bearable.*[12]

One such "perceptual trick" is our homeless policy. Prodded by a local billionaire who runs a surveillance tech company when he's not funding a right-wing anti-woke startup called the "University of Austin," Austin voters chose to outlaw public camping in 2021 so they wouldn't have to look at the misery of the unhoused.[13] No more camping, broadly defined as "residing temporarily in a place, with shelter." No more *shelter* defined as "a tent, tarpaulin, lean-to, sleeping bag, bedroll, blankets, or any form of shelter, other than clothing, designed to protect a person from weather conditions that threatened personal health and safety."[14] No more visible encampments. No more embarrassing images on the news. No more guilt on the drive to work. No more confusion about capitalism being broken or Austin being unkind and maybe even uncool.

If you think my critique of Austin is too harsh or is simply a product of Gen X nostalgia that can't let go of its youthful encounter with a smaller version of the city that was literally the set of *Slacker*, I'd point out that a backlash is growing. After enjoying a musical festival weekend during the slightly cooler months, many coastal transplants moved here during the early 2020s but were then shocked to experience the brain-boiling reality of a six-month-long summer in Austin, where the number of hundred-degree days are projected to climb from 80 in 2023 to 160 in 2100. Although MAGA-friendly transplants may have embraced the harshness of Texas politics and its distinctly non-coastal flavor, gentler souls must have looked around and wondered *WTF*?[15] The city has also started to slip in "best city" rankings that it used to dominate. In 2019 a *Forbes* headline asked, "Is Austin the Best City in America?" while *U.S. News and World Report* made it the top urban destination in the country for three years running, but by 2022 it had fallen out of the top ten, before eventually landing in fortieth place in 2023.[16] One sign of trouble was when the local musicians were weaponized against their will. By 2023 the allegedly rad musical festival known as SXSW started partnering with the U.S. military and weapons manufacturers because nothing says "Live Music Capital of the World" like Raytheon. Legendary local artist Thor Harris said, "We, the musicians, are soft capital, and we don't want to be used for one of the most disgusting things about America, which is our war machine."[17]

Even the hundred-year tradition of the University of Texas being a relatively safe space for nonviolent protest was crushed in May 2024. Courting favor with a Republican governor angling for a slot on Trump's ticket, President Jay Hartzell invited militarized state troopers onto campus for the first time ever, resulting in an escalation of violence against peaceful protesters that traumatized hundreds of students and made me afraid that another Kent State was about to erupt around me. I've never been terrified on a campus I've known for forty years, but that changed when I saw the intensity of the police assault against the mere *possibility* of the students creating an encampment on the lawn in front of the English Department. Students, staff, and faculty were getting hit, dragged, and arrested for simply being in the way of roid-raging cops whose disdain for the students was palpable. At the same moment when cops were pushing and striking my colleagues for only filming these abuses and a senior colleague was being struck with a baton for the crime of watching from the sidelines while Black, I found another scene one hundred yards away: seemingly oblivious to the campus chaos, a sorority was hosting a genteel soirée with cocktails on the veranda. Once the creative and intellectual heart of the city, the university was under siege and not just from riot police enacting PTSD-fueled scenes out of *Call of Duty*. Massive anti-diversity firings, the billionaire-inspired creation of a new college dedicated to nonstop free market jubilation (isn't that what the business school is for?), and a state-level hostility to bodily autonomy, trans rights, and queer identities had already pummeled the campus. Looking for jobs in other states, longtime employees wanted out of Austin for the first time, and department chairs worried about trying to recruit people willing to take their place on a campus—and a city—that was losing its progressive sheen. What was once a dream job in a dream city had become a shit show.

Even *Texas Monthly* gave up on its hometown in January 2023, when this longtime supporter of most things Austin bemoaned "how a funky little college town became the unbearable-traffic, unaffordable-real-estate, insufferable-tech-bro, inanely-precious-restaurant, expensive-BBQ capital of the world!" After blasting the spiraling costs, extreme gentrification, unaddressed homelessness, blatant segregation, over-hyped weirdness, and general disappearance of organic local culture in favor of trendy shops and slick chain restaurants, the magazine offered a blistering assessment: "There's something broken in this place's soul."[18] Other than the people who are getting rich off the rapid changes to the urban landscape, pretty much everyone with some history here is wrestling with this sad, broken feeling in a place that used to be the best spot in Texas, the one place in the Southwest that really gave me hope that things were going to turn out *all right, all right, all right.*

2 Into the Wasteland

I had already experienced the end of the world when COVID-19 struck. Just a few weeks before friends and acquaintances began sharing news stories about a worrisome virus in a far-off place called Wuhan, I headed to Southern California to join nearly five thousand people at the world's largest postapocalyptic festival: Wasteland Weekend. It's a temporary immersive world inspired by the *Mad Max* films, and it attracts those for whom the apocalypse is a glorious utopian space. I had no idea that something like the real thing was only a few months away.

The location is deep in the Mojave Desert, five miles from a paved road that is itself five miles from a place called California City, which feels like neither California nor a city.[1] There's a golf course where old men hit balls into the harsh wind, a long main street with weather-beaten folks bouncing along the rocky shoulder in electric wheelchairs, and a diner facing the runway of the tiny airport where locals watch the planes take off and eat so-so cheeseburgers. The locals probably find me disappointing as well because I'm dressed like a twenty-third-century hobo with a duct tape fetish. Before I am allowed to enter the Wasteland, my clothes must be appropriately "distressed" and "on theme." I practiced for weeks in advance back home in Austin, applying coffee, paint, and even blow torches to my rattiest shirts and shorts. I knew I had failed at my first attempt at a doomsday ensemble when my emo teenager said I looked like a "Danish explorer," whatever that means. But eventually, I got it right, or at least good enough for a "war pup," a first timer in the Wasteland.

I've never been to Burning Man, but I imagine it's something vaguely similar, even if the people here in the Mojave look down on the Burners for being too corporate and somehow fake (although many of them have spent time there). Wasteland Weekend is a little more blue-collar in vibe, maybe because big guns and gas-guzzling custom cars are an essential part of the scene, and instead of gossamer rainbows and glitter canons and tech bros on ecstasy, the atmosphere is more like a heavy metal scavenger hunt with a shot of undrinkable vodka.

I'm shocked how good the Wasteland is. A small city of atomic survivors emerges for a week under terrible conditions, and it is a thing of astonishing beauty: costumes, characters, bars, stages, streets—just for a week, and it's gone. This is no dark Disney-style theme park with professional *imagineers* calling the shots on how to make it happen: instead, regular people hammer, weld, and rope together an insane assemblage of wood, steel, and tarps to make their own shelters and playscapes. What emerges from this epic toil is a temporary city of profoundly immersive cosplay, a place of DIY genius and endless pseudo-cinematic performance: even if you're not done up like Mad Max or Furiosa, you need to look and act like you might know them personally.

The amateur creativity of the built environment blows me away almost as much as the machinery, to which I respond with a fired-up passion that is unsettling to my Prius-driving soul. *Wasteland* might be the best custom car show in the world because these are wild homemade monsters: visually brutal, ecstatically loud, and terrifyingly cool. They rumble with a sublime nihilism that says, "This is the last of the V-8s," to quote the first *Mad Max* film from 1979, and as you wander around, you'll see reverential visions of Max Rockatansky's Pursuit Special come to life among other muscle cars, trikes, and trucks that seem assembled from the wreckage of the past by someone with a talent for meth-fueled welding. I'm there with my wife, Monti, both of us filming and interviewing on tiny GoPro cameras that can withstand the elements (we are shooting a documentary called *Who Killed the World?*). As we wander and talk to people who are mostly neck deep in character—learning about folks with temporary names

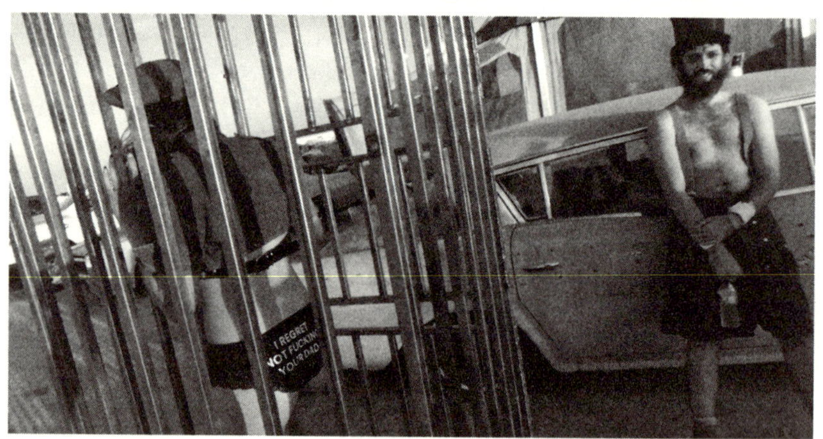

Fig. 2. One of the dozens of DIY muscle cars at Wasteland Weekend, September 2019. Photo by author.

Fig. 3. Participants at Wasteland Weekend, September 2019. Photo by author.

like Sprockets, Bomb Chel, and Rope—we obsess over the homemade cars, these deeply psychotic machines on endless slo-mo parade. Having grown up in the seventies when most cars were noisy boats of steel and leather, just before they got smaller and filled with plastic and computers, we can't help but glory in their atavistic rumble, the mad genius of their engineering. Life here revolves around these rude beasts: people hang on their hoods, on their roofs, even in cages dangling behind giant War Rigs, as the biggest trucks are known.

I talk to one young woman in a cage on the ground. Mostly naked, she looks like a pole dancer from a haunted house, complete with contact lenses that swallow up her pupils in milky white. Despite black panties that read "I regret not fucking your dad" across her bottom, she has a quiet, shy voice as we talk about the end of the world. She is typical, in that most Wastelanders look scary but are surprisingly gentle. I see much more kindness here than I expected, especially given how many heavy, realistic guns are floating around—all replicas, supposedly, though no one is checking. These simulated automatic weapons and small arms are rampant as is an endless array of DIY devices for (simulated?) self-protection. You would think people would be picking actual fights given the amount of weaponry and badass posturing, but I saw nothing like that, except in a sanctioned, regulated fight zone known as the Thunderdome.

Everything here transcends my assumptions. One father builds his camp around a shrine to his dead twenty-one-year-old son, a cocaine-and-fentanyl overdose. His wife has an autoimmune disease and is sleeping in the trailer. His sixty-eight-year-old buddy is in a fur loincloth and is the funniest person in Wasteland. He's a fireman from somewhere in Northern California, and he entertains us with stories and schtick for a good hour.

We go outside into the makeshift streets, which are something like *Deadwood* crossed with *The Road Warrior*. Everyone is covered in dirt and dust, the more the better, and no one is bathing as far as I can tell. People are shouting *Fuck You!* as a warm greeting. There is a wedding in progress that is quite sweet to see and a car made from a coffin with two spaced-out women cruising around being hilarious.

We visit the working radio station, a newspaper that prints a broadsheet each day, and the bulletin board that announces car shows and body-positive bikini contests. People hunt strangers as "bounty," often making friends when they find their "target."

Late into the desert night, we talk to people looking for homemade swill—instead of normal beverages, the camps hand out horrible concoctions that blend gin and pickle juice and mystery elements, and then we play homemade casino games with bottle caps. There is no "old-world" cash in the Wasteland. It's barter or nothing, and it's great to have a fantasy life outside of capitalism, if only for a week.

Wasteland invites a beautiful narrowing of attention to questions of survival: Where is the water, the food, the shelter, the tribe, the alcohol, the *gazzoline*, as they say in the *Mad Max* films? It's make-believe survivalism, a theater of bare-bones existence, but it's not entirely artifice because the weather is authentically fierce, and there is not much food and water that you don't bring for yourself. After an easy first day, forty-mile-per-hour winds start destroying almost everything. Compounds are blown apart; some people retreat to their cars. Conditions are truly rough.

Why does this immersive desert fantasy feel more alive, more real, more human, than the daily grind with kids and coworkers and folding laundry and eating burritos in the car? Why do people look more excited, and even more beautiful, in the shredded clothes of some gritty tribal future than in their normal outfits from the mall? Why are people so radiant and so damn nice here? We are not lonely in the Wasteland. Not passive. Not consumers. Not capitalists. Not employees. Here we are makers. We barter and give. We have tribes, each with an elaborate compound that celebrates our presence with shouts and bonhomie. We are semi-liberated from capitalism, though it does cost $220 to attend. I don't mean to sound snarky about the entrance fee because plenty of people barter a day's labor for a free pass.

Perhaps the answer to my questions is buried inside an even larger query. *Why is it that we are so adept at imagining our own obliteration as a society, often in dystopian films and novels, yet we are so bad at taking small steps, small measures, to save ourselves?*[2] That question loomed large over Wasteland Weekend but also over the pandemic. Is the answer in a kind of cultural self-hatred? If the work of cultural studies is to make visible the unconscious fantasies of our times, then perhaps the Wasteland is a product of a deep social despondency that says, *Please, please, please, put us out of our status quo misery and let something else arise, something raw and free, something that lets us work with our hands, not just on screens and keyboards.* As punk and goth musicians have long known, there is surprising beauty in imagining cultural suicide: the end can be a relief to the stagnation and suffering, and a new beginning is often filled with its own rough beauty and sense of limitless possibility. One thing is for sure: normalcy is a drag in Bummerland America, so much so that maybe we get excited to imagine its obliteration and are a little depressed to get back to the old routines.

Indeed, when my partner and I return home to our regular life in Austin, it's painful. Still a few months from the real onslaught of the pandemic, we experience the disappointing "drop" that the other Wastelanders are talking about online, using a word from the fetish communities to describe the big come down when you return to the regular world. Right away, we miss the apocalypse—or think we do.

By May 2020, a few months into the pandemic, the next Wasteland was canceled in favor of something closer to an actual apocalypse, and people got to experience a plague-infested hellscape whether they wanted to play dress-up or not. Everyone said the same thing about the early months of the pandemic: *This feels apocalyptic, this feels like the end of the world, this feels like a movie!* And it did, especially because it happened too fast to process with any degree of clarity, at least at first.

It was scary and disorienting—but also oddly grounding as well. For instance, as our worlds got smaller, we got frequent reminders about whose work is essential in a way that would make sense to Wastelanders. As Andy Russell and Lee Vinsel write in *The Innovation Delusion*, "The most unappreciated and undervalued forms of technological labour are also the most ordinary: those who repair and maintain technologies that already exist, that were 'innovated' long ago." Such "maintainers" are attuned to the constant processes of entropy and undoing, which requires what another scholar calls "broken-world thinking" to slow or halt the disintegration of the world. Maintaining the frayed wiring and sputtering machinery of various systems, not the introduction of novelties designed to confer status ($50,000 Leica M9-P Edition Hermès camera anyone?), is what really keeps "ordinary existence going."[3]

From this vantage the heroes are obvious and obviously underpaid: people who make, fix, or bring things that we need to survive the pandemic, like delivery drivers, nurses, internet technicians, grocery store clerks, and pharmacists. It turns out that these were the people we couldn't live without when COVID shut things down. Meanwhile, corporate lawyers, telemarketers, lobbyists, car salesmen, advertisers, bikini waxers, publicists, stockbrokers, golf pros, and celebrity influencers have much less utility at the end of the world. Wasteland prepares you for cleaving the world in two, between necessary and superfluous. It is a place where broken-world thinking is practiced as an explicit art form: how do you make something functional and even fun out of scraps of junk? That is the underlying challenge of the world they are making, albeit briefly, in the Mojave.

No doubt, they picked the perfect spot for Wasteland: so many utopian schemes have been plotted in the Golden State over the centuries, and there is something about the deserts of Southern California that is particularly appealing as a site of fantasy. As the crow flies, Wasteland is not that far from one of the last radical dreams to take root in this region, the early-twentieth-century socialist colony known as the Llano del Rio Co-operative Colony, whose founder was confident that it would "become a paradise on earth."[4] Despite "a sustaining conviction that one had broken out of an age-old prison and was marching, shoulder to shoulder, with loyal comrades, into a promised land," as the English writer Aldous Huxley described it, the residents of the colony witnessed its collapse in a few short years during the First World War.[5]

So far, Wasteland has fared better than its socialist predecessor. Despite losing a couple of years to COVID, it reappeared after the pandemic, and I'm sure the participants talked about how the event prepared them for living lean, how it made them into *maintainers*, and how it steeled their nerves for quarantine. And the films that inspired it all, the sublime *Mad Max* franchise, came roaring back as well. A new *Mad Max* film came out in 2024 because apocalyptic filmmaking goes on no matter what, good times or bad, fulfilling what film scholar Amy Murphy calls "the desire for a new more balanced relationship with nature; the desire for increased citizen involvement in planning decisions; and the desire for a more 'tribe-like' scale for one's community." All of those elements are clearly part of Wasteland Weekend, which is a cheerfully utopian project that looks like an apocalyptic hellscape.

Meanwhile, the real thing, the quasi-apocalypse of COVID-19 that arrives in full force in 2020, is far less exciting and much, much longer. It has no cool aesthetic, no cinematic alter egos, no immediate hope for a radical transformation of society, no timeline that we can count on. Eventually, as we get further into the 2020s, we hope that we're clawing our way back to some diminished semblance of normalcy, toward the memory of the way things were when we were *happier*, if not what you'd call *happy*. We have become maintainers of a different sort, struggling to keep the illusion of the good life from falling apart.

3 Waiting for Elon

Some crypto bros from Arizona cooked up a crazy scheme to get rich in 2022. They would build a giant metal statue of their billionaire hero, Elon Musk, on a gleaming rocket, truck it across the desert to Texas, throw a massive party, and then deliver their offering to the Tesla Gigafactory a few miles east of Austin. If Elon accepts the gift and tweets the name of their company to his gazillion followers, it will drive naive investors in their direction like wild horses into a desert canyon. At least that was their entire plan in all its beautiful goofiness.

I read about the rocket statue on a Sunday morning in late November when it was getting global coverage as just another quirky Elon story (this was a few years before his infamous "Dork Maga" leap onto Trump's campaign stage). I don't have much interest in billionaire statuary and even less enthusiasm for crypto, but I've spent a few years trying to figure out how the Tesla CEO became a cult hero for millions of people, especially young men zealous for Musk's anti-woke, techno-solutionist vision of the future. What do they see in this inarticulate, bullying billionaire that sends them into a frenzy of CEO fandom?

To find out, I drive with two friends to a Formula One track called Circuit of the Americas, where the Arizona crypto bros are assembling the Tesla faithful in preparation for a giga-pilgrimage to see the great man himself. Often doubling as a venue for acts like Elton John, Sting, and Megadeth (not at the same time!), the Circuit of the

Americas requires a half-hour drive from downtown Austin into a bland landscape of instant subdivisions and empty fields. My friends and I have no idea what to expect at this unprecedented event, but we relax when we pull into the parking lot and find maybe forty people milling around the tractor-trailer with the statue loaded on its back. A lonely DJ plays rave music in front of two rented buses, which mostly serve as a wind block for the three people who are dancing. A guy dressed like Big Bird on acid seems radiant in a psychedelic sort of way, but he turns hostile when my easygoing friend asks him about Tesla. For some reason this question harshes his precarious mellow, and psychedelic Big Bird heads off in a huff.

By a strange coincidence, most people are dressed like me, which is to say like a loser character from the 1990s film *Clerks*: cheap black sweatshirts, black pants, sneakers, sunglasses. The organizers are friendly young guys who give us nifty swag from their crypto company. Hoping it will make people relax when I talk to them, I put on a black ELON-emblazoned shirt and walk around a mostly empty field next to the parking lot, noticing that a dozen muscle cars are parked there, some with signs that advertise their own crypto companies ("the people's crypto"!). Someone is selling fourteen-dollar *slices* of pizza. Porta-potties wait in the distance for the tech bro hordes.

I walk up and examine the "monument," as they call it, which looks like a full-size ICBM missile ready to launch from the back of a flatbed trailer. It's enormous and well fabricated, some insane blend of Las Vegas and North Korean aesthetics with a massive bust of Elon affixed to a gleaming goat straddling a metal rocket aimed at the sky. Why a goat? Well, these guys hail Elon as the "Greatest of All Time": the GOAT!

Everyone is friendly to me, probably because I fit in better than I expected or maybe because I'm wearing a hat that says "Fartco." I'm surprised that no one asks me about my hat because I have a joke loaded about being the CEO of a company that's been blowing up. Instead, the crypto guys ask if we've seen their extraordinarily customized Jeep, luridly emblazoned with the name of their company. They must have wasted a few hundred grand to turn a normal Jeep

Fig. 4. Crypto bros and Elon fanboys waiting for the billionaire to accept their offering at the Austin Gigafactory, November 2022. Photo by author.

into a six-wheeled monstrosity, and of course they are very proud of it. I walk around the vehicle and nod, thinking, *Wow, this is like lighting a pile of money on fire.*

After my little interaction with the crypto guys, the vibe gets relaxed to the point of tedium. Our crypto hosts are surprisingly quiet. The closest thing to a sales pitch comes from a shy ten-year-old boy passing out fliers for his dad's rival crypto company. Meanwhile, a few young guys get eager to document their presence and ask me to take their photo with the monument. When his face comes out a little dark, one guy asks me to take the photo again. And again. Even a fourth time. I'm happy to help, though I'm amused by his vanity (or dedication to his hero on the missile). "Make sure you get the good light," he says.

Throughout the day I sense an undercurrent of desperation mixed with some big talk about getting rich and famous. When all else fails in contemporary America, I guess, there is always crypto. Our hosts have a fantasy that is almost childish: to make millions from a silly PR stunt to attract the attention of the world's richest man. But they're not alone in their aspirations for something magical to happen. In the background another fantasy roars past: it's a training session for amateur motorcycle racers on the mile-long winding track. Probably a bunch of middle-aged lawyers with Steve McQueen fantasies (younger people can imagine Keanu Reeves on his bike). Frankly, I'm a little jealous of them, but I have my own daydream: that I'm going to understand the weird cultural undercurrents that make this event possible and write about it in a way that captures its deeper reality. Surreally, in this crowd of forty people or so, I bump into a famous *New Yorker* writer who is doing the same thing. His black Mercedes coupe is parked next to the muscle cars.

For the next three hours, there is nothing to do: we can only wait and wonder about Elon. *What will he do? Will he come here to the track? Will he send one of his emissaries?* Rumors are flying. If nothing else, everyone hopes the caravan to Tesla's Gigafactory will do the trick. A row of cars behind two yellow buses and a tractor-trailer-mounted statue to His Muskiness—how could he say no?

Overhead we see planes taking off; a couple are exotic private jets shaped like lawn darts. Because someone on Twitter is always tracking Elon's plane, we think he's in town. But for how long? Every jet that takes off could be him, leaving us behind, just a crew of losers on the lawn. A few people look up toward the sky like anxious worshippers on the way to the BBQ trailer.

Five o'clock arrives, and it's time to roll to the Gigafactory. With fewer than forty cars, our caravan is a little sad but determined to get to the Tesla factory before dark. Frustratingly, because we're the last car in line, we get separated from the procession at a stoplight. My friend Jess knows the way to the factory, but even when we get there, we can't spot the rest of the gang. How can we lose a thirty-foot-tall metal sculpture and two yellow buses? Where could they be? The Tesla security guards won't say; instead, they are impatient for us to turn around and leave. We try some back entrances to the factory and are thwarted again. Eventually, security follows my friend's Subaru and

Fig. 5. Tesla's vast Gigafactory near Austin, May 2023. Photo by author.

records our license plate like we're some kind of nuisance or threat. We are definitely not getting on Tesla property.

Not sure what to do, we drive in circles for thirty minutes before we finally discover everyone huddled on the side of a public road adjacent to the Gigafactory. The grand offering is happening here, on an embankment that puts us at eye level with the second floor of the second largest building in the world (by volume, it's surpassed only by Boeing's Everett factory). It's my first time to really look at the endless form of this low-rise Death Star, and I'm impressed: the building hums with potency. *This is where something big is happening.* But our little parade is not part of that—not unless Elon makes an appearance and gives us his blessing. So, everyone waits awkwardly on the embankment, perhaps a little surprised that Elon can't be bothered to wave from the window to his fans and their $600,000 gift to his ego. After a while it starts to get boring. Despite all the media attention, the reality is just sad. We wait on the side of the road until it's dark, and we feel too hungry to stick around.

Reddit goes nuts the following day with denunciations. The consensus is that these guys are scammers and losers who made crypto look foolish. They didn't know how to honor Elon appropriately. The whole thing was "cringe," which is internet slang for the deepest level of uncool.

Yet it's not a total waste of time. I feel like a witness to a new kind of capitalist fervor, almost erotic in its contours, that stodgy CEOs of the twentieth century would never have elicited. Compared to Lee Iacocca or even Bill Gates, Elon is something new in the boardroom. These young men with their ICBM offering are typical of his fans who love everything about him—how he slouches, how he jokes, how he controls the narrative, how he dunks on his critics, and how he sells visions bigger than anyone since Columbus asked Queen Isabella for a boat. I suspect these men love what Elon represents because it's what they want for themselves: a magical transformation by which an ordinary human male undergoes a metamorphosis from unloved wanker to glorious tech god soaring above the multitudes. Living a life without limits, free from government regulation, social critique, or "woke" gender politics—that is the new (right-wing) manly ambition that Musk has pulled out of the ether of possibility. To his legion of fans online and off, he is the vagaries of capital made irreverent, cool, dope, sick AF, and worthy of emulation. Like Donald Trump, an obvious kindred spirit whom he claimed to despise not long before he embraced him like a brother from another mother, Elon stands for domination of the trolls and a magical unlocking of extraordinary male prowess; unlike the unstudious Trump, Elon adds a "revenge of the nerds" will to power and salvation by providing masculine engineering to the mix. *If only he would come to the window and wave! Elon, we're here! Let us in!*

No matter how much he sinks in public regard for his vile comments and authoritarian practices, especially in the wake of DOGE's assault on the federal government, Elon remains more than a capitalist success story to his admirers. To them he is a new kind of superhero who is even more ambitious than a fictional billionaire like Bruce Wayne, whose alter ego, Batman, is an urban superhero fighting one villain at a time (what a limited strategy for crime reduction!). The only analog for Elon's epic ambition is Superman, the one caped crusader who can do it all, on land, sea, and sky, so much so that you don't really need other superheroes. Elon wants to dominate the land (Tesla), the underground (the Boring Company), and the sky (SpaceX)—not to mention our minds (Twitter and Neuralink). To his admirers, he is the techno-savior of a world he wants to lead to Mars *and* a model of individual transformation from nerdy subservience to limitless grandiosity. He is performing the role of sacred prophet *and* platitudinous lifestyle guru; towering tycoon and dope-smoking *bro you gotta know*; inaccessible plutocrat and an intimate mirror of what you could be if you're willing to embrace the spirit of techno-transformation and *Be Like Elon!* Spinning half-truths in his inarticulate low-key manner, Elon stimulates the adolescent male imagination in a frazzled and desperate society.

Writing about Elon is like writing about a mercurial king who lives in an impenetrable castle and whose world can only be ascertained from weird echoes that bounce through the valley of ignorance. I wanted him to come out of his Gigafactory and at least acknowledge the surreal gathering outside, but maybe he saw through their scheme or decided that it somehow undermined his own brand. Maybe he was in the bath. Maybe he thought it was all too cringe. We'll never know.

4 Plastic Passion

Imaging falling in love with a robot. It shouldn't be too hard if you remember the blend of loneliness and tech-dependence that characterized the pandemic and its aftermath, a period in which 47 percent of Americans expressed the belief that sex robots will replace human lovers and 48 percent expressed an interest in visiting a robot brothel for a rendezvous with a plastic lover.[1]

I was initially put off by these statistics—all I knew about robo-love came from a weird smattering of pop culture images. I remember coming across a video clip of a malfunctioning Japanese robot that dental students in Tokyo were using for practice and thought it was the most disturbingly intimate thing I had ever witnessed. This might be a strange thing to say about a rubbery machine made to look like a distressed young woman with floppy hair, but the short clip still haunts me. At first the robot looks like a real patient staring up at the aspiring dentists, a willing vessel for their scraping and drilling, with multiple gloved hands reaching into her gaping maw. But then her head twists into action, her mouth starts chomping unnaturally at the air, and her mechanical eyes reveal a weird lifelessness that somehow seems very alive. The whole scene is super creepy and ominous, and when you're watching it, the singularity of machine sentience seems much too close—and much too freakish to embrace. And yet that is exactly what will happen: we will embrace the machines in an increasingly literal sense. In fact, we're already doing it.

Not very different in appearance from the dental practice robot, a new wave of hyperrealistic AI sex dolls now sells for upward of ten thousand dollars. With creepy visions of artificial love dancing in my head, I'm tempted to write it off as another failure of the sad American 2020s: *human intimacy is being phased out!* But I don't think this is the case, and if anything, I've been unfair to robo-lovers in my more pessimistic moments. From a more tolerant perspective, the rise of robo-love during an epidemic of loneliness seems like the most natural thing in the world. After all, the pandemic cut the living flesh out of our lives and left us with screens and buttons to satisfy our needs and those of our employers. Maybe it's not so bad to snuggle a bot?

It turns out that Texas is the perfect place to ask this question. Of course, the conservative state might seem like a strange place for AI erotics, but it's been a key location in at least two ways. In 2018, with considerable fanfare, a Canadian company tried to open a robot brothel in Houston—it would have offered customers an unprecedented chance to rent one of the high-tech dolls in room specially built for robo-romance. But local politicians fought hard to stop the brothel from staining their chaste and gentle city, calling it "weird" and "gross." Houston's city council went so far as to ban its citizens from having sex with an "anthropomorphic device" at a sexually oriented business—leaving open the legality of screwing a robot at Arby's.

Houston may have said no to robo-lovers for hire, but Austin is where they're often born: it's home to one of the main manufacturers of sex robots, the Real Love Sex Dolls company, whose website I encourage the curious to peruse. It can be off-putting at first, because at the top of their colorful home page is a list of options on sale: "FREE 2nd Head/Eyes/Wig! FREE Gel Breasts! Free Boltless Standing Feet! Free EVO Skeleton." I don't even know what an "EVO skeleton" is, but the whole thing sounds like the work of a deviant Dr. Frankenstein who needs to take a gender studies course. Clicking on the gallery of robot paramours does not reduce my general queasiness: one after another, the dolls look like department store mannequins dressed like porn stars. It's very techno-tawdry.

It is not until I read the 563 customer reviews over the course of a long, strange afternoon that I get over my robo-prudery. "I'm a 41 yr old, 150 lb, 5'2" woman & my male doll is over 100 lbs & almost my height with no legs," one woman posted. "I have a wonderful method of giving him bed baths & I adore having him next to me." Not what I was expecting. Another woman exclaims: "I have never been happier! He was the solution to what my life was lacking! . . . I sometimes forget he's just a doll when I'm lost in my own little fantasy world with him!" I can feel the ick factor receding as I hear the humanity in their comments: "He's a comfort when I desire, a sex object when I please, a body to cuddle, a companion to chase away the lonely days & nights, a distraction when I need it, he's everything I wish him to be when I want him to be." Someone named Abry says, "I wish I could love someone as much as I love this doll but this is fine—I'm going die alone [and] my corpse will stain the floor." A male customer explains his point of view: "You cannot resist touching them. Nor can you deny the very beautiful silent personality they soon begin to develop once they settle into your home . . . They are not something to be ashamed of or stuffed in a closet. You will want to dress them sharply, and proudly have them on display for all to see. They are literal works of art."[2]

Inevitably, a few male reviewers hit an off-putting note. "The artists who make these dolls are INSANELY TALENTED and I hope they receive even a modicum of the respect and appreciation they deserve . . . They produce a wide variety of appealing shapes. Boob lover's paradise. Only downside is they're often heavy and don't clean themselves." But most comments are surprisingly chaste, sounding no different than satisfied descriptions of food processors or shower caddies on Amazon. Many are quite moving because they hint at a life of isolation and social anxiety. "My doll is a perfect companion that loves to cuddle every night in bed," says one man. "It is definitely worth the investment if your date game isn't strong lol." Another man echoes this sentiment—"perfect for cuddling, I recommend it!"—while another sounds a note of resignation in describing his robo-crush: "She is very heavy, and hard to move around, but she is alright." (Survey data suggests that men comprise the majority of purchasers, but women are a vocal minority in the review section of the Real Love Sex Doll's website, and in surveys about artificial love, more than 30 percent express real enthusiasm.)[3]

I see all this plastic passion as a case study in the ethics of ick, which are often based on assumptions and misinformation, not to mention media sensationalism. What if the realm of lifelike sex tech is not a cause for alarm but, instead, a savvy human adaptation that should be admired? Indeed, maybe we can imagine scenarios in which sex robots are not perpetuating the objectification of women (at least not primarily), as is sometimes feared, and instead open new forms of human tenderness and meaning making.

What if we imagine a scenario like this? Everything is perfect for an evening of passionate cyberlove between a shy middle-aged customer (pick your gender) and a sexy young robot (same) on a chilly autumn night in 2029. The drone-delivered candlelit dinner has just arrived piping hot from the Amazon ovens, and the lighting has been dimmed automatically. The robot has prepared a superbly curated list of subjects for conversation, thanks to the precise data mining of the customer's online behavior: in short, the device knows *everything* the customer likes, from politics to porn, and it speaks sensitively, persuasively, inquisitively, on any subject the human finds appealing. When the customer's interest begins to wane on a particular topic, something the machine can judge by pupil dilation, it is programmed to segue to something that restores enthusiasm. After an hour or two of talking and imbibing (it can consume liquid but not solids, which are stored for later disposal), a real connection has emerged between robot and human. It smiles at the customer like a megawatt movie star, which makes sense because it was based on a well-known Hollywood personality. The customer compliments the robot's attractiveness once again, almost forgetting its mechanical nature, and the machine offers a simulated flush response that seems very real. The customer feels calm, hopeful, confident—none of which they can feel with a human being in any context but especially a romantic moment.

All this perfectly engineered flirtation culminates in a tender walk to the bedroom, and after some shy fumbling, the main act begins.

Yes, it's the moment for some flesh on latex canoodling. Unlike robot companions that customers warm up with blow dryers and hot towels, so as not to activate some primal revulsion toward necrophilia, this model includes self-regulating temperature control and lifelike body warmth sensation. And unlike actual dates with actual human beings, everything goes *perfectly* for the customer. The money was well spent, they think with boundless satisfaction. It's the carefully controlled intimacy they wanted. It's the passion they anticipated when they put down all that money, almost enough to purchase a used car.

Although I struggle not to spoof the weirdness in my hypothetical scene, I tried to paint it with some compassion to suggest that *robo-love doesn't have to be gross, exploitative, and hollow*. Could people treat sex robots in ways that would be unethical or even illegal if done to a human being? Yes, it's very possible, but so are the happier outcomes. As Nancy Jecker, a professor of bioethics at the University of Washington, told one interviewer, "The great advantage of robots is that they can provide sexual services without violating the basic human dignity of other people." She makes what she calls "dignity-based argument for sex robots" for older people in particular, noting that "not only do older adults face ageism and ableism in the communities in which they live but also healthcare professionals typically do not broach the subject of sexuality, and medicine is peppered with examples of ageist beliefs about later-life sexuality." Although not perfect in their current form (there is, for example, a preponderance of porn-inspired young female robots), sex robots could become a means for restoring human dignity for all sorts of vulnerable people.

Pandemic isolation opened the door ever wider to new sorts of techno-intimacy, and it wasn't necessarily a pretty sight. When technology offers something like love, tenderness, and connection in a box, fashioned entirely from circuits, wires, and plastic, it might seem heartbreaking or bizarre at first. But when I consider the cultural impact of sex robots, I'm trying to focus on what is possible, rather than what seems creepy. After all, for people with disabilities, individuals with severe social anxiety, or older people suffering from isolation or bodily challenges, sex robots could become an important tool for emotional and physical satisfaction. Will it still be a little creepy to find a grandparent getting busy with their robo-lover? Yes, a bit. But it's not any worse than discovering Grandma behind the Olive Garden fondling the busboy. In fact, the robo scenario might be preferable to Grandma's fondness for "unlimited breadsticks."

I remember the first time I heard about "furries" who dress up in something like a sports mascot outfit for their erotic gratification and social bonding. I thought it was extremely silly and said as much to friends, until one day a woman responded, "But . . . what if it's fun?" It stopped me cold. *Yeah . . . What if it's fun?* Who am I to kink shame? In a world filled with exploitative behavior, two people dressed as giant squirrels seems so innocent that it's almost quaint. I was dead wrong about furries, and my initial impulse about sex robots was equally wrong. In an era of AI replacing artists, social media companies promoting hate, and crypto bros swindling our savings, robo-brothels are the least of our techno-problems.

5 Healing Inc.

It's one of those unendurable years that I hope you haven't had. I put some of it down to bad habits mixed with bad luck or whatever makes a person sick enough they want out of the grim hustle of Bummerlife, but mostly I blame the American health care industry, a sick system in every sense of the word. At a time when I was sinking to the most vulnerable state I could imagine, I had to trust fall into a crazy patchwork of for-profit medicine, holistic healers, and Big Pharma predation, all of which promised a restoration to good health and a positive outlook as long as I could pay the bill. Where I landed with a thud was not where the uninitiated might expect and might help you understand why my eyes crossed when I overheard an inebriated Philadelphia MD boasting about how "American health care is the best in the world" while she was on vacation in a small town in Mexico a year or two before anyone heard the name of Luigi Mangione or wore a T-shirt that promoted his canonization. This medical nationalism is one of the most pernicious myths about life in the United States, where health care is too often a harsh, for-profit guessing game that I call "Healing Incorporated."

At the time it was hard to explain what was going wrong with my health, even to my friends. Some dudes said nothing other than *Hmm* when I told them that I'm, you know, knocking on heaven's door with a deranged ferocity. Others resorted to dim positivity—"Hey, at least it's not cancer!"—which is an awful way to talk to the massive chunk of the global population struggling with chronic pain, mental health issues, and suicidal ideation, all on the upswing in the uneasy American 2020s. Remember how much things began to slip during the first year of the pandemic? Prevalence rates for depression and anxiety in the United States increased sixfold between early 2019 and late 2020, while prescriptions for medications, counseling services, and "unmet need for mental health services also rose significantly."[1] And things didn't get better in the post-pandemic era. Neither the care of the broken body nor the burned-out mind has been thriving in the contemporary United States, which the almost gleeful reaction to the UnitedHealthcare CEO shooting made clear in 2024. There is a deep strangeness to the "healing" landscape in 2020s America.

For me it went something like this.

At the beginning of 2022, I'm already as anxious as a dog in a crate from my normal life challenges, but I somehow get worse, month after sweaty month, setback after setback. By fall I discover that I'm entombed in something I can't understand: the jittery mind goes to eleven, as they say in *Spinal Tap*, and then keeps going until I'm unfit to drive. At that point, perhaps not coincidentally, an insidious wave of chronic pain arrives deep in my core and sabotages my mind and my sleep. Soon it's spreading throughout my body: lower back pain, prostate pain, sacrum pain, piriformis pain, hand pain, shoulder pain, foot pain. Headaches that never quit. Some of these are familiar problems from a few years earlier; others are unexpected. By October I can't sit. By November I can't sit, stand, walk, or type except in very short bursts of essential movement. From then on, feeling like I'm stuck inside a pain coffin, I don't know what to do other than endure the explosions of unfathomable discomfort and anxiety that set my brain on fire. I pull away from friends. I have a panic attack about a weather forecast. I numb out with social media, dumbscrolling (like doomscrolling, but dumber). I lose interest in things that I used to count on. Standing in the water on a beautiful beach in British Columbia, I feel nothing except regret about spending so much money to feel so tired and burned-out. Worst of all, I am not looking forward to *anything*, which is the most unsettling part of depression spreading its wings and taking over your life.

Maybe because I'm an American studies professor who is always looking for patterns in the world around me, I start to feel like a metaphor for America in its dysfunctional, uninspired present. Instead of grand ambitions for the future, I'm only scared of getting stuck in endless pain loops, losing more of my hearing, remaining in a cruel and hostile part of a cruel and hostile country, and eventually retiring to a new kind of social nothingness far from the modest social life I have on campus—or more likely, never being able to stop hustling for rent and bills as I slide into old age. Everyone has those fears as they get older, but in the right combination, with the right circumstances that include a history of PTSD and neurological troubles, they'll knock you flat.

Some of the pain is inadvertently self-inflicted. Six months before everything imploded, I went off some meds for nerve pain, depression, and anxiety, happily assuming I didn't need them anymore. Unfortunately, one of the meds, an SSNRI called Cymbalta, is notorious for withdrawal agonies, a fact that psychiatrists prefer to gloss over, and as the drug leeched out of my brain, I began to slowly unravel in a new way. Alone in the bedroom one evening, I uncharacteristically threw a lamp against a wall, and it pierced the sheetrock. After that I was hanging on by my fingertips for six months that included that summer trip to British Columbia, one of the prettiest places in the world to miss seeing because of your mental health. I was there but not really.

The chronic pain hit hardest when I got back to the Austin heat, and I slid into my third bout of *agonizing curl-on-the-bathroom-floor-and-yell* pain in a five-year span. Is it something in my spine? Sacroiliitis? Sciatica? Frozen shoulder? Carpal tunnel syndrome? Tendinitis? Fibromyalgia? An oxygen deficit due to sleep apnea? Pelvic floor syndrome? A nutritional deficit? The ghost of Bea Arthur? Who knows? Some of these problems are familiar from years past; some are new possibilities. Four MRIs, three CT scans, and a bunch of X-rays provide conflicting evidence. Maybe I need surgery; maybe I need PT; maybe I need ayahuasca? Maybe I need to quit my job at Bevo, Inc., a cold corporate university if there ever was one, and find a quiet place to live without the one-two punch of Texas heat and politics?

Keep in mind that I'm what passes for "lucky" in the modern medicine sweepstakes. I have relatively good insurance, good referrals, good research skills, and a good enough income that I can keep trying new treatments. I'm not in a rural area where it's impossible to find a specialist. I have a supportive partner who can drive me to appointments while I lay flat across the backseat and gasp from the pain. But no one knows how to fix the cascading problems in my body—or even how to mitigate them. I'm crashing and burning into the best that American medical care can offer, with the possible exception of the concierge doctors reserved for the uber-wealthy in places like Malibu, where people get three-thousand-dollar full-body MRIs "just in case." Always good to take a looksie inside the 1 percent! The rest of us can wait and wonder about what lurks within. As the Soup Nazi from *Seinfeld* might say: "No full-body scan for you!"

Every MD has a confident diagnosis and a quick prescription for me—I *never* leave without a new drug. If you put all my medications into a giant medicine ball, you'd be dead before you could say "the Sackler Family." I remember Ativan, clonazepam, diclofenac, diphenoxylate, duloxetine, hydroxyzine, hydrocodone, Gabapentin, Lunesta, Lyrica, meloxicam, metoprolol, Metronidazole, Prednisone, Prozac, Rexulti, Seroquel, Sonata, Tramadol, Trazodone, Trintellix, Valium, and Zoloft. Some of these are not very strong; others would coldcock a rhino; but in reckless combinations that were generally unmonitored, I got a trip to the far edge of human endurance without having to leave my couch, all thanks to Big Pharma and its medical minions.

My descent into the cold bureaucracy of Western medicine goes something like this. I meet a conspiracy theorist foot doctor who brags about using military-style weapons to shoot pigs on his friend's ranch; he gives me super-powerful opioids and sends me on my way (I wanted a better podiatrist, but PETA's worst nightmare was the only one available). I meet a highly rated hand surgeon who never even touches my hands before recommending surgery—he brags that he's a "hammer" and that every problem "looks like a nail." Pretty soon I'm getting nailed all right, but not in the good way: I say yes to his first surgery, get no benefit from it, and say no to his second surgery when I realize that he's clueless about anything other than carpal tunnel. Next I meet a tall Nordic neurologist who has the bedside manner of a depressed mortician; like a nineteenth-century physician, she merely taps my knees and tells me to balance on my toes before declaring, "Well, the problem is not neurological." I meet a frat boy urologist who waits a year too long to perform testicular surgery, a fact that he confesses to me after the operation, while strutting past my wheelchair and heading to the hospital parking lot to retrieve his red Porsche 911 (Is that a stereotype? Yep. Did I witness it? Yep). I meet the rude, spaced-out receptionists who are living their own nightmare alongside my own. I get it—I, too, would find little joy in ferrying urine samples around a building that looks like the set of *Severance*, but I would try not to make the patients feel bad about their little peepee cups of shame. I also meet the staff of the world's worst sleep clinic, where I get conflicting advice on a life-threatening matter depending on who I see on a particular day—*they can't remember if I have the thing that will kill me or, hey, maybe not?* I meet the well-published hand specialist at the university teaching hospital who chuckles away severe pain with stories about his wife's arthritic foot—"Gosh darn it, we all get older, and you just get used to it!" *Thanks Jethro!* Later in the same hospital, I meet a team of three doctors who review my worsening situation. They know that replacing medicine X with medicine Y sent me into a depressive torpor. So, they disappear to confer or maybe smoke a blunt and watch an old episode of *Mr. Belvedere* and come back with a brilliant suggestion. *Uh . . . what about going back on the first medication?* I'm very tempted to say, "No shit, Sherlock, have a banana!" but I'm too tired and scared to sass the white coats.

Some treatments help a little, some make me worse, and no one cares enough to call and ask: "Did that work? Are you feeling better?" Yet as my bulging mailbox will attest, *they always remember to send the bill.* I know I'm lucky in one sense: the financial impact is not enough to push me into bankruptcy like millions of Americans, but I'm still sweating the endless copays, high deductibles, and out-of-network fees, not to mention the interpersonal weirdness that MDs like to generate. I see at least twenty doctors over a two-year period, and maybe five were kind and thoughtful. Only two of them gave problem-solving a real shot. The rest were less ambitious, preferring to hand me drugs and fob me off on physical therapy that offers cookie-cutter exercises with colorful stretchy bands. Although some physical therapists are brilliant and far more hands-on than the MDs, I don't get much time with the good ones, who are expensively out of network. Instead, I'm sent to four different low-quality, "in-network" PT centers and make little progress, though I assemble an impressive collection of red, blue, and yellow stretchy bands. And because it's harder than ever to find a good primary care doctor to quarterback all these treatments, I'm figuring everything out on my own: who to see, who to trust, and what to try next in the nightmare alley of for-profit medicine.

The people who work on my mental health are better. I meet a young psychiatrist who guides me through six weeks of daily transcranial magnetic stimulation sessions to ease my depression and pain. I derive some benefit and suspect it would have worked wonders if my body wasn't collapsing into a vortex of sorrow during the same six-week period. Meanwhile, I work with three good talk therapists in a row, but two of them go out of network in the first months of treatment. I hit the jackpot with the third one, who does EMDR, a form of trauma deprogramming. Although for months I'm too "dysregulated" for a potentially destabilizing treatment like EMDR, I stick with her and pray she doesn't go out of network.

Finding a psychiatrist in network is, uh . . . *the craziest part*. There's a six month wait in our prosperous technopolis for an in-network appointment, so I can either stick it out or spend $550 for an out-of-pocket intake session and $250 for each follow-up. Ultimately, I see a shrink who does nothing more than review a short questionnaire without looking up from his desk. He gives me something that doesn't help very much but requires me to return every three months to swear I'm not suicidal (sometimes I fib). I switch to another psychiatrist, whom I expect to wind up on *America's Most Wanted* for either Medicare fraud or roadside bestiality—*he's disturbingly weird*. Seeming super high on his own supply, he makes inappropriate jokes about the meds he's foisting on me. Contrary to what he appears to believe, sarcasm is not what patients look for in a doctor's bedside manner. Frustratingly, I can't point out the obvious (he's a dick) when I might need what's on his prescription pad.

And what about natural remedies and alternative care? After what I've described about mainstream medicine, surely holistic healers will save the day? Well . . . I was crazily desperate and would have tried anything. If someone wanted to reset my energetics, spark my quantum healing, unblock my chakras, scrub my spirit animal, splash my sacred waters, tickle my "starseed," or put some mushroom tea on the kettle, I was willing to try it. I'd do the breath work and activate my intuition. I'd wear a magnet bracelet and a pyramid hat to channel the healing powers of the pharaohs. In other words, I was 100 percent down with the patchouli-scented alternatives to corporate medicine *in theory*, but in practice they often shared the limitations of their mainstream counterparts: false confidence, one-size-fits-all solutions, and a rancid undercurrent of greed. Because few of these holistic folks take insurance, they often seem to view me as a human ATM. One physical therapist who looks like a fading soap opera star puts me on the exam table, decides that I really need Jesus instead of an MRI, and prays over my bare torso before taking four hundred dollars for an hour of nothing.

I disentangle from her and run for the hills—literally, because I hope to find better healers in the rolling hills of West Austin, where the rich people live and get their treatments. That's where I find a slick "chiropractor to the stars" who wants me to commit to a $2,400 series of spinal adjustments that improve the pain for about twenty minutes. (After one treatment, I say *no thanks* and slink away.) I try another chiropractor, who injures my ailing back on a mechanical "drop table" deployed without warning. Then I meet a manic paleo nutritionist who urges me to eat more ham despite being told that I'm a vegetarian. He evangelizes about the wonders of ham just in case: "Most days, I'll have a ham for lunch, I'll have some more ham for supper, and if I wake up and need a snack at midnight, I'll have more ham!" I also check out a high-end CBD store that gives me a sales pitch that sounds pretty scientific, but I get nothing out of their expensive balms and tinctures, which is not surprising if you look at the flimsy evidence about CBD for many conditions. And speaking of anecdotal evidence, I develop a special loathing for "natural" pharmacists who sell homeopathic snake oil alongside legit medications. When I ask about the lack of scientific evidence for their wishful-thinking concoctions, often based on the hilarious notion that *less* of a substance makes it *more* powerful, they always offer the same idiocy: "Well, a lot of people say it works for them," which could also be said about guardian unicorns and lucky rocks. Sometimes I buy their products out of desperation but just feel poorer and more gullible afterward.

People in agony are suckers for certainty, and these alternative practitioners have as much bravado as the "hammer-nail" hand surgeon or pig-hunting podiatrist. Without exception they promise they can fix me even though the last person failed. It takes me a while to realize I'm going broke from a $230 an hour bodyworker who swears they can solve the problem in one session, though I end up seeing them eight times with little to show. Another clinic offers a pain-free guarantee (eight sessions for $1,500!) that turns out to be an empty sales pitch. I try three or four acupuncturists, all of whom put the needles in the same generic spots that yield momentary calm but nothing more. Thinking that I used to respond well to acupuncture and just need a better practitioner, I switch to an expensive Korean doctor who has her own idea about where to stick me: she slams needles right into a pain center near my sacrum, causing a vicious flare-up that lasts for five days. She talks up her special machine that wiggles your torso (pleasant but dopey) for $150 an hour, hawks her special magnesium powder for the inflated price of $60, and seems disappointed when I cut my losses and take flight. Eventually, academic friends point me toward a wiry Chinese acupuncturist who insists that I buy his herbal supplements at the end of each appointment even though they seem to do nothing and could clash with my prescription meds (who knows? No one even checks). I know he always forgets where he put the needles because twice I find them in my socks later in the day, but he always remembers to brush against my junk when he's doing his reiki hand jive between needle insertions.

Speaking of junk brushing, I encounter a lot of massages therapists from China and Thailand who offer sex for cash when all I want is relief from debilitating pain. In the middle of a session, one even says quite sweetly, "You know, you can give me a massage!" Because their English is sometimes nonexistent, I struggle to convey my reluctance to make a sexual transaction. "No come?" one asks in consternation like I'm turning down a party invitation. I'm not sure how to respond to her unusually formatted question and just wave my hands and say, "Uh . . . No come!" "But you like!" she insists. "Uh. . . . no thank you," I say quietly, but she is persistent: "YOU LIKE!" I only succeed in making my point when I utter the embarrassing, racist-adjacent phrase: *"Wife no like!"* What can I say? It was a spasm of white guy awkwardness, and I was simply trying to follow her syntactic lead. To be fair to the scared, sleep-deprived, drug-addled, brain-fogged person I was, it's hard to understand the unwritten rules that govern "whack shack" economics. Some of these women are autonomous hustlers maximizing their profit margins; others are vulnerable immigrants trying to survive creepy dudes, crooked cops, and human traffickers until something better emerges. One woman told me she was saving up to open a Thai restaurant in Dallas, and I discover that my conversations with these women are quite warm after they realize I'm a "good guy," as they put it, though a few look annoyed with me for wanting "only massage" and not the more lucrative option. Fortunately, not everyone is a mercenary when it comes to their lewd advances during "healing" sessions. A handsome young male masseur offers to rub my, uh . . . swimsuit area *for free*, but I demure with a plausible explanation: I still remember how to do that on my own. I realize this part of my not-so-healing journey might sound like I was cruising the dark web for some euphemistic version of "massage services," but I was just a desperate person looking for a bargain to loosen a shoulder, neck, or back problem. Was I wandering some back alley with a fistful of cash? Not at all. These salacious misadventures happened in normal-looking businesses that had legit reputations on Yelp or recommendations from seemingly upstanding friends and colleagues.

All I wanted was an affordable session with a skilled bodyworker, one of the few things that can ease the suffering from chronic pain and even restore trust in a malfunctioning body, but I generally couldn't afford them. So, instead of forking over $220 for an hour-long massage at a fancy day spa, I was looking for $60 an hour bargains in strip malls when the pain got bad enough that I needed a massage twice a week. Some of these places were legit and provided a healing touch that didn't include an aggressive proposal for cross-cultural wankery, but you never know what to expect in the unregulated Wild West of bodywork. Of course, none of this would have happened if insurance generally covered massage in the United States like it does in some European countries because I could have afforded ten sessions with a well-trained therapist. Instead, I'm living another version of the American dilemma that pushes chronic pain sufferers toward street drugs like fentanyl or heroin because they don't have access to care or their doctors have overcorrected from the bad old days of OxyContin for all.

If this book is not a posthumous publication (check the back cover to make sure), you can assume that I didn't try meth, fentanyl, or crack in desperation. However, I did turn to psilocybin and ketamine for pain management. Wherever I looked, I saw these drugs heralded as the radical new breakthrough cure for, well, pretty much everything from smoking to sadness—and that hyper-inclusiveness should have been a giveaway that something was too good to be true. At first my psychotropic hopes were higher than a hang gliding Timothy Leary, but a large bag of psychedelic mushrooms offered no lasting relief, even if I enjoyed talking to a plastic squirrel in a waterfront park one afternoon in British Columbia. I try a few months of microdosing, which feels quite pleasant in the way that a cold beer might offer, but it's not very effective in the war against pain that I'm fighting. That's why I got more excited about the old horse tranquilizer known as ketamine, even if it was hard to find an affordable route into it. Most ketamine clinics charged $3,000 for six sessions in 2022, but I eventually found one that my insurance covered. I was ecstatic and arrived with high hopes, though the office was nothing like Haight-

Ashbury in the sixties. The clinic looked like any other doctor's office, with beige furniture, dim lighting, and busy nurses. One of them led me to a room with a soft recliner aimed at a television with relaxing nature footage. She took my vitals, inserted an IV, and gave me the thumbs-up. Within seconds I was shot into space on a psychic rocket ship without a navigation system—I felt like I was blasting off in six directions at once. They didn't tell me how to manage a psychedelic experience as powerful as any LSD; they simply pump Special K into your veins and set you loose on the freakiest interior journey of your life. I saw waterfalls. I saw monkeys. I saw my brother chatting with me in the womb (we're not twins); I looked over some kind of divine horizon and felt like I was glimpsing the secret nature of the universe; I felt awed and terrified in alternating waves that sloshed through my system. And then, an hour later, it was pretty much over, and I was walking to the car, telling my wife that *wow, ketamine is the answer . . . it's so great!* I told her that I had finally found something to unlock the grip of pain on my body and mind, something beautiful, hopeful, and transformative! Another half-hour passed as we drove on the freeway, and I was feeling semi-normal but also strangely spent, like I had given birth to a prehistoric pain baby through my shamanic third eye. For the next few hours, I was shaky but still optimistic. Some kind of portal of possibility had opened, and I was praying that these healing vibes were more than a synaptic blip.

But then it happened. That night I got hit with side effects I wasn't warned about and wasn't prepared to handle. No one told me that ketamine is a well-known bladder irritant and that you shouldn't take it if you're having urological issues, but again, I found out the hard way. At 2:00 a.m. I shot up, feeling like a nail was lodged in my bladder. I felt some deep interior switch flip, and all the positive energy of the past twelve hours evaporated and then some. Suddenly, I was spiraling in a new way. My brain felt crazily depleted, and I was having trouble forming thoughts as waves of severe pain overwhelmed my system. I gritted my teeth on the couch until the next day, on an endless Sunday that I'll never forget, when I moved around the house in a kind of waking death state, feeling the slide toward suicide with an unprecedented intensity. I have never felt so exhausted, confused, scared, and lost: my brain had become a hyper-mobile kaleidoscope of bizarre, anxious images, some of which I could still see when I opened my eyes (just for a second but still, not a good sign). I held my gut while my wife talked me through increasingly sharp stabs of pain and scoured the internet. No one was answering the phone at the ketamine clinic on Sunday, but we finally got through to a nurse who acknowledged that I shouldn't have taken the treatment because of my urological condition. *Well, thanks for telling me now*. Such risks weren't addressed in the screening process whatsoever, which is perhaps not surprising in retrospect: this unregulated clinic was one of a dozen that had set up shop in Austin in the early 2020s, pumping teenagers and grandparents alike with a powerful psychedelic drug with little preparation. Could ketamine work for whatever ails you? I hope so. It's an incredible experience if you're prepared for its intensity, and I can see the beauty and possibility in it. But because I landed in a poorly regulated, for-profit version of psychedelic therapy, it was a spectacular and disorienting failure.

My lowest moment of my ketamine crash was when I walked through the sticky November heat (welcome to Texas!) to the Turkish restaurant where my daughter works. I often walk to ease the pain, but the tangled synaptic mess called my brain was kicking around a darker option: that I was walking to say *Arrivederci*. I wasn't going to make an explicit announcement that "this was it" because I love my daughter and don't want to mess her up, but I had a voice in my hyper-medicated brain that sounded like it was coming from an underwater sound system: it was wavy, garbled, and ominous as it made the sales pitch for oblivion. When I tried to talk to my daughter in front of her restaurant, I had trouble standing and started sobbing. My kid was scared, but I tried to explain it was the pain and meds and sleeplessness and that dad was going to be okay, even if I didn't believe it. Ketamine had landed on top of dozens of prescription meds and months of sleep deprivation, adding crazy fuel to the crazy bonfire, and the agony was more ferocious than ever. Too many meds, too much dread, too much pain in too many places, too much suffering with no real guidance—instead, it's just a cafeteria of choices, some good, some bad, that you have to figure out on your own.

Only those who have lived with it can understand chronic pain. If that's the case, I hope you *never* understand it—not really, but I can tell you this much: it's a savage companion that haunts you like a demon. There is no OFF button, no relief other than fitful sleep if you can manage it. In my case the pain lingered and festered for months, fueling depression and anxiety like wind on a prairie fire. All throughout the fall, I had to keep going even if I didn't want to, and I now carry the sad knowledge that without my family, I'd be gone. Months of sharp, constant pain, the yawning vortex of depression and getting older, savage drug "interactions," skyrocketing anxiety and the echoes of PTSD, the isolation of office life in the Zoom age—it's too much for anyone. Too much for me at least. But I kept going out of a sense of obligation to the people who love me and the hope that on some future day I could barely imagine, something would shift, the pain would subside, and I could feel like a person again. I wanted to know what it would be like to grow old with my incredibly loving and hilarious wife. I wanted to see my daughter find her way in the world. I wanted to keep talking with my brother and bothering my friends with memes. And I wanted to outlive the forty-fifth/forty-seventh president so I can visit his tomb and take some selfies.

To survive, I often lived on top of an ice pack, sometimes unable to think a single meaningful thought other than *fuck pain fuck pain fuck pain*. Eventually, I landed in the office of a friendly pain doctor who runs a clinic filled with rough cases: if you're in there, you're in a bad place. After prescribing a few medications that made me feel even worse and trying a failed nerve block procedure in my spine, he shrugged and told me to try cannabis, which would be fine if it worked. Crazily, I'm in the minority for whom THC intensifies rather than easing the condition, something I learned one night when I ended up in a hospital at 4:00 a.m., unable to vanquish the agony crescendo until they hit me with the big opioids. Giving up on weed for at least a couple of weeks, I searched the internet for other solutions but only found terrifying accounts from people whose bodies were nonstop war zones. Every website had an endless supply of medical war stories from people who sounded worse than me, and it's something you don't ever want to read but especially not when you feel like your body and mind are breaking down.

One sadistic old friend recommended shock therapy, which made me wince because it had fried my Scottish grandmother's mind when she was in her last decade (I have great genes!). Even if I'd tried everything else known to medicine, both in its legit and quack forms, I was reluctant to go full *Cuckoo's Nest,* although it can't be much worse than helplessly layering medications with midnight recklessness. One night, maybe a month after the ketamine disaster, the pain was spinning me around the room, and I was slamming a cocktail of edibles, muscle relaxers, benzos, and opioids, all prescribed but not designed to commingle. The combination almost did me in. By 5:00 a.m., whacked out from sleeplessness, pain, and my all-you-can-eat buffet of medications, I disintegrated. The intensity of the pain, terror, and disorientation boggled my brain. Breathing hurt. Sitting hurt. Standing hurt. Lying down hurt. Sleep hurt. Life hurt. And because the American health care industry doesn't really know what to do with pain, there was nowhere to go in such a moment, unless you want to lie in a hospital bed and rack up debt.

I forced myself forward. Whenever the pain receded an inch or two, I put on my mask of sober adulthood and play-acted a kind of normalcy in Zoom meetings and, only when absolutely necessary, in the office. On the somewhat better days, I was putting on shoes, driving to work, talking to students, doing the shopping, being kind to my beautiful wife. With my hands shaking from an essential tremor (another new problem!), I wasn't doing any of these things very well, but it's a marvel I was able to do them at all. I kept hearing the same voice in the back of my brain that got me through a bad acid trip when I got thrown out of a club in South Austin in the late eighties and walked through the night like a slacker zombie. I told myself, "Keep going," until you find a friendly door that opens and someone takes you in. So, I just kept stumbling in constant agony, hoping and waiting for an opening. Sure enough, after a few more months, the pain started to subside: *God bless pure good luck.* No new doctor, no new treatment, no apparent reason—I just started improving, one bodily location at a time. As the pain receded, I stopped my desperate mixing of random meds and started sticking to what was prescribed. I even cut back on some of the dosages. I got more serious about my talk therapy sessions. I kept going to the pool and letting my body float. All that made a difference, and six months after the ketamine disaster, I started to have moments in which I thought: *I'm okay.*

I'm okay. It might not seem like much of an achievement, but I tear up when I type those words after too many months of putting the pain on one side of the scale and my will to live on the other and watching it teeter. *I'm okay.* We assume we want happiness, wealth, recognition, and love, but ultimately, we only need those two words.

I learned a few survival strategies that might help others stuck in the pain-fear spin cycle. For me it helps to move if you can—any movement is better than none. It helps to get in water—bathtub, pool, ocean, whatever. It helps to have physical contact—from a loving partner, a dog at the park, or a massage therapist. And it helps to aestheticize the despair. Goth music is crucial for me because, paradoxically, the bleakest records soothe the pain. The minor key dirges of The Cure and Bauhaus have saved my soul a few times, and I probably owe lead singer Robert Smith a thank-you card for the early Cure records that imbue disintegration with a somber majesty.

I still am not *entirely* okay. Even in summer 2023, nine months after all this came to a head, I was still slipping into the darkness. And by the fall, when a doctor yanked me off a low-dose opioid and switched my antidepressant *four times in four months*, something went seriously wrong in my brain. Every bad thing came roaring back with a psychotic fury, wrecking my body and mind for another nine months. Feeling stuck and cosmically punished, I sank into a bitter funk. More doctors, more drugs, more PTs, more agony. Once again, I couldn't sleep without pain drugs, and I spent mornings in a druggy haze, stretching and icing my glutes, shoulder, and hands for hours until I was able to stagger out of the house. It was horrible for about six months, but this time I caught a break: I found some ingenious bodyworkers who tracked the worst misery to problems in my neck and back. Focusing on overlooked muscles that were often far from the pain, they applied an unbelievable amount of pressure until it relented, a process that can take five minutes in each agonizing spot. I saw stars during the treatments, but I was happy to make a testimonial video for their clinic and their unorthodox form of myofascial release. In some ways it was a gloriously simple solution, but that undercuts the expertise involved. It was not something that anyone else knew about, at least not the way these people did.

By summer 2024 I had lost two full years to this mental and physical chaos, but I was slowly healing once again. As I took the semester off for the first time in twenty years and got some distance from whatever was triggering my intense burnout, the prospect of a full recovery in body and mind didn't seem delusional. Endlessly grateful for my wife's patience and compassion when things were falling apart, I was connecting more deeply than ever with her. As always, we talked nonstop during the day and then slept tangled up in each other's limbs like teenagers. We covered the dining room table with art supplies and joked around. Eventually, I started laughing again at sitcoms and stand-up. I started drinking less, eating better, losing most of the forty pounds that had accrued over a few years of not being able to endure a gym or bike. I no longer felt like an old building in the first seconds of the demolition process, that long moment in which the explosive charges have detonated but the building hasn't yet fallen.

I survived the worst years of my life with very little help from the "greatest health care system in the world," which was more often cruel and destructive than humane and healing, and I guess that's not surprising if you see Healing Inc. fundamentally as a profit center for people who like expensive cars. I recognize that some of the dysfunction is my own bad luck and bad genes. I know I have a set of risk factors that are my own—depressive mind, sedentary job, dysfunctional family, generalized anxiety disorder—but I wonder how much of my depression and chronic pain is sociological in origin. After all, I feel stuck in a world that seems engineered for maximum disenchantment, a society that prizes dumb domination and acquisition over creativity, community, and kindness, a society that is moving too fast in all the wrong ways, a country that seems antithetical to my ethos of *smaller sweeter slower lighter*. Invidious forms of social media and high-tech productivity measures only add to the problem, making us even more miserable, because now we know how many steps we didn't take, how many emails we didn't respond to, or how many Instagram vacations we didn't get to enjoy. The old phrase from Don Draper's midcentury world, the *rat race*, no longer makes sense because the average rodent seems lazy compared to our manic pace: checking emails while we use the toilet, multitasking while we drive, inhaling a quick lunch at our desk. A more apt comparison for our frantic, illness-producing, sadness-stimulating 2020s lifestyle is the intense, mindless scrubbing of a meth head on a bender, cleaning the same refrigerator over and over. We're all tweakers now.

6 Testosterone

I'm sure future historians will look back on Americans in the 2020s and say, *They were a wonderful, wise group of people—especially the men!* I say this after watching a popular Instagram video that was posted in the dog days of COVID in 2020. The star is a stem cell injecting, machine-gun-wielding, CBD-selling, poker-playing, trust fund–spending early-middle-age white guy who looks something like the Terminator version of Hugh Hefner. In this video he stands grinning in the desert near Las Vegas, shooting pumpkins in the dark with giant automatic weapons, smiling in alpha male bliss. As in all his videos, the trust fund Terminator is not wearing much clothing and is surrounded by a large number of women in nothing more than bikinis and heels. Eventually, the women get to shoot the pumpkins too, though the camera focuses on their backsides as much as their solid shooting form. To their credit, I suppose, everyone seems trained to shoot these monster weapons; these are not guns that someone can just pick up on a lark.

In most of his videos, this mega-MAGA alpha male is shirtless and looks like a stunt double for the star of a swords and sandals epic from the 1950s: impeccable definition on his abs, pecs, and arms but a little short to be the leading man battling it out in the Colosseum. He's a well-known influencer of sorts, a man who lives to boast and posture online—strong jawed, testosterone jacked, and conspicuously consuming, he revels in over-the-top straight guy lifestyle porn. Guns, bikinis, mansions, muscles—that's what has made him a hero to millions of young men. That's what you get in an endless loop of hundreds of photos and videos on Instagram and YouTube. He shoots the videos on yachts, on the Amalfi Coast, in Costa Rica, in various deluxe restaurants, often with lots of bare female flesh positioned in a semicircle around him, almost as if the women are worshipping at the altar of his well-oiled masculinity. Of course, he is the highly visible brand, while the women are nameless bikinis, always young and slender except for vast silicon orbs that offer pneumatic bliss to the teenage boys who leave comments in every language. "You've got the best life bro!" says a typical one. I can't properly translate the dozens of comments in Farsi or Hindi, but I can see that fifteen million people have watched this short video about nothing—nothing except the campy glamour of manly destruction in the Nevada desert. I won't put his name here because if he's anything like his favorite Republican president, and I'm not talking about Warren G. Harding, I suspect the one thing in the world that he cannot stand is being nameless.

7 White Lies

He's the dauntingly mythic Texan in the family tree. Tall and imposing, with his dark hair brushed back like Robert Mitchum, my grandfather was an illiterate East Texas logger with impossibly rigid ideas about how to survive his demons—maybe because, deep down, he knew he had some of that darkness in him.

Was it murder or manslaughter? I'll never know. What I do know is that he killed a man in the logging woods in the 1930s. This fascinated me as a boy, just as it fascinates me now, in part because I never saw him do anything meaner or wilder than rolling a Bull Durham cigarette or fussing at a dog. Of course, I only knew him much later, when his hair was white and he spent the hot part of the day sitting on a rawhide chair in front of a ramshackle cabin. Even though he didn't say much, he occupied a great deal of mental real estate in everyone around him. I guess the constant threat of violence has that effect on people.

I always had trouble making sense of my grandfather and his world. I'm a half-stranger in these woods for the past forty years, which is a big part of the problem. Despite spending summers in East Texas and landing in Austin for college, I grew up among clamdigger Yankees on the Jersey shore who didn't make a favorable impression on me either, but because of my East Texas mother, I grew up being called "sonny boy" and have a flood of cousins and aunts and uncles down here, a mix of one-footed loggers and part-time dog breeders, all talking about Trump and Jesus and Texas toast in the deep piney woods along the Louisiana border. One of my aunts worked five decades as a waitress in the same Texas roadhouse, serving chicken fried steak and gallons of iced tea into her late seventies. Add to that a first wife from Houston who was uncharitably dubbed a "loud-mouthed Texan" for being a small woman with large opinions when we were living in California and a family of origin that relocated to a dull nothing of a town in East Texas because my New Yorker father promised to bring his dirt road bride back home after thirty years away but then decided that two hours from her family was close enough, and well, all that puts me on the outside edge of insider when it comes to this strange state where my grandfather lived.

Until his death in 1987, Grandpa was a taciturn patriarch who ruled over a dozen kids, eight of them girls he tried to keep from entering the twentieth century in any way—no pants, no makeup, no television, no dating. You couldn't put it down to piety because he was unbaptized and unchurched, which became a big problem when he died—my grieving mother, thinking about the man he killed, asked her pastor what would happen to his unbaptized soul. With unspeakable cruelty, the pastor explained that her father would burn in hell. Not for the death he caused but for missing his chance to dip in the River Jordan and take the sacred splash. The pastor was unaware that white lies are the most artful form of mercy.

Although he was named after Robert E. Lee, my grandfather was no southern grandee. In his rough-hewn way, he provided for my grandma Flossie and their twelve children, but his domestic regime was oppressive enough that his eight daughters were driven half-mad—or entirely mad in one case. My mother is one of the luckier ones, but even she talks about going under her childhood house to strike her own head with a rock and cry. That sounds over-the-top even for a depressed teenager, but it wasn't any more so than the general conditions at their crude homestead at the end of a three-mile dirt road where flea-ridden dogs were dipped in vats of kerosene and water moccasins slithered across the stock tank.

As I got into my twenties and beyond, I still struggled to understand what Grandpa was all about. Probably more than anything, toward the end of his life, I remember him eating Cool Whip straight from the container. He would happily eat the whole plastic tub, that distinct blue-and-white bowl, like it was gourmet ice cream. For eighty years he had only eaten chicken-and-biscuit farm food, and he had almost never been in a restaurant—indeed, he'd never left East Texas except to cross into Louisiana for some untouched trees—or maybe something else that I'll explain later. But he found magic in that white chemical fluff.

Decades earlier, before he married my kind, raspy-voiced, fire hydrant–shaped grandma, he had been a rowdy bachelor with a taste for liquor and an eye for dancehall girls. I said he *almost* never left the county where he had been born, but there was one exception: to dip into Louisiana to see a burlesque dancer named Jewel. We don't know if she was the cause of the violence in the woods because he would never say, and I didn't dare ask, but sometime in 1935 he beat a man to death, hid the body, and was never caught, never charged, never punished. That's the story I grew up with.

Back then, this part of Texas was an island unto itself: the mechanisms of government hardly existed so deep in the piney woods that sunlight struggles to reach the ground. Sometimes I hear hints of this darkness in songs that make me think of my grandfather, including one that seems ripped from a tale like the one I'm telling. After killing a man in Northeast Texas in 1918, the blues musician Lead Belly spent a few years in Huntsville prison, not far from my grandfather's land in East Texas, and eventually released a song often known as "In the Pines" (he retitled it "Black Girl" for a 1947 track that Kurt Cobain helped to popularize when Nirvana covered it). Although the song was probably written about the hills of Appalachia long before Lead Belly got his hands on it, I imagine him channeling his hard time in Huntsville when he sang the chilling chorus: "In the pines, in the pines, where the sun never shine, I will shiver the whole night through." (The rest of the song is about a brutal death in which a severed head is found a half-mile from the body.)

According to my mom, her father was haunted by what he did, something I learned when I interviewed people who knew him for a short documentary film about the killing. He lived another half-century filled with poverty and violence, until, as a faint shadow of his former self, he succumbed to emphysema in a Lufkin hospital, still eating Cool Whip like ice cream straight from the plastic tub.

In the decade before his passing, I spent some afternoons in his front yard while my cousins and uncles shot snakes out of trees and talked about things that were foreign to me, but I liked riding in Grandpa's old green Chevy pickup with the bullet holes in the back window that no one would ever explain. I would give anything to have that vintage truck now, but poor families don't have heirlooms or assets to pass down, only stories and questions about what happened and why it was so awful. I have literally *nothing* from my grandfather. Although my sweet grandma Flossie was keen to write me letters and send modest gifts when I was young, Grandpa never gave me a present, couldn't write me a letter, and certainly had nothing for me to inherit. What little he had (land and cattle) was mostly split between his sons, as my mom and her seven sisters found out. I'm not saying he lived a small life because I'll never know the full story, but the only place I ever saw him was at his house or in his truck on the way to pick up hay bales.

Stuck in the cowboy past, he was unlike everything I wanted to become. But he tolerated my ambitions even if he couldn't understand them. He lived long enough to know me as a graduate student, but with his third grade education, he had no idea what that meant. So, my mom cooked up a useful fiction—we told him I was a lawyer because it was something he could imagine that might bear some resemblance to my funny world of books and papers. It was a white lie worth telling. After all, he seemed pleased that someone in his family was getting out of the woods where so many wretched things happen. But one of the strange things about getting older is the realization that we share our path with all sorts of ghosts: part of me is still in those woods, dogged by the weight of familial experience that is both impossibly distant from me and utterly central to who I am.

It is in this curious, melancholy frame of mind in the first summer of the pandemic that I pull some Cool Whip off the top shelf of the fridge and give it a try. From the first taste I shudder and recall its origins in a food scientist's lab somewhere along the New Jersey Turnpike and imagine how, if left in the sun long enough, the white stuff might decompose back into a shame syrup of crude oil and albino Velveeta. Its essential fakery shines through when served as just one noxious dollop on an old tablespoon—yet for a second, it still helps me imagine some connection to my grandfather, and I dab a little on a cookie. An American Proustian moment: the cookie smeared with Cool Whip that opens up a whole world, a small pleasure in bleak times.

A medium-long time ago I made a documentary film about his guilt over killing a man. I was told that he was never the same, but there were other things that made him never the same: fingers cut off, a steel beam to the head, infant twins dying in the crib, twelve surviving children to raise. But I told myself: just because you live in a violent world doesn't make you a murderer. I told myself that I'll never know what happened in the woods that day, but I would prefer to think it was an accident, a fight gone wrong or something like that, even if the other possibilities haunt and confuse me when I wonder what I have inherited from him.

And this is where it sat for a couple of years, with me wondering about the vagaries of family history and trying to form a hopeful vision of a man I hardly knew. But on Mother's Day 2024, I did my mom a favor by visiting one of her sisters struggling with cancer in a small West Texas town—the only one of the twelve kids who had forsaken the piney woods to live west of I-35 simply because her husband took her to where he wanted to cut and sell cedar posts. Over lunch in a little house that had fallen into extraordinary disrepair, with yellow wiring exposed to the elements alongside the front windows and a kitchen floor that sagged like a hammock, it became clear that she knew more than my mother had told me about my grandfather. I soon realized that my aunt remembered more details than the people I had interviewed for the documentary film, all of whom my mother had steered me toward twenty years earlier. Mom had never suggested that I talk to this particular aunt, whose memory and savvy were obvious. Even at age eighty she had bright-red hair and sounded like Dolly Parton with a smoker's huskiness. She was a nonstop talker with a kind of country charisma that was hard to dislike.

On this Sunday afternoon it was just the three of us at the kitchen table: my wife, my aunt, and me. We were talking about her cancer treatments, her children, and the job that she quit just a few years earlier. Then, in the middle of a lemon cake she had whipped up for the occasion, she cocked her head funny and looked at me: "You know he kilt that man with an ax?" I blinked. I didn't know what she was talking about. "Oh yes, he kilt that feller with an ax and got himself five years in the penitentiary over in there." She pointed toward Louisiana, some four hundred miles away. "I mean, after it happened he was gone five years—*five years!*—and he never talked about where he was and what he was doing, not one time never. That's why when we was growing up, us kids figured he'd been locked up over there." She pointed toward the east again. "But we didn't dare ask him."

I had never caught of a whiff of this before—and there was more to hear. That Grandpa didn't give his kids Christmas presents. That his sisters were lifelong prostitutes in between stints of marriage. That he beat his kids with a metal-tipped belt until a teacher put together a petition for him to lose custody, but no one would sign because they were too afraid. That he threatened my sweet grandma. "Go get me that butcher knife from behind the couch," she told my aunt one time when they were cooking at her little house in the 1970s. My aunt asked why the butcher's knife would be hidden behind the couch. Grandma answered in her sweet southern rasp: "Oh, hon . . . he's been coming at me with that knife and I thought I best hide it."

Once I heard these stories, it snapped into place: I'm an orphan by necessity. I was right to cut myself off from both sides of my family at the age of eighteen. I knew then what I've tried to rewrite since: that there is something irredeemable in the family tree. That the past hurts. That sometimes we're better off not knowing. That family history is no Daughters of the American Revolution parade of historical grandeur if you come from poor folks with unhappy lives. That family sucks and tears, just as often as loves and supports.

I wish I had learned something redeeming about my grandfather. That he was gruff on the outside but thoughtful and reflective within. That he was kind to his children and animals. That he helped his neigh-

Fig. 6. My East Texas grandfather in 1963. Family photo. Photographer unknown.

bors bring in the hay. That he was admired for his wisdom in his little hamlet. But he was none of these things. Just violent, backward, and mean. Add getting struck by the boom pole, which is a twenty-foot-long steel beam with a claw for loading trees onto a trailer, and he probably had a traumatic brain injury that amplified his rage. I know his logging crew thought he was dead when they found him in the woods and never thought he would live through the night with a gaping head wound. But he did.

In the past decade I've reconnected with a few relatives, and I'm glad; they're great people who didn't deserve my banishment. But I couldn't sort out the good from the bad when I was eighteen; that's something that takes maturity. I only knew how to cut ties, head across the country, and never pick up the phone. Besides, Grandpa never said two words to me, at least not that I could comprehend, because what came out of his toothless mouth was a muddy stream of grunts and syllables that sounded like the marble-mouthed Boomhauer on *King of the Hill.*

I have a clearer picture of him now. I've given up on redemption and settled on an uglier truth: that this hard man who happened to appear on my family tree is nothing to me. He is but a "rank stranger," if I can borrow a line from a haunting tune about thwarted homecomings that the Stanley Brothers made famous in 1960. I already knew as much about my paternal grandfather, an alcoholic pedophile dockworker from Liverpool, but now I added my Texas grandfather to the list. They are rank strangers to me.

Now, at age fifty-seven, I know I can stop looking back, something I've done with a kind of hopeful speculation since I turned forty and started trying to find something good in the family stories I had heard about the old days. I guess I was looking for something to call my own in the world of my mother, who came of age in a mid-twentieth-century landscape that might as well have been the eighteenth century, so different was it from everything I know—even though it happened not long before I was born, in 1966, the same year *Sgt. Pepper's Lonely Hearts Club Band* appeared on turntables and ushered in the era in which I feel at home. Instead, I discovered a harsh truth: I have inherited nothing from these men, my two grandfathers, and for that I am grateful.

8 Jewel Thieves

I'm in a quiet neighborhood a few blocks from a busy road with drugstores, wig shops, and taco joints. A six-foot cedar fence runs down both sides of my property, which makes it a nice, secluded spot for an oversized kiddie pool, a raised bed garden, and a garage that's been converted into a modest office with cool cement floors. Behind the garage, pretty much out of sight, is a wobbly chain-link fence that is the only thing between me and a construction site on a sleepy cul-de-sac. Back there, totally out of view, is the only place where it's easy to hop the fence.

Late one afternoon, in the first year of the COVID shutdown, I was in a Zoom workshop with a handful of people when I caused a minor scene. I whipped off my headset and jumped out of my chair because someone had moved past my window in a part of the backyard where I've never seen a soul. At first the brain imagines something benign, and I half-imagined a friend playing a practical joke, but I quickly realized that it was something stranger—an agitated young Black man only a few feet from my office window. He was looking over his shoulder and heading toward the wooden gate that goes into the main part of the backyard. Assuming he was a burglar, I started banging on the window, like "Hey, what are you doing?" Then I jumped toward the door to confront him, but even before I got out of the one-room garage office, he had sprinted across the backyard, hopped the gate to the driveway, and bolted for the street. I've rarely seen someone move with such mad-dash velocity, and I knew it wasn't because of an irritated professor in cheese-stained basketball shorts and Adidas flip-flops. Something else was propelling him to move at warp speed, and it weirded me out. Like in the movies when you see some dim character staring at the antelopes tearing across the savanna and then it dawns on him, *Wait . . . what are they running from?* And suddenly a giant lion bounds over the hilltop. That was me (the dim character, not the lion). Feeling some version of this Simba scenario in my bones, I stood stupidly in the backyard for a few seconds, a little confused and kind of pissed, just looking toward the street, when a second young man came barreling through the gate next to the garage.

Now I really didn't know what was happening. These guys were clearly on the run, and something about their agitated vibe told me this wasn't a low-key crime of opportunity like taking tools and lumber from the construction site. Something worse was taking place, and whatever it was, these two men, soaked with sweat and panting hard, were in high-speed escape mode through my quiet, fenced-off backyard.

I wasn't really thinking during most of this. I had a kind of calm, clear alertness that was a surprise after years of generalized anxiety, but it wasn't helping me think—I couldn't form any proper thoughts at the pace things were moving. I only had quick impulses. Like: *I think these two guys are in it together, not chasing one another.* And: *I don't think these guys are here for me, whatever that means. I'm just in their way.* Either way, I was in the middle of something.

The second guy, another young Black man in workout clothes, sensed me as soon as he exploded through the gate. He hesitated, taking me in while I stood and looked at him, face to face, maybe five feet away. It was too sudden for me to get scared, but I was making unconscious but important assessments. At some deep level most men are aware of the size and strength of the guys around them, so even without thinking, I knew I was bigger, but he was built like a tank, was thirty years younger, and looked like he knew how to leave bruises. I may have been annoyed and feeling vaguely violated, but he was in a frenzy of self-preservation and might have a weapon.

At this point I should have run or at least stepped back. I don't know if I could hear the helicopters and sirens yet, but I was starting to have a sense that these two had done something serious. Looking back, I realize I didn't have to stay put, and I certainly didn't have to talk to him. But I did. Without looking down, I knew he was wearing shiny red track pants cut at the knee and a jersey with no sleeves, and somehow this made me think: *Talk to him like he's an athlete. Talk to him like I'm rooting for him to get away. Talk to him like I'm a coach.* Which is a mode of address that is so foreign to me that it might as well have been in Gaelic. I have a fairly quiet voice that has, somewhat annoyingly, been compared to Winnie the Pooh, but somehow I leaned in and barked "GO! GO! GO!" like you would at a football game when a running back breaks a tackle and sprints downfield.

In that second, I genuinely wanted him to get away from the cops or whoever was chasing him as long as he got out of my space. Like some stereotype of a bleeding-heart liberal, I already felt sorry for the Black teenagers on the run. Unsettled though I was, I still thought: *You're about to find yourself in the mindless viciousness of the Texas Department of Corrections. You're not even old enough to buy a beer, but here you are, running your last sprint under a blue sky.* I didn't know until a few minutes later that he had shot a security guard several times in a jewelry store robbery four blocks away and that he had also pistol-whipped a woman in the store.

After a faint micro-pause in which he got his bearings and made some sort of snap judgment, he stopped looking at me and bolted toward the street. He could easily have backed me into the office to hide from the cops or done the same in the house, where my wife was enjoying an otherwise quiet afternoon. But instead, he flew, just as fast as his friend, another kid who was about to be found by a SWAT team in a carport four houses down.

I watched him until he reached the street, and then I sprinted into the house yelling "Armed robbery!!!!!" to my wife, Monti. I don't know why I decided to say "armed" when I hadn't seen a weapon. At this point we had been together five very happy years and had never been through something like this. *What do you do? What is the protocol?*

It's like those CPR classes you take with a dummy in high school; you always forget the urgent thing you're supposed to remember when you really need it. Monti had to tell me to call 911. With our small home suddenly feeling very porous and flimsy, we locked the cheap hardware on the doors, and I grabbed the most lethal weapon I own: a small rolling pin. Then we spent the next two hours talking to 911, watching for updates on Twitter and the Citizen app, getting better info from neighbors on the Nextdoor app, and reading that there were five suspects on foot in the area—which meant some of them could be hiding in my garage or in the old camper in our driveway. That was when the fear finally hit.

I didn't want to have to look under the camper or behind the doors of the office, but I got tired of waiting for the police to come back to clear the property because they were too busy scouring the entire neighborhood with cars and dogs and copters. So, with my wife watching and ready to call 911 again, I checked the trailer and then went into the garage with the rolling pin in hand to make sure we were alone and safe. I must have looked like a very angry pastry chef. I almost never want a gun, but at that moment I wished I had something that at least looked like one. Maybe everyone needs a replica pistol that looks scary but can't drill a hole in flesh and bone. I don't know, but I remember feeling naked and vulnerable while the cops were running down the street with automatic weapons and Kevlar vests.

It took forever for things to settle down. We were in a blocked-off perimeter for several hours, scrambling to figure out if we were safe. Finally, we heard they had caught most of the five suspects, and we went out in our car to try to see what was really happening in the neighborhood. We counted more than twenty cop cars at the jewelry store four blocks away and another dozen in the streets around our home. Cops were acting like it was a mini-9/11, maybe because Austin doesn't get much violent crime for a city its size and the police get a little too excited to wear body armor and the rest of the military gear that has devolved to local police departments in recent decades.

Back at the house, we spent a lot of time just looking out the front window. German shepherds and tactical gear look odd in a part of town that is half–weird old-hippie Austin houses with yard art and half–gentrified mini-McMansions with Volvo SUVs out front. Our sleepy little home suddenly seemed charged with randomness and unpredictability in a way that was unnerving, but some neighbors took it in stride. Because the family next door has a baby and fat chickens too, my wife warned them that the canine unit was coming their way. "Okay, we'll put the chickens away," the neighbor said calmly.

The next day our other hippie neighbors said it was the most exciting thing to happen on the street in twenty years. At some point Monti searched the backyard, hoping to find a ruby necklace or a bag of cash. I'm pretty sure that any loot a person finds on their property in the state of Texas is "finders keepers," but we had no luck, or none that I would admit here.

And that's how it all went down when the jewel thieves fled through my backyard. As the days went on, I kept hunting for news reports that offered the full story, but local journalism is now so starved that you get nothing more than quick sketches and clickbait written by interns. At least I kept hearing semi-useful things from neighbors. My mechanic said that the FBI was still looking for CCTV footage a few days later. I also heard the jewelry store security guard, an older Black man, was recovering from his injuries—he had been hit with the butt of a shotgun and then shot with his own gun. Then I learned that the suspects were in my backyard only because they had wrecked their getaway car nearby and were pinned down by cops while I was wearing headphones for my Zoom workshop, living a life as conceptually distant from armed robbery as one could imagine.

More worryingly, I learned that the suspects were professionals. Apparently, low-level crime had declined in our city during the pandemic, but more aggressive criminals were making up the difference. Violence had exploded across Texas, especially in the largest cities, like Dallas and Houston.[1] A detective told my neighbor that these were not "a bunch of scared kids but an experienced crew from Houston." Apparently, the security guard wasn't the first person they had shot, and detectives from Houston and San Antonio descended on the city with their own charges against the crew. They still looked like scared kids to me—police reports said they were barely in their twenties, and two were teenagers who had made a profoundly stupid choice about how to survive the pandemic. Stupid, for sure, but not inexplicable.[2]

In the subsequent days, I obsessed over what had happened. Was I starring in some kind of NIMBY parable, a story about inner-city violence penetrating a largely white neighborhood? Probably. I found myself inside an old trope, doing the best I could to represent what happened without stigma or stereotype. Was it a story about two kinds of masculinity coming into contact? Definitely. After all, most American men are raised to jump into dangerous scenes like jacked-up action heroes (well, hypothetically), even if most of us spend our lives washing down Doritos with Mountain Dew and doing nothing more heroic than cutting the grass when there's a chance of rain. That's why I still felt compelled to assess my own response on the Texas man-o-meter. Should I have done more? Should I have wrestled the intruders to the ground and announced a citizen's arrest in a manly voice? Should I have channeled my inner Chuck Norris into a roundhouse kick? *Uh . . . only if I had a death wish.* I was lucky to skate through this encounter with two guys who were supremely amped up, probably still armed, and obviously desperate to escape the scene where they had pistol-whipped and shot people.

Once in a while, even much later, I still search for updates about the young men and what they did, but the news doesn't cover the sentencing and incarceration of jewelry thieves; it only likes the part with helicopters, guns, and chases. All I could find out was that they grabbed more than $200,000 worth of Rolex watches and caused $150,000 worth of damages to the jewelry store. The three arrested were ages eighteen, nineteen, and twenty-one. What really struck me was learning that they were all eligible for life in federal prison for robbery, conspiracy, and the use of a firearm during a crime. I hate the idea that I saw these two young guys in their last moments as free men—running from the cops in the middle of a pandemic that was making almost everyone extra crazy and desperate, running straight into a brutal system of incarceration that has given up on the notion of rehabilitation. Of course they need to go somewhere where they can't pistol-whip and shoot people for a good long time, but I can't see how keeping them in jail for sixty years until they rot makes any sense unless you're the kind of white person who can look at them and their crew and only see their race.

9 Our Degraded Chaplin

Dr. Steve Brule may be the necessary clown for our fetid times. He comes from the sprawling meta-humor universe of two forty-something filmmakers known as Tim and Eric, whose creative partnership has been enormously influential in weirdo comedy circuits for two decades and counting. In 2010 they created a series of short programs about the goofy Dr. Brule, who is embodied to perfection by the actor John C. Reilly. Nominated for an Academy Award for his work in *Chicago* and revered as much for his performances in Sam Shepard plays as in broad comedies like *Talladega Nights*, Reilly is one of the most gifted actors working today—which makes it even more spectacular that he has invested much of the past decade in a recurring role as a shambling, buffoonish man-child obsessed with bodily secretions.

In the worst moments of the pandemic, I turned to Dr. Brule for an unusual kind of comedy that is real, heartfelt, ironic, avant-garde, and idiotically lowbrow all at once. With his ill-fitting dirty-brown suit, unstylish spectacles, and puffed-up, receding Afro, Dr. Brule plays the host of a dopey human interest program that often requires him to muse about the meaning of life or interact with real people who are not in on the joke. A childishly know-nothing know-it-all, he is a tender but obtuse oaf who is set loose on unsuspecting civilians in a way that is more dada than disparaging. Unlike the Cambridge-educated Sacha Baron Cohen's comic creations, notably his fake Arab hip-hop interviewer Ali G and his quasi-Muslim idiot Borat, the Dr. Brule character is rooted neither in racism nor privilege. Instead, Dr.

Steve Brule is more of a goofball punk rock creation: the pudding-faced clown making a shambles of expertise, pretension, and certainty while on some desperate quest for love and acceptance.

Part of the joy of Brule is purely aesthetic. The look of the program is brilliantly inept, with the good doctor constantly staring at the wrong camera, which often seems to malfunction. Shot on digital video, the show is processed through a VCR in post-production to imbue the tape with a quivering 1980s verisimilitude (apparently the editors bang the top of the VCR to rough up the footage and give it the dated, shaky amateurism that is a hallmark of the program). Producer Tim Heidecker has said: "It's a show that genuinely feels like this guy made it himself. It's as if it's 4:30 in the morning and he had snuck into the studio to make this show without getting permission. It's bare bones. Lots of technical problems. Just a mess. The whole thing is a big mess. A big, beautiful mess."

The formula is bizarre but simple: take a Mr. Bean–like doofus, add brilliantly mangled English, and aim the character at various experts whose mastery he clumsily assaults with crossed eyes and hilarious malapropisms. The result is a kind of comedy that is so around the bend of idiocy that it comes out on the horizon of brilliance. What emerges is a cringy update on the comic fool: he is our degraded Chaplin, our Three Stooges on quaaludes, our Laurel and Hardy with surrealist farting and dada drooling, He often blurts out inappropriately raw and disturbing information about a childhood in which his mother tried to slowly poison him and generally seems like someone who is too wounded to thrive in a modern world that is clearly terrifying to him.

In his guise of an access TV interviewer wandering the streets for a story, Dr. Brule often encounters the kind of self-styled experts featured on local TV news. Although they seem willing to deal with him for the potential exposure (all views are good views!), they gradually realize that his goal is to perform a Rabelaisian waltz on their egos. Churches. Burn 'em. Priests? Ruffle them. Wizards? Deflate them. Intellectuals? Confound them. Children? Kill them. Wait, that was a typo. Dr. Brule is a kind of holy fool who doesn't have a violent urge in him.

Half the fun is purely linguistic. When he meets a sushi chef, he calls wasabi "guacamole" and burns his mouth like a dim child. *Puppets* become *pruppets*, *jackpot* becomes *jackprot*, *bingo* becomes *bringo*, *Christmas* becomes *Chrimbus*, and everyone is warned, *Don't be a dangus*. Perhaps his most famous line is the almost correct declaration that "Bill Grates Invented Michaelsoft [*sic*]." Brule is sloppy, childish, unattractive, obsessed with being first-rate but ashamed of being horrible, fixated on his mother but convinced that he is unloved, a numpty daydreamer, a shoddy broadcaster, but also a true American innocent who yearns for the status and allure of being cool even when he knows it far exceeds his capabilities.

I am clearly one of the experts that he would lampoon, but at the risk of being a *shrushi-eating dangus* with an outrageous analogy, I would humbly suggest that he is not unlike (wait for it!) . . . the Pompidou Centre in Paris, where the postmodern architects decided to expose the plumbing and ductwork for the first time in architectural history; likewise, Dr. Brule is an inside-out broadcaster, with the guts of the system on full display. He reveals the childishness, the secret longing, and the general ineptitude of a society that is very good at hiding the fact that it's sad, superficial, wounded, and not very good at most things. What would he say about the pandemic? According to Tim Heideker, he would tell us, "Wash your hands, you dummy"—otherwise, you'll get "the Crovid."

In this sense Brule feels perfect for the pandemic moment and its anxious aftermath, the same way *The Simpsons* felt like the embodiment of something essential about America in the 1990s and just as *Team America* and *Human Centipede* did in the early 2000s. With his awkward self-exposure and yearning for virtues he will never possess, he is the new American everyman, and no, the character would not work the same way as a woman: it requires a hint of smug white male privilege that can be dramatically deflated, forever confining the character to a tragic position in which he can only dream of normative masculinity with doltish wonder. Outmatched and probably out to lunch in a world dominated by the beautiful, the cynical, and the slick, he is the innocent loser, the scared child, the earnest flop, the ugly duckling, the awkward soul, and he is all of us.

10 The Aging Process

Your grandma's house didn't always look and smell that way. It took many years and many small increments for the full elder effect to get locked into place. I know it's hard to believe, but Grandma wasn't born with the smell of Vicks VapoRub wafting from her polyester house dress while she soaked her feet in a vibrating pink plastic tub, just as Grandpa didn't always have those Dumbo-like ears with more hair than a Yeti. Like the Gobi desert or the various *Police Academy* sequels, it had to evolve over time.

But *how*, you may ask, no doubt with some trepidation if you're of a tender age not yet schooled in such matters? Well, it begins with small things designed to soothe an aching body, encourage deeper sleep, or prevent a cardiac arrest and gets filled in, piece by medical piece, as the human odometer approaches sixty, seventy, or eighty. After that, who can see the dashboard—and where are you going anyway?

People say fifty is the new forty. It's not. You don't feel forty or thirty or twenty when you've lived a half-century, even if you work out five times a day and wear the same clothes you wore on your BMX bike in 1982. Like facelifts and Spanx, age-inappropriate clothing is not much protection from the creeping immolation of time. I'm only fifty-six (!), and my bedroom is already filling up with life-sustaining gear that surely can't be mine: I thought I was relatively healthy, fit, and youngish when the pandemic started. Now I know that for me, as much as the nation in which I live, the great descent has begun.

It starts small enough, nothing more than a mouth guard to prevent my anxious jaw from converting my teeth into a fine powder of bone. Then, of course, you need the heating pad for the aching back. The humidifier is important for soothing desiccated nasal passages, which also demand that you purchase a whooshing air purifier. Then comes the heavy artillery: the CPAP machine because who wouldn't want to look like Darth Vader with asthma? Nothing says sexy like CPAP!

All this came into view when I woke up one shapeless pandemic morning, uncomfortably aware that "waking up" is less of the discrete event it once was and more of an extended process that unfolds over several stages of painful stretching, noisy joint de-cricking, and sore finger rubbing. The full elder effect includes many more degradations that I have yet to encounter, but I expect them to arrive soon like a FedEx package from a mortician with a sense of humor. I guess it can't get too much worse than the day when I drank denture cleaner (by accident, thank you very much). I was using it to clean my calcified mouth guard but was exhausted and the toxic solution looked like a glass of delicious Gatorade. The next thing I knew, I was calling poison control and trying to explain that *yes, I'm the same person who called last month because I accidentally ingested my dog's tranquilizers.*

I don't know how it happened, but I know this much: aging in America is terrifying for all but the very rich. The rest of us are not allowed to stall out because we need money for rent and medications no matter what our age; we must keep working just to keep the lights on. Amazingly, *The Guardian* reported that the number of American workers seventy-five and older will increase by 96.5 percent by 2031.[1] I know my dad only retired at age eighty-one because he could no longer hear the customers on the floor of the Home Depot where he had worked in the tool department for fifteen years (masks undermined his lip reading).

Yet lifestyle magazines, conservative thinktanks, and batshit bloggers are already repackaging this neoliberal endurance contest as a glorious jaunt, reframing American elder labor as incredibly good fortune. I just read a blog with the horrible title "WHY YOU NEED TO WORK FOREVER AND NEVER RETIRE," and I wanted to cry. The general tenor of these pieces is bizarre: Isn't Grandma lucky to have free air-conditioning during her shift at the Walmart? Isn't it great that Grandpa's job at the Burger King keeps him nimble? What's next in the grand repackaging of decline? Maybe, thanks to science and delusional marketing, in our lifetime we will be forced to witness the *very first superhot one-hundred-year-olds . . . Playboy* or *Esquire* will have a cover screaming THE HAWT HUNDREDS . . . Videos on Pornhub will promise "100 Reasons to Come," while the headlines about new trends on Grindr scream, "Seasoned to Perfection!" and "Move Over Daddy—Make Room for Great-Grandpappy!" Young people will compete on dating apps to "do a century" by seducing smooth-cheeked centenarians whose flawless outer beauty, puffed up by Botox and expert craftsmen, will be quietly betrayed by inner rot and decay, leading to a disturbing new phrase entering the language: "humpbrittle bones."

On the more hopeful side, all this extra living should produce some sort of insight, perspective, or intergenerational generosity. The humility of losing your youthful swagger must yield some loftiness of spirit, some deeper understanding of the human comedy that is good for something other than working at Costco and then watching *Matlock* reruns, right? Why has our culture demeaned aging while celebrating eternal youth? In Japan the old are volunteering to pick up radioactive waste to spare youthful bodies from cancer that will set in ten, twenty, years later; in the United States elders are an untapped resource for national reinvention. Rather than worrying about irrelevance, medical bills, and the grave, they could tutor, teach, mentor, and inspire if given the chance (or the resources and support). But instead, we are stuck in the American way of aging and dying: relatively alone, underappreciated, with nothing more than big TV to distract us from oblivion. It's a uniquely American tragedy, this cruel devaluing of the old.

11 Subdivision

I sit in warmish water, my feet dangling between limestone boulders and curious brown perch that make their home in this little man-made lake in the hills west of Austin. Above me is a hazy August sky—the air is gray and gummy. Here, in the midst of a particularly fetid summer, I can almost feel Texas expanding, puffing up like a balloon that swallows you whole. There is no way out when you're this far in.

I have spent most of my adult life in this vast oil and cattle kingdom where fantasies of secession still get lip service. Technically, the state can't secede and form its own country, but suburban Republicans and actual cowboys like to pay homage to that old fantasy of independence—and I can understand how someone might think that Texas could be its own nation, mostly because a person can drive all day at eighty miles per hour and still find themselves stuck inside its excoriating heat. Plus, it has a long history of doing whatever it feels like doing—talking loud, spending big, and boasting plenty—though that gets old pretty quick if you're not into that sort of thing. All of which may explain the complicated feelings I had when I left the lake and flopped into my car for the ride home.

On the long drive back into town, I whiz past exclusive subdivisions squirreled away in the gorgeous hills, some of them almost totally out of view, with nothing that could serve as a good landmark—and nothing with any style or verve or eccentricity, just some Republican signs, boats on trailers, and a lot of expensive late-model cars in front of hulking houses on half-acre properties. Out here, where the unadorned

Texas Hill Country can still dazzle you with its charms, the grandeur of the land has been concealed by generic calm and tacit exclusion—and that is entirely by design. Along with the wealthiest suburbs outside Dallas, Fort Worth, Houston, and San Antonio, this is the prosperous part of Texas that keeps hard-right Republicans in statewide office, tyrannizing trans people and generally making life miserable for progressives, despite the fact that Texas cities lean pretty blue. Out here an elite realtor can sell a hundred million dollars' worth of property in a single year. The top realtor in the fancy hills west of Austin is (of course!) a glamorous, toothy blonde who must have been president of Tri-Delt at Southern Methodist University in the aughts. In a full-page magazine advertisement, she boasts that she sold more than $130 million in houses in the previous year and that her career total is over a billion dollars. Think about this. A single person has sold over *a billion dollars* of mansions in gated subdivisions and waterfront properties where you can land your seaplane on the Colorado River and taxi up to a private dock—all in a career that couldn't be longer than fifteen years.

I love the land out here. A heavily treed geography of rolling hills that is considered the dividing line between the American Southeast and Southwest, the Hill Country is one of the undeniably gorgeous parts of the state. But in the last twenty years, new tech money and old-money Texans have conquered and altered its charms. What is emerging is much different than the pretty, unpretentious landscape that attracted Willie Nelson to build his ranch here a half-century ago. Instead, the land west of Austin has become an exercise in Neo-Gilded Age containment: the creation of a "safe space" for opulence that makes the best land inaccessible to the rest of us.

A lot of things aren't present in these super high-end suburbs (economic diversity, used record stores, people of color). They could've done anything with all their wealth, on all this beautiful land, but instead they've created a perfect habitat for what the kids call *basic*—a kind of suburban white hyper-affluence that revels in pumpkin spice lattes, J. Crew ensembles, cold-pressed juice, and fleecy Ugg boots. I don't object to anyone's chosen footwear or coffee concoctions, of course, but I worry when they seem attached to wasteful consumption patterns and reactionary politics. These blandly grandiose McMansions, aggressively vast lawns, and high-end Land Rovers are not innocent choices but often somewhere on the spectrum of fascist aesthetics that is creeping into American life. To be clear, I'm not saying they are fascist per se, but these lifestyle choices are often *authoritarian adjacent*. If you really think about the implied philosophy of the elite American suburb, and not just the gated ones, it represents a serene form of domination over nature and sociology. It brings the landscape to heel no less so than the gardens at Versailles and the aristocratic passions of yore, just as it keeps the great unwashed (me!) from accessing its loveliness. The scarcity of public hiking trails or public access to rivers is appalling in the Hill Country. One time I rented a Jeep to see if I could find a nice spot along a river where my wife and I could swim. We drove for a few hours, hunting for possible access points, before giving up and driving to a San Marcos strip mall for a fro-yo. Almost all the good land is private in this part of Texas.

So much of unconscious American MAGA privilege looks like this now: flocks of white people in SUVs racing to town from their suburban homes, each one a portrait in unsustainable living, each one chasing a single-serving dream of security and safety while fleeing from a meaningful engagement with racial, cultural, and political diversity. As Austin has boomed crazily for the last two decades, these curated suburbs have quickly covered the recently pristine landscape with the architecture of waste—thousands of toy castles of sheetrock and foam (literally) for orthodontists and software developers and eventually, by the 2020s, celebrity "cool" dudes like podcaster Joe Rogan and tech titan Elon Musk. It feels soulless and friendless to me, but that's probably because I don't have any friends in 20,000-square-foot houses. These folks are not interested in bearded humanities professors even if I often teach their children, a fact that they tolerate rather than embrace. Out here in the luxo-burbs, I'm on their turf, and I keep my opinions to myself. Wacky professors, conceptual artists, social workers, banjo players, kindergarten teachers, freelance jugglers—they don't live out here in $2 million houses without an indie coffee shop in sight.

From an urban studies perspective, the upscale American suburb is easy to mourn or mock: the lack of public transportation, the low walkability score, the heavy weight of conformity, the stultifying whiteness, the environmental waste, and even the existential challenge of living in a bubble of sameness. But it's not hard to understand why people end up here when they have been programmed for a suburban outcome. When you make some real money, you're told that the only place you can find complete safety, green lawns, and good schools is in the 'burbs, not in the allegedly chaotic city center, with its rutted roads and endless thrum of diversity.[1] Austin has some closer-in neighborhoods that attract billionaires like the jewelry mogul Kendra Scott, but building in existing neighborhoods doesn't bug me the same way the conquest of the pristine Hill Country does.

And for what? These developments are ecologically and socially dubious; they don't have the interwoven, democratic feel of living in a small town or in a diverse urban neighborhood; they are filled with unethically grand estates—yet they're sold as the ultimate in safety and success for the modern upscale family.

Of course, suburbs don't have to be this way, and to the north of Austin, a different kind of suburban story is unfolding. As the historically Black and Latino neighborhoods of East Austin have experienced intense levels of gentrifications, people of color have been moving out and heading north to suburban towns like Pflugerville, Texas—so much so that Austin is the only major U.S. city to lose Black population in the past decade. Are people of color happily cashing out on their East Austin real estate and moving to a suburban dreamhouse with a large lot? Or are they being tragically displaced by white hipsters, speculators, and rising costs? It's a complicated story, one that defies the easy generalizations about gentrification, but one result is clear: what was a small ranching community in the 1980s known as Pflugerville has become a diverse suburb with good schools and relative prosperity.[2]

I don't see the same hope in the rich suburbs where Trumpism festers on manicured lawns that often feature an enormous Texas flag like something out of *Triumph of the Deep-Fried Will.* Driving to the top of a huge hill on the western edge of the Austin city limits, I gaze across a horizon of eerily similar houses in a brand-new development with one of the typical names: Brittany Oaks, Coldwater Canyon, Sycamore Crest, The Lakes at Hawthorne Trail, Somerset Crossing, Deerland Estates, Rhinoplasty Grove, or some other combination of impressive-sounding words that don't really mean anything (there is a website that will even name your subdivision for you). Whatever their faux English name might be, these massive Hill Country developments are the definition of unsustainable and wasteful: giant lawns that require endless watering, giant houses that require massive air-conditioning, giant commutes that require cars, fuel, and ever-widening roads.

These posh subdivisions are not ugly. They're more like a face that is superficially attractive but somehow off. Like the face of Ghislaine Maxwell, the English socialite better known as Jeffrey Epstein's alleged partner in pedophilia. The "offness" is unsettling when mixed with beauty and wealth—like it's too easy to see under the perfect smile to some inner deficiency or rot. In the case of the super high-end hills of Austin, you have to look beneath the luxury veneer to realize that something unsustainable and undemocratic is hidden within.

I understand why people want to secede from the precarity-filled country we inhabit, and why they want to create their own private enclave yet still call themselves "Austin residents." We all need our buffer zones in the jarring 2020s: noise-canceling headphones, immersive videogames, deluxe SUVs, fantasy sports, VR headsets, or suburban bliss—they're all ways of blocking out a reality that overwhelms or unnerves. But we still have an obligation to choose the *least harmful buffer possible*, not one that is ecologically problematic, socially exclusionary, experientially homogenous, and ultimately antidemocratic. As the scholar Marco d'Eramo has argued about the "Senile Utopias" of Arizona and other suburban "lifestyle centers": "You don't meet the unknown much in a closed environment . . . . There's little chance of excitement or adventure in a place where everything's kept so tightly under control."[3] That's how I see these prosperous Sunbelt suburbs: as the opposite of humanity's greatest creation, namely, the diverse, cosmopolitan city, which is the closest thing we have come to semi-achieving a semblance of "spatial justice," a geographical concept that describes a place that encourages the equitable intermingling of classes, races, languages, and other factors, all the things that the high-end suburbs are generally designed to filter out.[4] Instead of bringing us together as citizens, these expensive subdivisions do exactly what their name suggests, separating and subdividing us by class, race, and political orientation.

What if we stopped subdividing ourselves? Better-designed cities would make urban living more appealing to everyone, even the high earners who have fled to the Sunbelt suburbs. Despite their imperfections, places like Copenhagen, Vancouver, and Singapore suggest it's possible, if you embrace the kind of measured urban planning that real estate developers and other commercial interests generally fight against. We could also reinvest in small towns that foster a kind of civic intimacy because when done right, which includes an attention to diversity that was often historically lacking, the American small town is a wonderful little machine for living. I grew up in a town of less than a thousand people, a place so small that we could live without a car, and I still watch *The Andy Griffith Show* and wonder if we could create a funkier, more-inclusive, somewhat punk rock version of Mayberry. And of course, given the dazzling natural beauty of our continent, we could even explore rural options that connect us to the power of the unspoiled land in ways that could be deeply sustainable. These are all noble ways of organizing human experience, something that the walled-off, super exclusive American suburb mostly is not.

12 Selma

It started, like so many things in America, with a movie. I was on a COVID tour of the Deep South with my wife, Monti. Cooped up for long enough to make a baby, if we were so inclined and twenty years younger, still afraid to fly for virological reasons but willing to drive, we headed in a new direction for a pandemic getaway, promising ourselves that we would minimize human contact and cooking up other rationalizations for a long road trip in the middle of killer plague chaos. That's why instead of shooting up the interstate that slices through Austin to see Monti's family in Wichita, Kansas, or heading northwest to the mountains we love near Taos, we went east through the high-speed swirl of Houston, stopped for a night in an unusually desolate version of Baton Rouge that was in COVID shutdown, picked up lunch in the charming miniature New Orleans that is Mobile, Alabama, and finally landed eight hundred miles away in Montgomery, Alabama.

Who goes to Montgomery during a pandemic? Or perhaps, who goes to Montgomery at all? One answer is *guilty white people* who have been reading about civil rights and queuing up inspirational movies set in the area, about which I'll have more to say later. But equally important is the fact that Montgomery isn't bad for touristy things. Despite its toxic associations with the segregationist governor and presidential candidate George Wallace, this attractive city has begun facing its difficult past, or at least parts of it, in an admirable way. Home to Rosa Parks, Big Momma Thornton, Tallulah Bankhead, Hank Williams, Nat King Cole, Zelda Fitzgerald, and for a while her husband, F. Scott Fitzgerald, Montgomery is layered with a complex history, both good and bad, that you can feel in its tree-lined streets and old brick buildings. Dr. Martin Luther King preached at the beautiful Dexter Avenue Church downtown, just twenty feet in front of the bus route where Rosa Parks refused to give up her seat in 1955. Less gloriously, in 1861 Jefferson Davis established the Confederacy's first "White House" (and how!) in a stately Montgomery home that belonged to Zelda Fitzgerald's grandfather. Not surprisingly, we had a surreal and moving experience there, exploring three painful moments from our perverse national pageant.

The first stop was 1932, a moment like the present when assumptions about work, life, safety, and stability were getting banged up hard. Thanks to the corporate magic of Airbnb, we stayed in the home where F. Scott Fitzgerald wrote *Tender Is the Night* and his wife, Zelda, finished her only novel, *Save Me the Waltz*. We assumed the house would be filled with Jazz Age exuberance and groovy flapper vibes, but their year in the house was a miserable one. They fought and drank too much, and she ended up in a mental hospital for the bipolar episodes that dogged her until her death some years later in a hospital fire that killed nine patients caged inside their rooms. When she was identified only by her expensive slippers, her famous husband was already long dead from a heart attack and wild living.

Upstairs in their Montgomery home, we made pasta and checked email in handsome rooms that looked not so different from when the glamorous young couple lived there. Downstairs is a small museum dedicated to Scott (of course), not the overshadowed spouse he liked to plagiarize.[1] During our few days in the house, I discovered that the quotations plastered around the property revealed an emerging truth: that Zelda's voice is freer and more contemporary in the 2020s, while F. Scott's sounds stilted and immature in his fixation on wealth and nostalgia. Although I have a Gatsby-obsessed friend who will argue otherwise, I think Scott might need to forfeit his comfy chair in the pantheon of American letters and let Zelda take a seat.

Don't get me wrong—it's still an amazing thing to sleep in Scott and Zelda's old joint, even if sometimes they strike me like the Kardashians of 1920s literature—as in, famous for being famous. And I was going to say, "And for being good looking," but check the photos for yourself. As Larry David would say with a shake of his head, "Not so much."

One morning, in the spacious front yard of the Fitzgeralds' elegant brick home, I opened a tiny glass door to a mailbox-sized lending library that offered *The Sisterhood of the Traveling Pants* but no books by the former residents. Nearby I read a historic marker with a ponderous quote from Scott. In the slightly purple-tinged prose that always strikes me as his Achilles heel, he talks about the inability to feel the world around you as you age: "Now once again the belt is tight and we summon the proper expression of horror as we look back at our wasted youth. Sometimes, though, there is a ghostly rumble among the drums, an asthmatic whisper in the trombones . . . and it all seems rosy and romantic to us who were young then, because we will never feel quite so intensely about our surroundings anymore."

What a load. He was only 35, not 102, when he wrote this. He may have felt cut off from the pleasures of his reckless youth, but it was probably a deficiency that was unique to someone who filled expensive hotel rooms with empty bottles, because even as I'm moving further into the final third of my life, I experience the world just as intensely, often painfully so, as I did as a morose teen with a general vibe of hurt feelings. If anything, sensations wash over me now in a way that wasn't even possible when I was young because I know more about suffering, longing, and sacrifice, both on a personal and collective level. And as my wife and I set off from the Fitzgeralds' house for an encounter with the legacy of racial exclusion and violence in America, I worry about letting the full force of emotion wash over me. Which is to say, Fitzgerald didn't know much about getting older.

We were going next to 1895, where we found one small sliver of the long history of lynching in the United States, a brutal practice that finally received its first museum and memorial ever in downtown Montgomery in 2018. The Legacy Museum is compact but powerful: it should be one of the first stops on any itinerary for so-called American history buffs, who spend far too much time on Civil War battlefields and presidential birthplaces that only confirm triumphalist narratives about American ingenuity and exceptionalism. But as important as the museum is, the most substantial impact, aesthetically, politically, emotionally, comes across town within the new lynching memorial, whose grim sophistication and conceptual eloquence is evocative of the Holocaust memorial in Berlin. With its hanging steel boxes, each roughly the size of a coffin and engraved with the name, date, and county where someone was murdered, often with the force of law behind the killing, the space feels like a cemetery elevated to the level of extraordinary political art. I stood beneath many of the boxes that hang overhead, and I looked for ones marked for Texas. As you can imagine, they are not hard to find. Moving uncertainly through the sprawling memorial, I paused before the two names engraved under the perversely named Liberty County: John Cherry and Alexander White. I do not know their full stories other than what some vague newspaper accounts allege about them murdering a man, but I know their names and the date of their demise: "06-10-1895." The county in question is just outside of Houston, and I later realized that I knew someone whose great-grandfather was sheriff there around 1895. Maybe I should have asked her about it, but I didn't (mostly because this person is an anti-racist scholar who has enough trouble with her own family history for me to add another unsettling possibility). Anyhow, one of the by-products of civil rights tourism for white people is realizing that what might seem distant is in fact close to home.

Our final stop was 1965. Sitting in Scott and Zelda's living room, on a green velvet sofa amid other period furnishings, with a large portrait of the author gazing down on us from above the fireplace, we did something the famous writer had failed to do: we reckoned with the pain of American apartheid, if only for a couple of hours and in a very circumspect and privileged way. With my laptop open on the coffee table, we watched the 2014 film *Selma* with uncertain expectations. I heard that it was just "okay." After a friend told me that, I expected something maudlin, dull, and preachy, but that is not the case. It is a powerfully acted and directed film about a crucial moment in the civil rights movement when Dr. Martin Luther King, John L. Lewis, Bayard Rustin, Ralph Abernathy, Coretta Scott King, Viola Liuzzo,

Fig. 7. Selma's National Memorial for Peace and Justice, dedicated to the four thousand African Americans lynched between 1877 and 1950, December 2020. Photo by author.

James Reeb, and other men and women crossed a bridge lined with racist cops in Selma, Alabama, in order to march to the state capitol in Montgomery and demand the unimpeded right to vote.

I almost never use the word *hero* when teaching courses in American studies because it seems dated and dorky. Besides, Americans looking for heroes are usually looking in the wrong direction: Washington, Jefferson, Teddy Roosevelt, and others have been mythologized into something they never were, and it often serves a purpose that is problematic, if not destructive. But the people who strategized and marched in Selma seem like heroes to me. Mostly ordinary people (I'm not sure anyone could call Dr. King "ordinary"), they were risking their lives for equal justice under the law. Despite a brutal police response and the usual forms of state repression that have made anti-Black violence one of the defining features of the American experiment, the march over the Edmund Pettus bridge became a turning point for many reasons, in part because the enormous media coverage it generated compelled the Johnson administration to pass the Voting Rights Act later that year.

The bridge itself is nothing special and looks much the same today as it does in the old footage that appears in *Selma* and documentaries like *Eyes on the Prize*. Famously, it's named after a Klansman and Confederate general who deserves little more than oblivion or scorn, but his name remains for some interesting reasons. One we heard was that Black Jubilee dancers take pleasure in stomping their feet on "Pettus's bridge" in the name of African American freedom. Others want to keep the name because it's been transformed into a symbol of resistance. As Representative John Lewis argued: "The irony is that a bridge named after a man who inflamed racial hatred is now known worldwide as a symbol of equality and justice. It is Biblical—what was meant for evil, God uses for good."

On the east side of the bridge are some homespun memorials to the events of 1965: high school student murals, small rocks painted with sayings from John Lewis, a hand-lettered sign that reads TOMB OF THE UNKNOWN SLAVE, and other items that are powerful in their sincerity but still haphazard and temporary in a way that doesn't match the significance of what happened on the bridge. On the south side of the Alabama river, there is no official memorial or museum, no expensive federal complex, only a closed storefront for the Bridge Crossing Jubilee Headquarters and Souvenir Shop, which, despite some earnest murals on its side, looks pretty sad.

On the north side of the bridge, which spills into the main drag of Selma, we found a small visitors center that was empty except for a tall, friendly man working the desk. Seeming delighted we had arrived because visitors were rare during the pandemic, he pulled out a map with places to explore in the city, and so out we headed. We expected the kind of sights we'd found an hour away in the much larger Montgomery, with its blend of stately homes, a prosperous-seeming commercial district, and impressive museums. That is not what we found in Selma.

Selma is not thriving. We walked the main street and saw vacant stores with strange things left behind—old mannequins, a gun range target with bullet holes in the neck of the figure marked "Susan," and a bizarre metal statue of a white-sheeted spirit (a strange allusion in these parts) named "Jeffrey the Ghost" that was a failed attempt to attract tourists, from what I later read.

Past the edge of downtown things got worse. I've been all over the United States, but I've never seen such dilapidated buildings, most of them half-imploded for several blocks in every direction, and this was even before the tornadoes of January 2023 swept through the city. Dozens of graceful buildings that must have been beautiful a century ago were now boarded up to die, most of them worn and sooty. The metal used to shutter ornate arched windows had rusted dark brown on buildings that were probably erected around the time of the Civil War. In 2016 a Black worker was paid twenty dollars to spend half a day helping to demolish a Selma cotton warehouse built in the 1870s, recovering five hundred bricks. He told a reporter for *The Guardian* what he thought of his demolition job: "This is slave work, that's what it is, but the only work around. Kind of funny when you think about it, because them bricks were probably made by slaves. That is Selma for you, though: still a city of slaves."[2]

Fig. 8. Downtown Selma during pandemic, December 2020. Photo by author.

Amid this near-total dead zone were a few signs of life: stooped old men wandering the sidewalk, a kid on a bike, a mysterious building with some sort of clientele coming and going. Later we drove to the white side of town, where we found some middle-class homes and even a small country club, neither of which erased the feeling that Selma feels broken. Racism wrecked this city, and it hasn't yet found a way to recover.

We drove out of Selma feeling somewhat shaken. Five hours later, in Jackson, Mississippi, we did what we had done before on our COVID tour of the Deep South: pick a hotel chain that promised extra health precautions. And indeed, our hotel had put a bold blue sticker with a COVID pledge over each door, but this was just superficial quarantine theater: in reality the staff and guests wore no masks (or half-wore them), and no one seemed to have gotten the memo about the pandemic. The worst offenders are often the rowdy white guys who seem proud to strut around maskless. To them it's an act of heroic defiance, as if they imagine themselves storming the beach in Normandy on the way to magic liberty land because they won't wear protection against a lethal disease. Local conversations and AM radio alike provide a worrying sense of southern stereotypes coming true: callers are complaining to the host about the "China flu" and slinging the name "Obama" like a cuss word. As I moved around the dull hideousness of suburban Jackson looking for something to eat, I kept hearing The Smiths' song "Girlfriend in a Coma" in my head with my new lyrics: *Redneck with a death wish. . . . Oooh ooh oooh, it's serious!*

It's pitiful but not surprising how little most white people know about the deeper mechanics of racism, which is the essential fact of life in the United States (if you say, no, it's "liberty," you are a stone-cold moron or a grifty ideologue). People don't know what to do about structural inequities that have given them a lifetime of benefits (albeit without much contentment in many cases; privilege without satisfaction is a paradox that is little understood). As much as I try to wriggle toward the light, I know I'm ultimately in the same camp.

A day later, after driving across northern Louisiana, we stopped near my parents' small town outside Tyler in East Texas. I looked out my hotel window and wondered what kind of soulless maniac builds a gleaming new six-story hotel that overlooks a shopping center parking lot the size of Rhode Island. Of course, the front of the hotel had a normal parking lot, but I'm talking about the back, where most of the rooms were built facing a kind of consumer oblivion, with no trees, no grass, no rivers, to contemplate; across a half-mile of asphalt, nothing was visible but Petco, World Market, Ross, and a dozen other chain stores. Only in America.

13 Pigeons

We're cutting from the heart of Texas to the Colorado Rockies, doing what everyone does to get across barren stretches of desert: *driving way too fast.* Why not slow down and savor the view? Well, we're in a rough part of a rough state. Take a denuded dust zone and add slaughterhouse stench and spent mobile homes and yawning dead towns and multigenerational hopelessness, and you can start to envision this grim landscape of flat land, rough little burgs, and endless drives. This is real West Texas, which isn't anything like the converted art town known as Marfa, where you can find a few minimalist boutique hotels, three or four fancy restaurants, some 3D-printed houses that list for $2.3 million, and a few dozen half-million-dollar ranch homes painted to look like art galleries. Nor is it the stunning desert kingdom of Big Bend National Park, the gentle mountains around Fort Davis or Alpine, the arid border charm of El Paso, or the dusty glamour of the chaotic border town called Terlingua. No, this is the other 90 percent of the region, which isn't cool, isn't pretty, and isn't getting hipster visitors from New York City looking for Claes Oldenburg sculptures and Donald Judd boxes. Here a desert ferocity extends pretty much from the Mexican border all the way up into the geographically distinct northern tip of the state known as the Panhandle, where you can find some of the largest slaughterhouses in the country, not to mention one of the world's tallest crosses, a two-hundred-foot-tall, privately erected structure along the interstate that can be spotted from twenty-five miles away—or thirty miles if you're a true believer.

Out here the wind blows so hard it sucks, and life is unspeakably hard on rural people in a way that the film *Nomadland* revealed to some audiences (*Sacre bleu! Hardworking poor white people in America!*) but which has always been obvious to disenfranchised folks living anywhere on the arid soil that stretches a thousand miles from West Texas to the Pacific Ocean (and I include my sweet Aunt Helen in this category because she worked fifty-five years as a waitress in the same West Texas roadhouse, serving chicken fried steaks and guiding patrons to a salad bar made from a converted bathtub). Not always, but generally speaking, what you see out here is ugly in a way that is exhausting. The smell of death feels like it's everywhere, thanks to industrial abattoirs, along with the haunting feeling that if you ran out of gas, you could just disappear into a landscape that literally provided the backdrop for the Coen Brothers' dark desert noir, *No Country for Old Men*. One particularly galling example of the brutality in these parts: in the Panhandle town of Dimmit in 2023, an explosion at a dairy farm killed eighteen thousand cows. That's about 20 percent of the number of cows slaughtered in America in a single day. (Yes, it was an "accident," but here's a grim fact that makes it seem less random: 6.5 million animals died in barn fires in the United States between 2013 and 2023).[1]

So, we flee this somber, dusty landscape, my wife and I, racing down narrow roads where the gas stations are fifty miles apart, speeding northwest until we cross the state line into New Mexico and ultimately Colorado a few hours later. Once in the mountains, we wind our way through desolate valleys dotted with old mining towns and even an abandoned utopian project from the 1960s where some artists thought they could create a counterculture utopia (almost no trace of it remains). Finally, many hours later, we reach Colorado Springs, dreaming of cool mountain breezes and groovier times.

It's not as stoner-crunchy as you might expect. Sure, you can take some gummies and mountain bike all the way to the natural foods co-op in your Phish T-shirt, but it's also the regional epicenter of Colorado's dead-eyed Trumpistas and angry suburban evangelicals, who spent most of the pandemic screaming that face masks are a Satanic conspiracy like fluoride, evolution, and ethnic studies programs. Like much of the American West, Colorado Springs is a paradoxical place—despite the tension in the air, the land is fantastic to behold. Few things are as spectacular as the unspoiled Colorado landscape.

The first thing we did was hike up a long dirt road to some gorgeous rock formations on the eastern edge of town. As you approach them illuminated in the golden sunset, they glow with otherworldly colors: blue, turquoise, yellow, red. But as we walked up and got closer, we realized that their only true color was red—the rest of it was nothing but spray paint. Thousands of cans of spray paint, more than you would need to tag an entire subway system, had seeped into the stone and earth. Wherever we looked, Technicolor proclamations of love and stupidity have altered what was once a sacred place, a natural cathedral of stone more than one hundred feet high and five hundred feet across. Dozens of spires and stone outcroppings, even trees, leaves, and gnarled roots, have all been shat upon with the human excrement of spray paint. In our lesser moments as a species, we are little more than pigeons.

We hike back to the car and leave for food. Winding up a mountain road, rimmed with glorious peaks and ridges, we stop at a restaurant that looks more like an abandoned massage parlor than a place for food. Is this where zombies get postapocalyptic hand jobs? It's awful; it's gross; it's creepy—a ruined-looking building with no sign of life. Unsure what to do, we drive slowly to the backside of the place and notice an open door to the kitchen. I get out of the car and look around. No people; nothing. "Hi," I say quietly through the doorway, which somehow scares the daylight out of the young woman inside making pizza. "Everyone sneaks up on me" she sighs. I say sorry and order a pizza that I tote back to the car. It's greasy and heavy, and soon we've planted the seeds of revolution in our bellies. Too much Coke and gooey-gross pizza mixes poorly with the anxious zeitgeist of the 2020s.

Now here we are, looking for hope and restoration in one of the most beautiful mountain ranges on the planet. Despite the occasional spray paint vandals, the Rockies are still sublime in a way that can feel mystical. It's a place that should be sacred, not scarred with fast-food

Fig. 9. Spray-painted trees in the mountains above Colorado Springs, July 2020. Photo by author.

joints, evangelical mega-churches, and schools of war (the Air Force Academy is nearby). A sublime landscape deserves better than the crude extractivist ideology that has been imposed on it. Maybe in some parallel universe, the magnificence of the American continent would infuse its occupants with a spirit of nobility and wisdom, elevating their schemes for living above the level of crude hustle or dumb delusion, but not in this one, at least not since colonization and conquest.

Here's my claim about the great American derailing. I say, we've made a mess of it on almost every level: ecology, economy, culture, infrastructure, ideology, you name it. Of course, we've made beautiful progress in a few parts of civic life, but overall, we've been doing donuts in the Walmart parking lot of American politics since the sixties. If we were in *Easy Rider* on our choppers in 1969, we would say, "We blew it, man." We just blew it. Could we rebuild the engine and start over? Sure, it's always possible in theory, but in the reality of the 2020s, it seems pretty unlikely. Corporate marauders and white privilege dead-enders will never relent, never surrender an inch without launching a thousand-year grudge against people with demands for equity and compassion. Good luck to whoever inherits our collective detritus. Maybe they'll do better, I think with an uneasy stomach, putting the car in gear and heading down the hill to town.

I need cheap socks and razors at Target. Along the backside of the shopping center, we drive past a beefy old white man moving across the parking lot on an electric Rascal scooter. He looks like Peter Fonda if he had survived the shotgun blast at the end of *Easy Rider* and lived into his Trumpy senior years. We roll past him like he's a threat, which is not implausible in the land of random shootings—and of course, there is something unnerving about people who radiate anger for their own private reasons. Coming to the front of the Target, we park next to a beat-up SUV with a large white decal in the back window. It depicts a wild and angry woman looking over her shoulder and saying, "If you're gonna ride my ass, at least pull my hair!" That seems like a fair request.

14 Sensitive Man

There is a cult of sensitive souls around the fifty-something singer Bill Callahan, especially where he now lives in the center of Texas, though his fans are in the cracks everywhere. I think his work bears deep listening and, like a good Leonard Cohen record, feels right in moments of burning melancholy and loss.

For me, after a half-year in the pandemic doldrums, getting sick of waiting for a change of scenery, and on a day when I was feeling the sadness of an empty nest parent for which no counsel can really prepare you, I started digging further into his catalog. With his voice sitting high on top of the mix, he can sound elemental, almost like an indie folk version of an Old Testament prophet who likes to drink Shiner Bock and tell stories about the mysteries of life—imagine a resonant voice with the authority of Johnny Cash. Other times his artful phrasing evokes Willie Nelson in his jazzier moods, albeit with a deeper baritone and more wistful way of being. Sometimes there are even jagged avant-garde shards, sudden strikes of discordant guitar, that seem pulled out of Tom Waits's discography, a holdover from Callahan's noisier roots in the lo-fi nineties, when he performed under the name Smog.

For all these distant echoes, he's always his own thing, which is no small feat when you're just using a couple of guitars, drums, and a big but tender voice that seems to hold the world. Increasingly over the span of his three-decade career, there's a lot of space in his songs, which float along on wisps of slide guitar or soft brushes across the snare. But I think it's the quality of the lyrics, strong as poetry on their own, that really sets him apart: "And father left at eight," he seems to remember about his childhood, "Nearly splintering the gate." Other times he settles on the power of nature (birds, horses, rivers) in a way that is common in eco-fiction but not in American songwriting.

What I like best is when he captures the sense of failure in ordinary life almost like a proletarian novelist from the 1930s. He's often got that weird old Americana vibe, like a wise, timeless character who's been wandering the land and taking notes since the time of Lincoln. How many songwriters would make a list that is straight out of Howard Zinn by way of William Carlos William? Like this from his epic song "America":

Afghanistan!
Vietnam!
Iran!
Native American! America!
Everyone's allowed a past
They don't care to mention America!
America!

Though I don't feel much doubt about where his sympathies rest, he is able to embed whatever critique he has inside something that feels cut free from the usual moralizing. I guess moralizing is okay if it's not "usual"—you want it with a twist of lime or something that makes it fresh.

Notably for me, Callahan has a song from twenty years ago called "Bowery" about his Irish American grandfather dying on the streets of New York, a drunk and an addict coming up for "his last breath from the river of methadone." It made me think about my grandfathers, both hard working-class men, lifelong laborers who died worse off than they started, as if the American dream was some kind of trick of the eye. I'll tell a story about the English one, which fits with Callahan's song. A Liverpudlian immigrant dockworker, he did things in Brooklyn in the 1940s and beyond that would've gotten him locked away in more enlightened times. An alcoholic brute who preyed on children, male and female, even in his own family, he was a failed human on every level. That's why it's probably our family's collective loss that he didn't die on the Bowery, although around 1955 he was found unconscious and bleeding on the dockside streets of Brooklyn, with a loading hook lodged in his rectum (which may have been a pointed statement from his coworkers about his sexual predation). After he molested several of his own grandchildren in the 1970s, my father and his two brothers went full Sopranos on him—they took him for a car ride and explained that they would absolutely, positively kill him if he transgressed again. The good news (I guess?) is that they didn't have to kill Grandpa. Instead, he died in a cheap motel at the age of eighty-two, separated from his Glaswegian wife, for whom the phrase *long-suffering* must've been invented, with a little booklet of McDonald's coupons providing his only sustenance. These were very poor people who got very little for their suffering or the suffering they inflicted on others (just to be clear: he was cruel; she was kind). It was a bum deal in every sense of the word, even if it wasn't literally on the Bowery.

In songs like "Bowery" and many others over his long career, Callahan sounds like someone who has it all figured out, something that eludes me in general but especially when I think about family history. Not all of his songs have this sage-like quality, but I associate him with a kind of Olympian vantage on the grim hazards and fearsome unruliness of life that I admire. I appreciate this cool knowingness in him and Cat Power and Neil Young and Courtney Barnett and a few other artists with a wry, meaningful, philosophical take on the world, but I worry why the white guy who is exactly my age, in exactly my city, is the one who resonates so deeply. I think it's an imaginative shortcoming on my part. Maybe that's okay, since at fifty-seven, my goose is mostly cooked, but we're expected to question such affiliations nowadays. I'm not really looking forward to the moment when music is mostly made by computer and we don't have to worry if the human being who crafts the song is nice to his kids or whatever, but I'm also embarrassed that my heroes are simply better versions of myself.

15 Killing Us Softly

It happened fifteen hundred miles away from where I live in Texas, but we felt it everywhere. People stared helplessly at screens, watching something that wasn't *supposed to happen* but was also completely predictable. The attack on the U.S. Capitol was unlike anything I've ever seen.

What's been exhausting in the months and years since is the nameless intensity that we're stuck with. It's this feeling of democracy unraveling, the end looming, chaos churning, anger rising, options narrowing, climate changing, sinus aching, desire fading, dreams blurring, interest accruing, paper jamming, ice melting, haters hating, and players running out of replays because the game is finally over (and this is before Trump's astonishing, appalling resurrection in 2024).

This nameless intensity is one of fifty reasons my hands are still trembling when I get out of the 250 gallons of warm saline solution in a sensory deprivation tank. I'm a little disappointed the experience hasn't transformed me into a prehistoric ape-man like William Hurt in *Altered States*, a 1980s science fiction film that introduced much of the world to flotation tanks. For eighty-nine dollars the supernatural soak is supposed to calm and center me, but nope, afterward I'm as jittery as before, and like the dying criminal in the punk rock comedy *Repo Man*, "I blame society!" His friend, the cynical young Angelino played by Emilio Estevez, is having none of it. "That's bullshit," he tells the dying man. "You're a white suburban punk just like me." With melodramatic sadness, the dying man explains, "Yeah, but it still hurts."

And it does. *It still hurts*. And this is probably because the historic moment in which we are living is filled not just with anxiety and uncertainty and baroque forms of immiseration but also an atmosphere of looming heaviness that is hard to explain without getting as far-out as a sci-fi cult film.

So, let's call it an invisible pressure system, a pseudo-barometric force that silently operates on our bodies, our nervous systems, and certainly our imaginations, and drives us into tight corners of bad feelings. This was true before, during, and after the pandemic, but *now*, right now, in January 2021, it's *bad*. There's a high-pressure system of abstract feeling in the traumatic days of COVID spiking and insurrection brewing, days in which being far from the action was not much of a buffer (glad, though, I was not to be inside the Capitol with the make-believe Viking and the dimwit brigade that brought a DIY gallows to hang the vice president).

Maybe the reason these events feel so miserable is that the individual and societal are interwoven in our bodies, ever more so as we become cyborgs with iPhone appendages and a dozen other means of embodying new technologies. This argument pops up a lot in an academic field known as Affect studies, but sometimes, when things go wrong in just the right way, you don't need a book: it just hits you heavy in the face like a bag of sand. At such moments I wish the Second Amendment slogan of "Don't Tread on Me" was understood as something more than a gun lover's cri de coeur because the threats to our freedom and dignity are more diffuse than some bureaucrat taking away Bobby Joe's thirty-aught-six on the eve of deer season. We're being tread upon in a thousand different ways—is it any wonder depression and anxiety are at record levels? In ways that the average therapist will rarely suggest to a suffering patient, these are politically induced conditions in many cases. They are contextual diseases, and right now in America, the context sucks.

So that's what we're wrestling with, this broken-nation feeling that's hard to shake. What should we do? What experience can we draw on? What collective solutions are possible in our hyper-individualistic society? We have to ask these "we" questions to get out of the haze of disappointment; otherwise, we'll atomize and isolate, falling back on the single-serving remedies that we're always pushed toward. We'll tell therapists what our mothers said when we were small rather than blaming the systems of capital and bureaucratic degradation that are always hard at work, weighing us down. Or maybe we'll tranq out on opioids and TikTok. Maybe we'll drink too much. Or shop too much. Or space out on meds for reasons that might be more political in origin than mainstream therapy tends to assume.

I'm no different. Few Americans are. And it's for a simple reason: we're living in a 240-year-old bait-and-switch scheme. We grow up assuming we're part of something grand and noble, but unless you grew up with an ideal demographic profile in some prosperous wonderland, it's not what we're promised in our deluded civic life. Foreigners see us more clearly: that we're a nation built on union busting, extreme militarism, regressive tax policies, extractive eco-violence, stark racial division, cynical regulatory capture, class stratification, and a general ethos of selfish acquisition. Not exactly the kindergarten mythology in which America is a magical land of opportunity, a shining beacon of democracy in an unjust world, a gee-whiz super swell place where nifty dreams come true by the dozen. Most of us aren't blind to the dark underbelly, which we remember whenever we're slammed with cognitive dissonance because some soulless politician mouths words like "The children are our future" while voting against Head Start, paid family leave, affordable childcare, and school lunches.

In the final scene of *Killing Them Softly*, one of the most fascinating political films of the past decade, a hitman played by Brad Pitt approaches his mob boss to ask why his payment is light. Slumped over a sad-looking bar in New Orleans, the boss, whose style is more State Farm than Tony Soprano, mumbles something about "recession prices" and points to the TV over the bar, where President Obama is giving his 2008 victory speech at Grant Park: "This is the moment . . . to reclaim the American Dream and reaffirm that fundamental truth—that out of many, we are one."

"You hear that line? That line's for you," the boss says, shaking his head at the hitman's cynicism. Like a cheesy shift supervisor at the

Dollar Store, the boss implies that a "team player" should take less money—after all, we're all "one" in this great country.

"Don't make me laugh," the hitman scoffs. "One people? It's a myth created by Thomas Jefferson." The boss is surprised. "Oh, now you're going to have a go at Jefferson?" he asks.

Pitt's character responds with one of the great closing monologues in contemporary cinema. In a close-up blazing with contempt, he delivers a caustic sermon:

> My friend, Thomas Jefferson is an American saint, because he wrote the words "all men are created equal," words he clearly didn't believe, since he allowed his now-children to live in slavery. He's a rich wine snob who got sick of paying taxes to the Brits. So, yeah, he writes some lovely words and roused the rabble and they went and died for those words while he sat back and drank his wine and fucked a slave girl. [He points to Obama on the TV.] This guy wants to tell me we're living in a "community"? Don't make me laugh. I'm living in America, and in America, you're on your own. America's not a country. It's a business. Now fucking pay me.

We see Pitt's face in the dive bar's amber glow for one cool second, then the director cuts to black and hits us with Barrett Strong's 1959 Motown classic, "Money (That's What I Want"), with the lyric:

> The best things in life are free
> But you can give them to the birds and bees
> I need money (that's what I want).

This is the sad truth: we are on our own, solo performers alone with the formidable problems of American life, generally with few resources and little preparation. Right now, as we stumble into the mid-2020s like exhausted refugees from the recent past, the one thing we are truly a part of is this weird intensity, this great electric freak-out, that characterizes this herky-jerky American decline in the digital century.

We're wired up for failure, jolted into submission, then shocked by our own ignorance of what is going wrong. *And it hurts.*

There is an inherent cruelty to a society that fails to prepare its citizens for reality.

16 Behind the Pine Curtain

I know some Black people won't drive through East Texas unless it's an emergency. Even before the mysterious death of a Black woman named Sandra Bland made national news in 2015, when she perished in police custody somewhere between Houston and Brenham (and yes, I'm defining East Texas more expansively than some), Black people in Dallas, Houston, or Austin knew this was one of the most dangerous parts of a dangerous country. And if you're gay or trans or anything other than a straight white conservative with a bumper sticker that says *My Other Truck Is Jesus*, you probably won't feel safe in the rural parts of East Texas. If you must get off the interstate, just keep the windows up, the tank full, and stay under the speed limit.

Outsiders probably don't know much about East Texas, but people with a dark sense of humor call it "behind the pine curtain" for a reason. It's hot, poor, overwhelmingly white, rabidly right-wing, and walled-in by thick stands of trees that invite a kind of claustrophobia of the soul. Those who drive I-10 between Beaumont and Houston have only seen a thin slice of it, namely the ugly Gulf Coast turf the oil industry has turned into a toxic badlands, a poster for environmental racism. Just beyond Beaumont, on the way to the Louisiana border, the town of Vidor was long feared for its Klan violence; in the 1920s whites drove their Black neighbors out of the town for good, it seemed, and for seventy years, as the Texas journalist Mimi Schwartz put it in 1993, "not only were there no blacks in Vidor, but there was no trace of black culture." The ethnic cleansing was almost total: "There were no black beauty products in the drugstores; no copies of *Ebony* or *Jet*; no black churches; no black civic officials, lawyers, doctors, or garbagemen; no black high school students, teachers, waitresses, cashiers, or shoppers," Schwartz wrote. "Most days, the only black people in town were on television."[1]

That's Vidor. Head north for a few hours, and you'll find the upper reaches of the region in places like Lufkin, Tyler, and Longview, with their gently rolling hills, majestic pine trees, and dozens of man-made lakes filled with powerboats, some trailing Trump flags in grand flotillas of resentment. Likewise, the more centrally located land around Brenham is quite attractive—the small city is known for its local creamery, Blue Bell Ice Cream, the source of delicious rocky road and vanilla, not to mention the listeria outbreak that killed three people in 2015 and resulted in criminal charges against the CEO in October 2020.[2] A cynic would say that their heavily marketed image of small-town wholesomeness was just another regional delusion.

The truth is that East Texas has often been less than wholesome. An early-nineteenth-century Mexican general decried its population of "fugitive criminals, honorable farmers, vagabonds and ne'er-do-wells."[3] Not so much has changed in the region, with the suffering, then and now, landing disproportionately on people of color. In 2022 the Southern Poverty Law Center mapped out the locations of seventy-two hate and antigovernment groups in Texas—almost all of them are peppered on the eastern half of the state, while the western half of Texas is almost entirely blank.[4] The region has always been a bastion for the Ku Klux Klan, which has killed hundreds of Black people in Texas since Reconstruction, the majority of them in rural East Texas in the late nineteenth and early twentieth centuries. More recently, in the 1980s, the Klan terrorized immigrant Vietnamese fishermen for simply working the Galveston Bay.[5] Of course, the Klan was powerful in nearby cities as well. In the early 1920s one out of every three eligible men was a member of the KKK in Dallas, prompting its main newspaper to label it "the most racist city in America" (admittedly, Dallas is just out of East Texas proper, but it's the hub for commercial activity for a good part of the region: you watch Dallas TV stations, listen to Dallas radio, and use DFW airport if you live in someplace like Tyler).[6] Nowadays, if you head east for an hour from Dallas until you wind up in rural Van Zandt County, you'll find "the largest racial disparity in the country" in drug cases—according to an ACLU report, Black people were *thirty-four times more likely to be arrested than whites for marijuana possession.*[7] A little farther east, in Tyler, where my parents have lived for the past four decades, the county courthouse features a monument to the confederacy that thanks "loyal slaves [who] raised cotton and grain" (and it was erected in 1963!). Head south for two hours, and you'll land in charming Nacogdoches, the oldest town in Texas, where my mom went to secretarial school in 1960—a 94 percent white police force rules over a small city that is over half-Black and Latino.

The only major city on the eastern side of the state is Houston, where a few million fantastically creative and hardworking people are trapped in a built environment that would make Jesus weep. There are plenty of things to love in Houston, but it takes hard work to uncover them. With a natural landscape whose most prominent point is a mere thirty feet, Houston hides its cool stuff behind a concrete explosion of freeways, "stroads," strip malls, and rutted streets. It was shamed as the ugliest city in the highly industrialized world in 2013, and at any point between May and November, it feels like the sweatiest.[8] It was ranked the second worst city for bikes in the United States.[9] It's also a terrible place for pedestrians, with below-average walkability scores, and a mediocre place for public transportation.[10] Thanks to long commutes, high crime, longer-than-average workweeks, and an uninsured rate that is triple the national average, Houston's workers had the highest stress levels in the United States in 2023.[11] In other words, *Houston, we have a problem—and it's you.* Even its defenders admit, "To love it is to do so despite everything that is Houston," as one *Texas Monthly* essay put it.[12] It's true that the urban core has a fantastic "gayborhood" in Montrose and some genuine charm in the Heights, around Memorial Park, and around Rice University, but they are no match for the unregulated sprawl of an ultra-humid city on Sunbelt steroids. The tragedy is that the Houston museums are sublime, the food is outstanding, the sports teams are exciting, the medical centers are world-class, and the Black and Latino communities have produced goddesses and geniuses like Beyoncé, Megan Thee Stallion, Chingo Bling, Lil Jon, and many more.

No doubt, Houston has more than its share of the fantastic and appealing, but thanks to its largely unregulated growth, its wonders are still a relatively small part of an unpleasant whole that blends Kuwaiti-style opulence into butt-ugly sweltering. As one local said while trying to explain the city's problems: "Cars, concrete, and lack of zoning. . . . Houston did not grow as much as it metastasized. I grew up there when it was a much smaller city. Now it's just a bewildering tangle of highways."[13] That infamous lack of zoning creates all sorts of strange situations that often make Houston as charming as a dive motel with black mold: sex shops literally next to department stores, new apartment complexes adjacent to ugly industrial sites, a crematorium nestled between houses on a residential street, high-rise towers overshadowing a row of modest homes, an insane tangle of freeways that get wider and crazier every few years, and even a five-story wooden roller coaster just a few feet from a house where the occupant must be losing their hearing and their mind at approximately the same rate.[14] It's an unsustainable mess that seemingly refuses to change, even though most residents think the city is headed in the wrong direction.[15] A third of the homes and businesses are at risk of flood devastation, which became painfully clear to the world during Hurricane Harvey in 2017. When flooding related to climate change is taken into account, the city has a real estate market that is inflated by ten billion dollars.[16]

Scale is a crucial element of the Houston problem. Fifty-two miles across, the city goes on forever in every direction—and you *have* to drive; even where light-rail does exist, Houstonians insist on crashing their cars into it in ways that are unique to the city.[17] But hey, this is car culture in extremis. Everything around the urban core is eight-, ten-, twelve-, or twenty-lane high-speed madness, with new lanes added every decade to allow new commuters to reach new suburbs filled with new strip malls and new tract homes for the same old fantasy of the suburban good life that has dominated American life since the 1950s.

And what fuels that fantasy in 2020s Houston? Surely, most people come to this oversized urban ATM for love or work, not the glorious vistas or the weather. There are a lot of good jobs in the city and even more mediocre ones: 37,000 people work for Walmart, making it the city's largest employer by far; another 20,000 toil for McDonalds; and energy remains a major player in the city—5,000 lost souls are part of Dick Cheney's Halliburton, which runs most of the world's fracking operations when it's not helping the U.S. military in wars or getting sued for the Deepwater Horizon explosion and oil spill. And of course, several of the world's biggest oil companies are headquartered here.

What else can I say about this vast, paradoxical city? It's flat, it floods, it lacks zoning, it has the worst humidity this side of Jamaica, and it has a serious sexual trafficking problem, with massage parlors filled with exploited immigrants whose passports have been locked away. It's an unsustainable urban studies nightmare, but at least it's never boring—its silver lining is that it's an *incredibly* cosmopolitan city, with large communities of color creating beautiful lives there, including waves of Nigerian immigrants who have built a thriving scene for the best Afrobeat music outside of Lagos. While Mexico provides a third of Houston's immigrant population, the numbers are surging from Venezuela, Iraq, Cuba, Afghanistan, Honduras, India, Pakistan, Vietnam, China, and Columbia. When the built environment of Houston wears me out and I'm choking on its high levels of air pollution, I take hope from the epic creativity of this majority-minority city. Somehow, despite all sorts of structural impediments, many Houstonians have created something worth savoring, something far better than the spiritual emptiness and political rancidity I see across the rest of East Texas, where Trumpian cruelty reigns supreme.

Leaving Houston behind, let's head north into the rolling hills and piney trees that stretch for hundreds of miles, a landscape that is beautiful in its pristine state and generally despoiled by what has been imposed upon it. Here is my modest claim about rural East Texas being the most brutal part of a historically brutal state, which, unless you are wearing chaps and rounding up cattle as you read these words, might deserve some consideration. Half of my large extended family is scattered across East Texas, starting with my kind, beautiful mother, who is from an illiterate logger's homestead at the end of a long dirt road in San Augustine County. She didn't use a phone until she was twenty, which was sometime in the early 1960s, and she certainly didn't have a television or any other contact with the outside world if you don't count the occasional magazine about Hollywood stars. Her family had burrowed deep into that county going back to the 1840s, which for white people in Texas is almost as far back as you can go without claiming Native blood. I'm not suggesting that my huge extended family tells the whole story of the region, but they've been there long enough, and in many ways are typical enough, to shed some light on life behind the pine curtain.

My grandfather, uncles, and cousins were mostly hard-luck country boys who raised cattle and logged the piney woods, which is one of the most dangerous jobs you can get stuck doing. As a boy, I could see where my grandfather lost fingers to a logging chain that suddenly pulled taut on his trailer. One uncle was hobbled from a missing foot, but now that I think about it, that foot was severed in an oil well, a few years before he ended up driving a logging truck back and forth from the woods to the softwood sawmill in Pineland. His brother was crushed by a vast timber-hauling machine called a skitter, and he spent the rest of his life as a paraplegic in bed, being abused by his wife and her assortment of new boyfriends.

It gets worse. A few relatives were what was called "simple" or "slow" in a hushed voice at family reunions, while others died from alcoholism and other substance problems. One was a serious drug dealer who would've gone to prison for shooting an AK-47 through his front door at a guy coming to collect a debt, but he was sprung from the local jail by a brown paper bag of cash that my uncle delivered in the dead of night. (The sheriff was so corrupt, he was profiled in the *New Yorker* for his misdeeds.)

If my East Texas uncles are all standard-issue good old boys, except the one who came out of the closet at age sixty, my eight Texas aunts are a mix of churchy and wild. The wildest one was always done up in that inimitable 1970s way: tube top, bleached blonde hair, too much makeup in a manner that was, frankly, awesome because she seemed uninhibited and uncontainable in her baby-blue Camaro. Less awesome was the fact that she married a child abuser who was in and out of prison for years. We kept our distance from him, while she worked as a cocktail waitress in a Houston dive bar and died much too young. Meanwhile, another relative had been a bad cop in Houston in the 1960s (how awful do you have to be to get labeled a *bad cop* back then?). His simmering racism was scary because he wasn't dumb; the fact that he was quick-witted made his resentments spark with danger, something I could feel even as a child in the seventies. He taught me how to shoot a .357 magnum revolver into the woods one afternoon when I was twelve. I remember the gun exploding like a canon after barely brushing the trigger; it probably wasn't the sort of thing a child should handle, but what else are you supposed to do on a hot summer afternoon in the piney woods other than massacre the foliage?

Almost all these relatives had mobile homes in the same county, and the mobile home seems like a perfect symbol of local values: discount living, even when you are earning a decent wage. When I learned to drive in my uncle's dilapidated truck on the eight-acre backside of our East Texas mobile home in the 1980s, I got it stuck in a soft spot in the sewer line and couldn't get out. Stuck in shit: I think that's what you call a full-on metaphor. A few years earlier I was practicing driving on a riding lawn mower and didn't know how to stop, so I ran it into the side of my uncle's mobile home with an aluminum bang. I'm lucky it didn't flip over, though I might have fit in better if I had lost a finger or a foot.

Perhaps this goes without saying, but fitting in was hard for me. I remember spending summers in East Texas and getting to ride in the logging trucks to the mills while my uncles drove giant 18-wheelers dangerously overloaded with 100,000 pounds of timber; I guess they were amused or confused by their moody New Jersey nephew who was trying to find a place in a world that was like a sadder version of *The Dukes of Hazzard*. When I was seventeen and bored in the Texas heat, my mother bought me a Winchester rifle in a pawn shop in Jasper, Texas, the site of the notorious lynching of James Byrd in 1998.

Trying very hard but not so persuasively to perform the role of *proper Texas man*, I used the Winchester to shoot tin cans and some animals that I wish I hadn't. In the summer of '83 I remember my well-fed cousin saying in a very high voice, "You wanna go to the dump and shoot some cats?" I remember jumping into his lifted Ford Bronco 4x4, which he drove illegally everywhere from the age of fourteen, and watching him shoot at the feral cats roaming in the dump. I don't think I shot one, but maybe I've blocked it out.

Sadly, I hit the armadillo that my uncle encouraged me to shoot on a deer lease where he was driving us in circles, just two lazy hunters going down a dirt road in the middle of nowhere looking for something to shoot. He was a Vietnam vet with ample charisma, and I didn't want to disappoint him. He probably saw the armadillo as a consolation prize for not coming across any deer because he told me to get out of the truck and shoot it, and I did, popping it right in the arch of its back. It ran away into the brush and may have lived or may have died, I'll never know. But I immediately felt—and feel to this day—that it was the stupidest, ugliest thing I've ever done.

17 Civil War

Three hours into clearing branches and raking leaves on a long, hot Saturday morning, I was feeling eager to finish up and go make lunch. Having moved the leaves onto our quiet street for easy sweeping up, I left my rake, broom, and shovel on the curb and walked up the drive to get some brown paper lawn bags. Yes, there was a midsized mess in the street, but it also looked like someone was still at work, very much in the midst of a project.

But suddenly, from the top of my driveway, I heard a loud and aggressive voice from the street. I couldn't see who it was, but as I walked back down the driveway, I glimpsed an older man on a bicycle bellowing in a stern voice: "RAKE YOUR LEAVES! IT'S AGAINST THE LAW TO LEAVE THEM IN THE ROAD." He couldn't see me, but I caught sight of him as he zipped away in a yellow reflective vest and gleaming white helmet.

I never know what to say when I feel attacked, but I ran into the road and managed a snarl of "MIND YOUR OWN BUSINESS," which feels like pretty weak tea—but hey, he had vexed me plenty with his blend of aggression and speed, all the more surprising given his advanced age. I wanted to share some choice language, but I've learned it's best not to let out my full New Jersey vocabulary because it's just not helpful to anyone, and it reads as sociopathic to Sunbelt people. It's overkill here, the profusion of f-bombs and whatnot.

So, I fretted and mulled and pondered for the remainder of the warm Saturday. Who rides through a neighborhood as the self-appointed yard police, Barney Fife division, and spouts off like that? Who would blast drive-by corrections at their neighbors? Would a person of color make such rude pronouncements about the yards of strangers? Would a woman shout angrily from her bike at an empty yard? I suppose there is a "Karen" for every occasion, but I still put my money on white guys of a certain age. You need a long lifetime of practice to get this sort of entitlement right.

The next day I saw him again, and he was still at work, keeping the city safe from some list of petty infractions that he carries in his head. A few blocks from my house, I watched him blow through a quiet intersection and still have the nerve to yell "STOP SIGN!" at two cyclists—two Asian American graduate students who had begun a sleepy rolling stop that in no way could have endangered the great white potentate of the spokes. Yet the geezer let loose just the same, hitting them with unwanted reminders about civilization's strictures like a father correcting wayward children.

An hour later I was surprised to see him again, stopping where a construction crew had set up a porta-potty in a driveway. He felt free to leave his bike propped against a phone pole and hustled up a stranger's driveway to relieve his itchy bladder. I was tempted to yell, "USE YOUR OWN BATHROOM, YOU BASTARD," but mostly because it amused me to think the thought.

I hate these random forms of conflict that have seemed to proliferate and fester over the past decade. Once Trump became the dominant force in American politics rather than some comb-over buffoon fighting bankruptcy in Gotham, civic distrust went into overdrive. Ever since he claimed victory in the 2016 election, people seemed on edge in a new way—they seemed distrustful of the other side in a way I had never seen before. Pulled into a psychological civil war, I started looking sideways at everyone who wasn't obviously on Team Randy (all six of us) and became paranoid about strangers who might have a red hat and a .45 in their closet. Maybe it would have been easier living in a blue state, but down in Texas, I felt like a target despite being a big straight white guy. If I was feeling it, I figured it was even harder on people with infinitely more vulnerability—trans, undocumented, unhoused, queer, immigrant, and so forth. Trump and his minions were pushing the revanchist view that diversity was pathological, dissent was unpatriotic, and garden-variety liberalism was the new communism. In this context tense little moments felt like something more than a flicker of interpersonal weirdness, and they would dog me, souring my whole outlook for hours or even days.

In the case of the mansplaining geezer, I felt vaguely assaulted and entertained thoughts of violence that aren't really me but are very much the men in my family; happily, I've learned to tamp down the atavistic urges that I inherited. I don't really want to knock him off his bike or challenge him to arm wrestle, box, or duel with battery-operated light sabers. All that manly stuff seems absurd. Plus, it's so expensive these days to fix a veneer on a front tooth. That's something I remember painfully well from walking into a tree branch while reading my phone during the Obama years, and I think about it every time I imagine punching someone, because people who get punched are often inspired to punch back. The subsequent hours and money wasted in the dentist's office are simply not worth the preservation of my inner caveman, who is obviously a moron who rightfully gets told to shut up and settle down by my better instincts.

Instead, I let myself breathe and wait and watch, and then, a few days later, I tried to instill in myself the voice of liberal tolerance. I asked myself, why shouldn't he fascinate me like an odd squawking bird that wakes up the neighborhood with its racket? Noisy, mildly noxious, but ultimately harmless. Then I told myself, *Remember how little I know about him.* I also told myself, *Remember how little you know about anything in general.* I tried to humble my rage, reminding myself that I might not have sketched him right; I don't know what meds he is on, what surgeries he has scheduled, what grief he holds onto.

Yuck. I hate this self-chastising liberal voice in my head—it's like the NPR version of Jiminy Cricket fussing at me with his smug insect do-goodism. Feeling like a grotty teenager forced to wear church clothes that don't quite fit, I wince at my lameness: obviously, I'm performing generic goodness at the expense of other raw and chaotic urges that seem far more real, in the same way that the flame on the gas stove is the realest thing in kitchen.

Ultimately, I ended up with a semi-satisfying perspective that is both philosophical and peevish: maybe his problem is not entitlement, or not just; maybe it's a kind of Tourette's that requires him to flail at a world that never listens. Maybe he's like a frustrated dog barking in a pasture at the other animals, like the goats who won't listen and the pigs who just lie around doing nothing, not even sweeping up the leaves that pile up around them. I have to remember that dogs bark for their own reasons, that he might have his rationale, even if I still want to knock him off his bike. I swallow my irritation.

I'm barely the good person that I am.

18 Big-Box Blues

There is blissful predictability to the Target experience. No matter which of their two thousand stores you stroll inside, you'll probably discover that everything is in stock, nothing looks dirty, and the clothes are pretty good for fast fashion (or at least I hope so because I'm wearing them). If you have a little cash to blow on a Bridgerton ceramic mug or a fitted T-shirt that says, "Soul full of sunshine," Target isn't a bad place for quick jolt of retail therapy.

That's the accepted wisdom about Target, and if I don't think about it too much, I'm happy here too. Its bland consistency is like soothing vanilla yogurt on my finicky consumer palate. Unique among its big-box rivals, Target possesses a kind of fluorescent Zen quality. Because it doesn't want to distract customers from scanning the shelves and filling their red plastic carts, Target is the uncommon retailer that doesn't play background music. Maybe this monkish silence is why folks are on pretty good behavior here. While viral websites like People of Walmart mock the exposed butt cracks and mulleted mayhem in the blue-collar alternative, Target shoots for a soccer mom vibe, which has allowed it to make $100 billion each year without the controversy or critique that its rival superstore attracts.

Yet something weird lurks under the surface in Target. Although not as fear soaked as other big-box retailers that are forcing their hourly workers to wear police-style body cameras, Target is paranoid enough to keep their socks and underwear in a locked glass case just like electronics and beauty supplies.[1] Are the nice Target people really

Fig. 10. Target parking lot, Austin, April 2024. Photo by author.

shoplifting pairs of socks imprinted with SpongeBob and two packs of Men's Golfer Print Boxer Briefs? Target thinks so. Staring at SpongeBob under glass, I'm puzzled. Is Target not what it seems? Does its sterile blandness conceal something? I look around and wonder how Target became so essential to middle-class lives? I grew up in a town with no corporate stores, just mom-and-pops, and now I'm Target bound whenever I need a frying pan, hair conditioner, or (sure, why not?) SpongeBob underpants. If you can gaze at the store like a quizzical space alien with no experience in big-box retail, Target starts to radiate a subtle glow of strangeness. What is underneath its profitable enactment of corporate "niceness"? Who makes all this stuff, and how does it get here? And most enigmatically, why do we want it? Why do we accept Target as a kind of neutral, unoffensive, semi-tasteful but still "basic" American style? And perhaps most importantly: *Why am I always here?*

Let me explain how I became troubled by the red-and-white.

I am wandering in the seventh month of quarantine year one. It's an endless Sunday in October, and I'm drained by the wicked heat that dominates Texas life until the kids put on their Halloween gear, sweating through their Spider-Man costumes and princess regalia. We've had nothing but the cruelest high heat for five months, and I've long since sunk into a mindset in which endless sun and humidity feel like torture: if the eighteenth-century libertine the Marquis de Sade lived here in Austin, he would have called his nasty book *120 Days of Sodden* and been too sun-desiccated to hump a horse or whatever else he did to get his French freak on. To make things worse, the kind of places that might otherwise cool us off—swimming pools, restaurants, museums, gyms—are shuttered now. Almost nothing is left for an air-conditioned stroll except the big retail spaces that will never die: Target, Big Lots, Walmart, Costco, IKEA, Lowe's, and Best Buy. They're the last thing standing.

I land in Target. If you need something to wear, it's better than Sears but worse than Nordstrom, which I can't afford. Target has the weird personality of a corporation trying to be open-minded, like your eccentric aunt who used to follow the Grateful Dead in college but now thinks "maybe we should give Trump a chance." It's also trying to be more tasteful than Walmart despite having almost the same dreck on display, albeit with a slightly classier presentation. Basically, Target offers middle-class people a more dignified atmosphere in which to browse for twelve-packs of paper towels, clunky costume jewelry, sweatpants, and phone chargers under a single roof. I appreciate that. And I am very grateful for the cool air because, like most Texans, my movements are entirely controlled by the flow of air-conditioning: no AC, no me.

Big-box stores can offer a kind of mindless pleasure as we poke around the aisles and ponder a new pair of basketball shorts or a jumbo box of frozen waffles, but living through quarantine is giving the experience a different hue. Today I am walking in a pandemic stupor, gazing at things like I'm trying to see the hidden green lines of code that constitute *The Matrix* of consumerism. For much longer than normal, I stare at the Shark UltraLite vacuum and the ZeroWater 5-Stage Filtration System and the Ninja Foodi and the nonstick, supposedly no-longer-carcinogenic skillets and the crudely stitched canine Halloween costumes that I want to put on my dog, though I know she doesn't want a stuffed monkey strapped to her back—she doesn't want to wear slutty angel wings, and she doesn't want to be a cool cosmonaut for even five minutes.

I'm not quite certain what to do while I push my red cart down the aisle and wait for my wife to find something. Aggressively red signage reminds me several times about a *free gift card*, which seems spectacularly insincere: corporations have no "free gifts" for anyone, not ever. There is absolutely nothing free in America whatsoever, and that is the truest thing that can be said about our country nowadays. Even freedom, as military propaganda likes to remind us, isn't free, so much so that it might be time to replace that hoary phrase with something more accurate like "Liberty is a luxury good whose price point, if you have to ask, is probably more than you can afford."

Places like Target are numbing but necessary if you want something from a store other than Amazon. This gives Target a weird centrality in my life, which is particularly strange during the dark days of COVID, when it feels like the store is the only thing functioning. I'm both grateful and appalled that this sterile red-and-white box is our last best hope.

What could I think about as I drift past oversized plastic cups that say *Sippin pretty* and *Me time*, down the long rows of frozen food and canned beans, past the end cap that says "Better for You" above salty snacks? It's next to a much bigger area for low-quality snacks that lacks signage but could easily be labeled "Worse for You." I walk on and admire the profusion of rice pots and woks and shower curtains and area rugs and dog collars. I own a lot of this stuff: it's where I get toys for my dog, patio furniture for my yard, and sweatpants that I barely take off for the duration of the pandemic. So many random things are on display, some of them seemingly as bored as me. The Instant Pots and the off-brand slow cookers seem to eye each other warily, like savvy fighters from two opposing ways of life. I wonder who wants a sleepy old crockpot when you can have a Smart Wi-Fi Programmable Multi-Cooker on your simulated granite countertop (the kind I just put in my house)? And old classics like Mr. Coffee are still duking it out with the newfangled Keurig pods: so many ways to make coffee!

Why am I here exactly? I'm not sure, other than the fact that it's hot outside and *it's not Walmart*. My friends get upset when I tell them I went to Walmart for something, as if red state belligerence is contagious and I'm going to come back in some camouflage hunting gear and a Chinese-made MAGA hat. I scare them when I cross these sorts of imaginary borders.

The same liberal friends tell me I should be saving money at the Costco across town, but in the spirit of my Scottish grandmother, I object to the membership charge. Paying a hefty entrance fee to a theme park or a concert is bad enough, but it's just pitiful when you're only getting access to 120,000 square feet of poured concrete with an array of metal shelves stuffed with endless stuff. Of course, that doesn't quite do justice to Costco, with its ocean of chunky bacon crumbles, rotisserie chicken meat, dark chocolate potato chips with Himalayan pink sea salt, eight-foot-tall plush bears, big bottles of store-brand vodka, faux leather couches, and even discount coffins in some locations. I'm looking forward to that last one—at least until Marshall's starts carrying "factory reject" coffins on an even deeper discount. Scratch and dent coffins seem like a good market niche for a smart COVID entrepreneur as the death toll is hitting the six digits and climbing fast. My friend couldn't bury his mom in Chicago for three months because the crematoriums were booked up with COVID deaths, and maybe it's the same with coffins.

Weirdly, at such moments I often hear a voice beckoning me to this other superstore, where we shop once or twice every few years in a vain effort to save money. It's always the same phrase, "Welcome to Costco . . . I love you," and it comes with a well-known visual: a large, sad man speaking with eerie blankness. Utterly devoid of feeling, he greets customers entering a cavernous Costco in a grim future where nothing works, and the American dream is sputtering like a broken leaf blower. Endlessly repeated and frequently memed, the phrase becomes an absurdist mantra for a consumer dystopia: indeed, that brief, bleak line sums up Mike Judge's ferociously dark 2006 satire *Idiocracy*. A Rip Van Winkle tale set in a degraded future in which a machine gun–toting pro wrestler is president, moronic corporations replace water with a sports drink, and Starbucks offers hand jobs instead of coffee, the movie was too dismal for test audiences, who found its vision upsettingly real even in 2006. Was it a goofy comedy or a stark warning from the future? By the time we hit the Trump years, the answer was clear.[2]

Even before the pandemic, everyone was making references to *Idiocracy*, which is unusual for a box office flop from a previous decade (though, to be fair, it had acquired a cult following almost from the moment it was released). By the time we crash-landed into COVID, it felt like *Idiocracy* was no longer a movie but, rather, was sheer prophecy about Trumpification and its discontents. The creator of *Beavis and Butthead* had done what QAnon could not: he had foreseen our new and totally unimproved reality in which we run out of toilet paper, reject basic science, and listen to our leaders ponder the restorative properties of bleach.

In this sense "Welcome to Costco, I love you" functions as the "I can't go on, I must go on" of the early twenty-first century, the tagline of our shabby-shoddy absurdist comedy in these not so United States. That line appears in Samuel Beckett's 1953 play, *Waiting for Godot*, and then gets an update at the end of Beckett's 1955 novel, *The Unnamable*, in which we hear: "I can't go on, I'll go on." Penned by the Irish writer in Paris only a few years after he helped the French Resistance defeat Nazi Germany, his lines possess a heroic existentialist quality: life is a horror, but we can face it with courage and grit and somehow survive with a shred of dignity. You could even look cool in sunglasses like Beckett and his Parisian friends.

Not any longer. Trumpland in pandemic is not cool. Trump and his worldview are the antithesis of cool (and soon we'll learn that Biden's administration isn't the resurrection that we needed). Too often we are reduced to the hollow, depressed consumerism that Mike Judge was mocking, and I suspect that a literal "Welcome to Costco, I love you" is just around the corner. Weirdly, it has the same rhythm, the same feel, and the same blend of resignation and determination that we hear in Beckett's phrase, but it's absurd, dopey, and empty. There is no love or dignity being offered in *Idiocracy*'s dirty superstore filled with loose goats and birds, where even the greeter is on corporate autopilot, sounding narcotized with some sort of heavy-lidded medication that you need to survive the nothingness.

But I'm not in *Idiocracy*. I'm not even in Costco. I'm in the toothpaste aisle of a bright, clean Target, which nowadays is just another stage for existentialist drama, viral anxieties, and consumerist angst in America. A few minutes pass, and I find my wife, slog through the self-checkout, and bag up our things with a deep sense of *this is how it will always be*. Wandering the big-box stores, trying to save a buck, taking home stuff you don't really love but are willing to accept as good enough—these are the experiences that are most fundamentally American in the 2020s, and I'm no longer sure if the country is capable of anything more majestic or grand.

A decade ago the anthropologist Daniel Miller wrote an upbeat book on consumerism called *Stuff*, in which he shows that "goods are utilized within an extraordinary and expressive field of cultural life, where we use them to help delineate our values, cosmology, emotional repertoires, and sense of sameness and difference, and as with other cultural forms, for entertainment, communication, and adding to our capacities within everyday life."[3] Even though Target-loving bloggers will swear that "it's the epicenter of all my life's needs and more importantly my escape from reality," I'm not entirely convinced it's a benign pleasure with a rich "emotional repertoire."[4] Big-box retail in contemporary America often seems more like an emotional and expressive prison than a playground of possibility. What Gods can be worshipped around the T-shirt rack at Target? What emotional range is possible on the cleaning supplies aisle? What signifiers of difference are available in the clothing section, other than the glittery

Pride T-shirts made in overseas factories where workers suffer human rights abuses?[5] I am grateful that Target is tidy, air-conditioned, and safe; I'm delighted that other people feel a modicum of joy in its aisles. I've perused the manic websites that list *dozens of reasons to love Target,* and I appreciate that "through focus groups, metadata collection, and volumes of demographic information, Target is able to understand their customer so well—creepily well—and anticipate his or her needs," but ultimately, I'm closer in spirit to the late sociologist Zygmunt Bauman, who saw consumption as a tragic fact of contemporary life because it leaves us in perpetual pursuit of the new, the novel, the latest, the greatest, which is another way of saying that we live within a "consumption system that is based on fostering permanent non-satisfaction."[6]

A monarch butterfly flits past the window as I type those words. Unbothered by the big-box blues or even half-built border walls, she's on her way to Mexico.

19 Under the Violet Crown

I am living through an extremely tense moment in a city known for being laid-back, funky, and upbeat. The weather may be perfect for the first part of 2020, but as summer approaches, the pandemic is gaining momentum like a tropical storm in the Gulf of Mexico. People are suffering, and parts of civic life seem unrecognizably quiet in what has been the fastest-growing city in the United States for much of the past decade. Rather than working out at the gym or gathering for drinks and music, my friends and neighbors in Austin, Texas, now spend their days inside, shut off from other people, often with a painful new awareness of their body's fragility. Generally excluded from our city's cult of exuberant youth, older Austinites are at the center of my thoughts, along with worries about the immunocompromised and the uninsured, as everyone slowly learns about COVID-19 and how it spreads. If we are lucky enough to still have jobs and houses as the weeks of slowdown turn to depressing months, we work and wait at home, watching too much news and texting old friends for comfort and distraction. Meanwhile, the streets of Austin are becoming eerily quiet, and some entire downtown blocks are boarded up as if the zombie hordes are overdue. Restaurants, bars, and clubs are silent; the music has stopped in "the live music capital of the world"; and the traffic has been cut in half. Friends tell me that the air feels cleaner, though I haven't noticed.

I have noticed how grateful people are for small interactions: self-isolation means that the dog walk becomes an important opportunity to smile at strangers, even from beneath a mask, and to check on neighbors from a good six feet away. *Six feet away or six feet under* could have been the motto of the anxious first weeks in Sunbelt semi-quarantine. After those early weeks, the city fluctuated between tense and slack, between total panic and ostrichlike denial, like a moody teenager.

No one knows what life will feel like after the pandemic, we tell ourselves in those naive early months, and no one can say how long it will take for things to feel normal again. And not everyone wants to return to the old status quo, even if it's possible. With the pandemic highlighting the disparities around us, some people are hoping that something better will emerge after our long months inside. Surely it will only be a few more weeks, maybe a few more months, and things will get better by the fall. We are so deluded, but how could we have known any better in the first half of 2020? Looking back a few years later, in the midst of Trump's second term, I have so much empathy for our early pandemic selves: we didn't know how bad it was going to get.

Back in 2020, as I was still feeling my way into the strangeness of the pandemic, I took some comfort from an interview with the novelist Anne Tyler, who was asked if she had difficulty being optimistic right now as the country recedes into ill health in more ways than one. "Not up close, if you know what I mean," she said from her Baltimore home after her book tour was canceled in spring 2020. "Up close you'll always see things to be optimistic about."[1] It's still early in the pandemic in the city of the "violet crown," so named for the purple glow of the hills at sunset, at least as nineteenth-century Texans imagined it. For now I am inclined to agree and even to embrace the hope that there is solidarity in solitude as well as in suffering if we know how to reach for it. What I don't yet appreciate is the fragility of my optimism.

20 Rage Lava

One of the things I hate about certain dudes is their willingness to spew rage lava whenever things aren't going just so. Fifty years have passed, but I can still remember someone pulling a rocking chair from underneath my three-year-old brother and throwing it down the stairs with such force that it impaled the basement door and simply hung there while my mother sobbed. I was five.

I've worked hard not to be like that, but I still feel the appetite for destruction when it comes to certain kinds of technology. I have had an especially rocky relationship with computer printers ever since the heyday of dot matrix. I have to remind myself not to kick or otherwise assail these contraptions even if it provides a kind of feral satisfaction. And I've made progress: I haven't given into this Dexter-like feeling in years. I've kept the Dark Passenger in check.

But I've been fighting headaches and fatigue for eight weeks. Tomorrow's the day when I have to go back to in-person teaching after two years of remote work, and frankly, I don't want to be in a room with the coughing COVID kids, most of whom won't wear a mask unless it's required, which the governor forbids.

And so, while feeling a little more helpless and overwhelmed than usual, I let it rip. Which means I removed the nonfunctional printer toner cartridge and hammered it so hard on the top of the printer that the cartridge shattered.

Smashing a printer cartridge is a comically bad idea. It's a plastic box filled with black inky dust that can shoot, and in fact did shoot, over everything, including my favorite T-shirt, my books, and my face, which I expected to look like post-explosion Wile E. Coyote or an Edwardian chimney sweep. I wasn't quite that sooted up, but the ink went everywhere else in a fine cloud that barely missed some vintage guitars while filling the cracks in the floor.

The cheap printer was the third one that I had bought in three years because they all crap out—this one had been dying even before I smashed it. Electronics are depressingly disposable items now, and I don't regret whacking it. I only regret that I embodied a gross familial and cultural stereotype: the testosterone-fueled baby-man, raging against his own limitations, against a general state of pandemic confusion, against various forms of institutional callousness, against the absurdity of teaching an underfunded and unwanted subject to often unwilling students, and against abject helplessness in the face of macro conditions that are punitive and cruel. Desperately angling for some kind of consolation prize in the free market Olympics, I performed manly violence for myself with a result that was more Mr. Bean than Chuck Norris. And now, with permanently toxic black ink mixed into my temporarily toxic masculinity, I have to clean up the floor.

21 The F-Word

Long ago and well before COVID, I thought it was overheated and cartoonish to talk about fascists in America like they were on every street corner or radio station. For instance, when I was in college in the 1980s, if you wanted to come off as a sixties acid casualty right out of *The Big Lebowski* or the worst kind of holier-than-thou Gen Xer, you could throw around the f-word to describe anyone who seemed intolerant or reactionary or hateful. Jesse Helms? Oliver North? Anita Bryant? *Fascists!* I was always doubtful about the wisdom of using this term as a daily slur. In dropping the ultimate f-bomb casually, even indiscriminately, I worried we were draining the meaning out of a political concept that had devastating importance in the twentieth century. Although I didn't think we would need the term for some urgent domestic purpose in my lifetime (silly me), I wanted to keep it vital and meaningful in the event we did: "In case of Fascists, break glass."

By the early 2020s the glass was broken, a fact that was painfully clear in the aftermath of the 2020 presidential election and the assault on the U.S. Capitol. Perhaps you saw that remarkable scene in *Greyhound*, the Tom Hanks film about a U.S. Navy destroyer on the run from German U-boats trying to sink a convoy? At one point two enormous ships almost collide head-on in the foggy night in the North Atlantic, coming so close that they scrape the rust off one another's hulls. As a goodhearted captain, Tom Hanks's eyes bulge as he watches the other ship grinding past, almost within arm's reach.

That's how close the United States came to a fascist coup in the chaotic months right after the 2020 election. The right went to war against two hundred years of flawed but vital democratic precedent, using lawyers, lobbyists, and the outrage machines of Fox News, Twitter, and AM radio. Soon the Capitol was filled with faux Vikings and rabid marauders carrying Zip Tie handcuffs to hogtie their political enemies on the Senate floor. Did we fully appreciate the seriousness of the danger during those months? I hope so, but the red hat brigade did not: a quarter of Americans thought January 6 was a legitimate protest against a "stolen" election at the time, and within a few years, conservative sympathy for the insurrectionists was much deeper and wider, thanks to years of revisionist PR. Equally worrisome is that the coup and related efforts would have succeeded if not for some lucky breaks that have been widely noted: a military that kept its distance from the election, a few civil servants who put professionalism over politics in states like Georgia, and a would-be dictator whose laziness and general dimwittedness somehow overshadowed his Kanye-sized mega-ego.

Lucky is the crucial word because those good people on the side of democracy didn't always react like peppy young Olympians after a cup of coffee. Probably because they had been battered into an apoplectic funk by four long years of norm gutting and general gaslighting, most decent folk could only fret and rage on social media through the waning days of 2020, never quite sure if the election denier movement represented an actual coup by an actual fascist or just more inexplicable nonsense by the unpredictable molester-in-chief. There was a lot of "Is this really happening?" going around.

Meanwhile, the right made hit lists with the home addresses of election officials in swing states and marched in the streets in black GI Joe cosplay ensembles that were no less menacing for their performative absurdity. They looked goofy, but I wasn't laughing. Hefty dudes in black paramilitary clothes and Rommel goggles are easy to mock until it's dangerous, even deadly, to laugh at them.

Nazi may have been the ultimate term of political derision in the United States for eighty years, but it has always had its implicit defenders in the fascist and fascist-adjacent ranks, where Trump found his most frightening allies. In late 2020 two high school journalists discovered that the Kentucky State Police had been using inspirational quotes from Adolf Hitler in their official training presentations for years (not to mention other quotes from Robert E. Lee), all designed to encourage cadets to become "ruthless killers." On one slide, over the famous photograph of U.S. Marines raising the flag on Iwo Jima, the state police had added the Nazi phrase *Über Alles* in bold. When confronted with this information, officials from the state police shrugged it off at first, claiming that it was perfectly legitimate training for their virile young "warriors" of the speed trap. (They like that word *warrior* a little too much in American law enforcement.) Even more egregious was that the student journalists were in high school in Louisville, Kentucky, where police officers had murdered an innocent Black woman named Breonna Taylor in her own home in March 2020, near the start of the COVID lockdown. Like Trumpland's sleazy denials of responsibility for the Capitol riot or the authoritarian legislation emerging in places like Texas and Florida in the 2020s or the mainstreaming of racist and fascist rhetoric within the American right, it is all part of a slow war of attrition against democratic norms and civil decency that culminated in Trump's reelection in 2024.[1]

In 1966, the year I was born, the Second World War was not some distant memory like the Battle of Antietam or the sinking of the *Lusitania*. Crazily, it was only a little more than twenty years since American and Russian tanks had rolled into Berlin, and memories of the war were everywhere etched into people's bodies and minds. I can even remember the actual Nazis in the neighborhood, as it were. On the Jersey shore on one hot summer day of my childhood, I sat on a sandy beach blanket with my mom's friend Helga and her uncle, a middle-aged man from Germany who had lost a leg fighting the Allies. Sitting on a beach with a limbless Nazi was not all that strange in 1975, though even as a boy I had a good sense not to share my potato chips with a brownshirt.

Nazis: you would think they'd all be dead by now, and frankly I'm a little disappointed it's taking so long. I have always looked forward to the day when the world could bury the last known old-school Nazi, which should be around 2035 if we can imagine a Bavarian kid drafted as a fifteen-year-old in the final months of the war who remained alive for another ninety years. Maybe I'm a sucker for antifascist symbolism, but I thought the world would be able to dance a little freer that day. But clearly, these antidemocratic impulses are hard to stop, and they are spawning imitators all the time. Worst of all, they're never as far away as you think.

A few years ago, I took my first visit to Berlin and saw all the historical sites that I had time to explore. One morning I sat with my wife in a cycling-themed coffee shop eating a vegan muffin and sipping oolong tea. I could've been a fading hipster doofus in any cosmopolitan city, but on this day I was trying to figure out if we were anywhere near the bunker where Hitler died. Using the handy Google maps app on my phone, I tweaked the screen with my fingertips, magnifying the little map while I narrated what I saw: *It looks like we are pretty close . . . uh, actually, we are* really *close. . . . Wait . . . we are on it!* With bug-eyed disbelief, we paid the bill, jumped out of our chairs, and rushed to the backside of the building, where a few Chinese tourists were reading a small metal sign, intentionally unimpressive to discourage neo-Nazis from using what was now a nondescript parking lot as a gathering point.

Maybe the best advice for surviving America right now comes from the late great George Carlin: "Think of how stupid the average person is and realize half of them are stupider than that." I get it, but I don't quite accept it. It's a funny half-truth that doesn't fit my daily experience, in which villains, rats, and morons are a tiny minority. Even if we have a disproportionate share of creeps running the show at the higher levels, the people I know and meet in the world are generally decent, kind, and relatively gentle—and often quietly bitter about the way American life is structured by dislocation, competition, and corporate compunctions, not to mention the unavoidable triad of race, class, and gender.

We deserve an infinitely happier fate than worrying about fascists on top of financial uncertainty, climate change, ineffective health care, and everything else that makes American life so challenging in the 2020s. In a better world, we would outlive all the old Nazis and the new ones too. They should be buried and gone, but somehow they keep sneaking out of the crypt and back into the halls of power. It's our job to put them back in there: collectively, nonviolently, but definitively. If our species is capable of killing the planet, we can certainly snuff out a toxic ideology.

22 Naked Lunch 2020

It felt like something bad was breaking loose, something uncontainable and impossibly dangerous. This bilious man just would not stop, would not relent in a televised event that only ran ninety minutes, but in my head it goes on forever. Sitting in my living room staring at the screen, I just felt lost and stunned while the Reichstag burned in gorgeous high-def. It was like nothing I've ever seen on TV, nothing I've ever found on the internet, nothing I've ever encountered in my long decades sludging through the torrent of images that I call home as a scholar of visual culture. Perhaps I should have been prepared for this gruesome "democracy jumps the shark" moment by the relentless strip-mining of the American mind over the past half-century: the Jerry Springer reruns and the "dank memes" and the swift boating and the prank videos of old women being thrown into pools and everything Tim Allen has ever done and the sequels and prequels for *Fifty Shades of Grey* and, well, the general miasma of bile and stupidity and species-killing obtuseness that has settled upon the continent since I'm not sure when. But I wasn't prepared. I was shocked.

At this point you are probably wondering which specific disaster I address? Could it be Rudy Giuliani and his Keystone Cops legal defense team in front of the Four Seasons Landscaping Company in Philadelphia? Could it be the fake Native shaman and the racist "Proud Boys" who invaded and looted the U.S. Capitol for the first time since the War of 1812? Could it be any of the public utterances of Lauren Boebert, Elon Musk, or Kanye West, one of the most prominent American artists of the millennium, who declared, “I see good things about Hitler”? No, I’m talking about something that now seems easily forgotten: the first presidential debate between the gelatinous orange demon and an irascible grandpa at the end of September 2020. I’m writing this four years later in a country still bruised from insurrection and chaos, wondering if the American presidential debate is a worthless charade. This long-hallowed institution was always an incomplete, insincere, and occasionally deceptive form of political communication, but Trump revealed the fragility and farce within these televised spectacles of pseudo-democracy. For all their flaws, I assumed these debates were the closest we could get to knowing the mind of the candidates. But in 2020 Trump showed something that he would reinforce in 2024: that stagecraft, bullying, bluster, and prevarication could turn the hoary rituals of our republic into an episode of *South Park*.

Watching the 2020 debate startled me like a home invasion, and I understood with painful certainty that whatever *maleficia* that you could attribute to the bellowing orange menace were actually an understatement. That night I saw something feral and unhinged in Trump’s face, like he was ready to do anything to stay out of jail, to retain his access to golden toilets, powerful lawyers, and grabbable pudenda. In the middle of the 2020 debate, I even thought about “Gimme Shelter,” the ominous Rolling Stones song, especially when Trump soft-pedaled the violence of the Proud Boys and the rest of the online racists itching to spill blood in his name. *Rape? Murder? It’s just a click away.*

Debate is the wrong word for what took place onstage in Cleveland. It was more like last-ditch marriage counseling for an abusive spouse who needs a padded cell instead of a therapist’s office. While Biden presented himself with the dull dignity that has often made American politics so sleep-inducing and uninspiring (only later in the campaign did he seem to wake up), Trump had the aura of a coked-up dictator from a former Soviet republic, some unpronounceable place where a violent oligarch goes through the pretense of an election for the little people with their make-believe ballots. All night he made his own truth like a stubborn child caught stealing, putting the black heart of modern American conservatism on full display: the only thing it's "conserving" nowadays is its own nihilistic self-interest. What was once a semi-coherent political philosophy that could at least be debated has turned into a cheap smash-and-grab operation that would have shocked an older generation of Republicans. Bob Dole, Dwight D. Eisenhauer, or Barry Goldwater, for whatever their limitations, were not cretinous lizard people willing to lie, molest, and steal; even the crooked antisemite Richard Nixon drew the line at sexual assault.

What would they have made of the chaos unfolding onstage in Cleveland? Two fussy old dogs growling and barking at each other, though only one seems rabid. The orange goblin makes the first presidential poop joke, telling Biden, "*You're* a number two!" He berates Biden's intelligence: "Don't ever use the word *smart* with me. There's nothing smart about you, Joe." He boasts nonsensically: "I'm the one who brought back football." He deflects on his income tax returns and bungles the language: "I was a private developer. I was a private businesspeople [*sic*]." When asked if he would condemn white supremacist groups, he equivocates, ominously telling the Proud Boys to "stand back and stand by," before adding the claim that the left is the real problem. He slams Biden's son Hunter's drug problem and mocks his son Beau's death. He claims that Biden had broken the military, given up on manufacturing, and would destroy the American suburbs: "If he ever got to run this country . . . our suburbs would be gone!"

YouTubers would later watch the catastrophe in Cleveland for its humorous qualities, not its political content, at least if I can judge from scores of online comments mocking the geriatric candidates. But it wasn't funny in September 2020. It was profoundly unsettling to watch a rancid game show host "winging it" to suit his whims, his titanic ego, his sadistic sense of humor, and his dwindling bank account (who can refill it now that rich daddy Fred is dead?). So, there he stood on that Cleveland stage, a bellicose, almost certainly COVID-contagious huckster, glowering and bellowing germs for ninety minutes straight, which at the very least deserves some sort of medal for Adderall-fueled endurance in the field of deceptive assholery. All evening he was once again planting the seeds that would come up in violence and hate in the ransacking of the U.S. Capitol on January 6, 2021 (among them the non-denunciation of the Proud Boys). Staring at his spray-tanned visage, I thought of a grim line from *Apocalypse Now* (1979), when a frustrated three-star general explains to his subordinates why Marlon Brando's Colonel Kurtz had become a menace to the American effort in Vietnam: "He's out there operating without any decent restraint, totally beyond the pale of any acceptable human conduct. And he is still in the field commanding troops."

As usual, the Twitter people performed outrage for one another or gave into mordant satire about the evening. Some made earnest lists of reasons to vote for Biden, as if facts could possibly matter to the mediated zealots huffing the cheap red, white, and blue paint from Fox News, which was still a few years away from the Dominion settlement that confirmed their cynical mendacity. Then or now, you could show "conservatives" a sober list of thoughtful reasons to get off the Trump train, and most of them would say *fake news, liberal lies, lamestream media!* Sunk cost fallacy suckers, the real MAGA voters will never, ever, let their man go; they've invested too much to admit their mistake. So, anything and everything will be brushed off; no charges will stick on Trump for as long as he is perceived as powerful. And along the edges, his grinning Proud Boys will say it's unfair to judge the man on his past and his present. *You don't know how the future will be? Why not take a chance on fascist romance?*

We can read a hundred plausible reasons in favor of a white-haired establishmentarian like Joe Biden. We can even watch him squaring off against a draft-dodging, silver spoon–sucking, spray-tanning, incest-curious fraudster misogynistic abuser fascist clown who survives off buckets of KFC and Diet Coke while spraying the gasoline of his ignorance on the raging fires of the pandemic and everything else already ablaze, all while he disrespects the American war dead, and still, somehow, millions of Americans will wonder, *Hmm . . . which one deserves my support?* Mind blown. Of course, this was four years before Biden froze onstage like Jack Nicholson in the winter maze at the end of *The Shining*, four years before the country stepped on the rake a second time.

The day after the 2020 debate, I am in the backyard garden feeling like the simpleton in Peter Sellers's film *Being There*, mindlessly pulling weeds and happy to feel the sun on my neck and not think about the news. But something foul is in the air. The combination of Trump and pandemic has brought something horrible to the surface of American life: the unrestrained cruelty in a political elite that had long hidden behind a pompous rhetoric of decency. This is how America feels in lockdown, six weeks before its most important election since the Civil War, with its political system starting to show some alarming fragility. Could it get worse?

It gets worse, so much worse, after that first debate and the crazily contested election of 2020, until we are rubbing our eyes and asking ourselves: terror on Pennsylvania Avenue? White nationalists rampaging on the Senate floor as the world looks on in dismay? A woman trampled to death on the steps of the Capitol while wearing a 1776-themed shirt that said, "Don't Tread on Me"? It was the sort of thing that *just isn't supposed to happen in America*.

But come on—*what did we expect?* Ever since Trump and his Slovenian robo-wife floated down that escalator to announce his presidential run, it's been an all-out war on teachers, immigrants, scientists, librarians, women, and artists, not to mention the queer, the nonbinary, the trans, the dreamers, the poor, the Black, the brown, the Asian, the Muslim, the olds, the littles, the in-betweens, the reformers, the joyful, and the decent. For all of them, the Trump regime was, as Rudy Giuliani grossly put it in his incitement to riot, "trial by combat."

My only surprise is that anyone could be surprised, me included. But I can't blame anyone who felt ill prepared for the full technicolor horror of it all. After all, we're bombarded with a progress narrative that tells us things are automatically getting better year after year, that each generation will exceed their parents' standard of living, and that prosperity and liberty are like tech stocks always going up, up, up! *Buy low, sell high!* As if prosperity and stability are our birthright.

But now our red-white-and-blue American liberty bubble is bursting like a soggy piñata, and I'm shorting the phony freedom market. Cash out while you can! After observing the riots in DC and the ice storms that shut down the state of Texas for a week, the African American soccer star Reggie Cannon, then playing for Portuguese team Boavista FC, said in March 2021: "Explaining to my teammates what is going on in the country is baffling to me. Explaining the America I have lived in to those who don't live in America, it feels like I am describing medieval times."[1]

Medieval indeed. I know it's depressing to admit that things are as bad as they seem. But perhaps it's time to replace our national progress narrative with its opposite, what historians call a declension narrative, the benefits of which I'll joyfully describe for you. Please understand that I'm not trying to get you to join a German nihilist society, even if I adore the Houston-based street artist who wheat pastes enormous razor blades with the vicious caption GIVE UP on random walls and billboards in Texas cities. I'm in the not-so-lucrative reality business, and when things are looking bleak, we need what I might call, with absolutely no respect due to the feelgood huckster Dale Carnegie, *the power of negative thinking.*

Here is one place, maybe the only place, where the uptight Puritans of seventeenth-century New England had it *almost* right. From the get-go, they had a sense that things were going into the newly invented crapper with a resounding splash. Remember that the first generation of dissenters came to New England in the early 1600s with a clear sense of purpose and commitment: they were choosing to give up everything they had known in England to pursue their own religious and economic goals. But their children didn't make those choices—they were Puritans by birth, not by choosing, and many of them grew up with much less dedication to the holy cause, so much so that by 1670, church attendance was getting spotty and Boston had a brothel in operation filled with horny *impuritans* looking for dirty deeds done dirt cheap. *Forsooth!*

Did church leaders try to conceal the unpleasant truth under upbeat rhetoric and civic boosterism? Did they rely on the power of positive thinking? Not for a New England minute. Instead, they went to the dark side and obsessed over their collective failures with a startling intensity. At first they thought simple fasting on special days might restore them to God's graces, but when this failed and things continued to get worse, they turned to an ominous new "fire-and-brimstone" style of sermonizing known as the jeremiad, designed to scare the wickedness out of the flock and put them back on the path of righteousness. As the historian Perry Miller wrote sixty years ago in a shockingly enjoyable article called "Declension in a Bible Commonwealth," these ministerial catalogs of the sins and shortcomings of New England society quickly became the "most polished, thoughtful, and impressive creations" of the late 1600s. "Year after year denunciations of wrath against vicious and unclean practices, against a lifeless frame and flaccid zeal, sounded in the ears of New Englanders; time after time they were exhorted to repent and reform lest God in His anger destroy them utterly, but still they declined."[2] But Miller points out that the ministers were incomplete in their criticisms—"They berated the consequence of progress but never progress itself. . . . They arraigned men of great estates, but not the estates." In other words, they fought a cultural war against vanity and wickedness, they excoriated individual choices, but they said nothing about the larger economic forces that drove these behaviors. When the Puritans put their wicked brethren on blast, they were missing the root causes (which is why I see them as "almost" correct).

That sounds painfully familiar. Today we might need to return to the jeremiad in an updated form, but we should make sure that we focus its rhetorical wrath on the true culprits—not individual sin but the systems of crony capitalism, blind nationalism, white supremacy, and other toxic beliefs. Because then . . . *behold . . . before your very eyes! Presto magico! Reality itself!* Yes, America looks very different when you take off the beer goggles of ideology that promise *more, better, faster, greater, all for the low, low price of free!* This is what "Naked Lunch" meant to midcentury writers like Jack Kerouac and William S. Burroughs, the latter of whom used it as the title of his most scabrous tale: once in a great while, you can glimpse things as they actually are and see the ugly thing on the end of a fork you would prefer to shove into your mouth on spaced-out autopilot. Which is to say that most of the time reality hides in plain sight; it disappears into pattern, repetition, and our sense of the normal. Over time we become "blind to the obvious," as economist Daniel Kahneman writes, but also "blind to our own blindness," which means we become tragically unaware of our own perceptual shortcomings.

But when we break through to the naked lunch moments and realize that the bleakness is, well, *bleak*, we can find a sort of liberation in the abyss. Julie Norem, a psychology professor at Wellesley, argues that pessimism is a better way of preparing for the future than its more celebrated opposite.[3] By letting go of the childlike optimism that typifies so much of American discourse and instead focusing on the horrible things that will probably happen, based on a fairly horrible track record, we can plan to meet these grim challenges with a healthy dose of realism. In similar research at New York University, psychology professor Gabriele Oettingen shows that "pessimism can be a better motivator for achieving goals than optimism," because excessive positivity can lead to complacency.[4] As *Psychology Today* put it, "People with a depressed mood may demonstrate more accurate judgment about an event (real or imagined) and a more realistic perception of their own abilities and limitations."[5]

So, friends, take a walk on the pessimistic side of American life and see where it leads you! Maybe then the inexplicable aspects of contemporary culture will start to make more sense. A second impeachment defense headed up by a blustering lawyer from "Phillydelphia," as he said to the Senate, who was previously known for representing a man who claimed to have bitten into a deep-fried rat at a KFC? Makes total sense if you are thinking in terms of the ludicrous decline and tragic fall of the American empire.

But the biggest shift will be in how we imagine the American project overall. If we get rid of blinkered sports fan nationalism (America, F@*# Yeah!), civilizational grandiosity, feel-good denialism, and cultural smugness, we can glimpse the outlines of a much different country than the one our politicians love to rapturously salute on the Fourth of July. We used to decry the Soviet Union as the ultimate example of a societal failure and tsk-tsk at Latin American countries going through coups and hyperinflation so quickly that the middle class would disappear with all its savings in a few weeks, and these things were undeniably tragedies at an unfathomable scale. But what about the ways in which the United States is failing hard and fast in health care, infrastructure, and even the basics of democratic governance? As one of my shivering academic friends pointed out in a week in February 2021 in which an ice storm crippled the Texas power grid and 246 people died from exposure—at least in the brutal, soul-destroying Soviet Union, people had heat.[6] And when it became clear in spring 2021 that some of my acquaintances were getting vaccines simply because they knew someone who knew someone with the inside scoop or because they had overheard something at their local Buddhist center or because the bungled Health.gov website didn't crash at the one moment they logged in, and that the official channels were clotted with incompetence and the grimy residue of corruption, my well-traveled friend, a Latin American studies scholar, told me it was just like living in Cuba twenty years ago, when Cubans almost couldn't get anything, not even food, without relying on informal, back-channel, word-of-mouth networks.

There is an infinite sadness to being an American in the 2020s—and even the most privileged among us must come to terms with that heavy reality before we can begin to heal from endless months of COVID stress and too many years of Trump trauma, both of which landed on top of all the intricately layered forms of suffering that came before. If you've had a terrible couple of years that felt like a tree falling on your house, keep reminding yourself: *I'm not depressed. America is depressing.* It's one case in which the old breakup line needs to be flipped: "It's not me, it's you."

23 Obscene Delirium

When the world was on fire during the first summer of a plague and a simultaneous global recession, it was hard to imagine that a good number of people once worried about the corrupting influence of philosophers and literary critics. I'm not talking about ancient Greece, which put Socrates to death for being a total *noodge*; I'm talking about America in the 1980s, when postmodern theory was a thing. Postmodernism, or Pomo, was like a cool underground party for bookworms that somehow blew up and went mainstream for about fifteen minutes. When it popped into view on college campuses sometime during the Reagan administration, it prompted horrified gasps, sensual moans, and cynical eyerolls in response to its alleged attack on all sorts of conventional wisdom, especially the belief in capital *T* truth. Competing forms of truth? What next? A belief that gender identity is not fixed at birth but is instead fluid and mutable? That the institution of marriage could adjust to accommodate homosexuality? That the pope was fallible and maybe even flammable? Oh, it was all too much to bear for the pearl-and-Rolex-clutching classes.

Perhaps not surprisingly, one of the arch-villains of this cultural moment was a French philosopher named Jean Baudrillard. "The secret of theory is that truth does not exist," Baudrillard whispered, seducing a few grad students in the humanities and maybe a few others with his gallic charm but hardly creating a mass movement like Amway or Mormonism. Nonetheless, Baudrillard was what passes for a gigantic rock star in my line of work. He was a rogue cultural critic, a provocateur, a serious philosopher, and a bit of a performance artist all at once.

Because academics are generally ignored outside of France, unless they are able to build weapons of mass destruction, I give Baudrillard enormous credit for getting under people's skin. In the 1990s he said cleverly annoying things like "The Gulf War Did Not Take Place," which was a great surprise to the Iraqi casualties who had been literally bulldozered into the sand. But of course, he meant something that was both more esoteric and more pointed about the U.S. invasion: he knew the killing was real but thought it was more "atrocity" than "war."

Perhaps if he were alive today, he might have written a similarly provocative essay claiming that *the Trump administration never happened* because whatever Trump was during his first four-year Washington rampage, he was not in any sense *an administrator*. A wannabe mob boss? A huckster? A scam artist? A chaos agent? A reality star? A Cheeto führer? An Adolf Twitler? He was all these things. But he was not doing administration per se in those gazillions of hours of "executive time" (such as watching *Fox and Friends*) between long days on the links. Trump and his minions had little interest in administration in any meaningful sense of the word; they were much more devoted to its opposite, which was neglecting proper management, hiring unqualified stooges, and generally running things into the ground in order to focus on plundering and posturing. *Administration* implies some awareness of rules and procedures, but the Trumpistas were famously unwilling to play by any inconvenient rules, to the extent they had any awareness of them. If anything, they were anti-administrative in their approach to matters of state.

Baudrillard would not have been shocked by the rise of Trump nor his sins. Even in the 1980s, he fretted about the future of an America in which depraved values and tastes were ascendent. "It is a world completely rotten with wealth, power, senility, indifference, puritanism and mental hygiene, poverty and waste, technological futility and aimless violence," he wrote, before adding darkly, "and yet I cannot help but feel it has about it something of the dawning of the universe."[1]

After learning to drive late in life, he rented a big fat car like a proper American and drove across the United States around the same time that Trump was getting famous/infamous in the 1980s for a ghost-written book touting his business genius, which was supremely ironic because he was fighting off bankruptcy and well on his way to being (literally) the least successful businessman in the past half-century of American life.[2] Utterly unlike the simulated business tycoon and future political schemer in both his politics and perceptivity, Baudrillard wrote a scathing, funny, peculiar critique of what he had seen in the Lower 48 during the Reagan years. "Americans may have no identity, but they do have wonderful teeth," he observed in his book simply called *America*, one of his best-known titles along with *Cool Memories* and *Simulacra and Simulation*. These complex books were unusual for appearing on coffee tables and in sci-fi blockbusters like *The Matrix* in 1999—not the norm for recondite texts about the vexing nature of modern life, with its slippery surfaces and uncertain depths.

Back in the eighties, Baudrillard was already attuned to the emergent world in which images were realer than real and media defined our interior lives with greater and greater precision. "The space is so saturated, the pressure so great from all those who want to make themselves heard," he wrote. "There is in effect a state of fascination and vertigo linked to this obscene delirium of communication. A single form of pleasure perhaps, but aleatory and dizzying."[3] It remains true today, where I live half my waking life inside the claustrophobic bubbles of corporate mediation with names like YouTube, Microsoft Outlook, Twitter/X, Reddit, Facebook, Instagram, and CNN. It's an exhausting way to live because it is draining something precious out—attention. In *The Matrix*, when Neo discovers he is called a "coppertop" because his energy is being harvested as he dreams, we are being offered a fundamental insight about the attention economy then in its infancy.

The obscene delirium of communication. Even during the early years of cable television and the videocassette revolution of the 1980s, Baudrillard intuited what would prove true in the coming decades: that media was becoming the nerve center of everything, and certainly the most important industry of our time. I always put it this way: whatever railroads were to the nineteenth century, what oil was to the twentieth century—which is to say, the thing that made everything else possible—that is what media corporations have become in the twenty-first century. (And here is the part where you should feel free to imagine Laurence Fishburne saying, "Welcome to the Matrix!")

When the political scientist Francis Fukuyama famously declared "the end of history" after the Berlin Wall came down three decades ago, he believed the epic struggle between capitalism and socialism was finally over because the markets of the democratic West had triumphed decisively over their collectivist rivals. But he was trying to call a boxing match that had quite a few rounds left. Socialism is quietly ascendant even in the United States in the 2020s, especially among young people, and the greatest economy of the past thirty years is micromanaged by the vicious authoritarians in the Chinese Communist Party. The real victory wasn't capitalism over socialism, a battle that remains unresolved—it was the triumph of media, especially new media, over any opposition to its total domination of human life. Say it again: *the obscene delirium of communication.* The profits and ethics in the modern communication industries are certainly obscene, but the delirium is equally real: we are driven to distraction by email, social media, surveillance capitalism, streaming services, and the twenty-four-hour news cycle. Increasingly rattled and anxious, we live in a world built for the benefit of algorithms, not human beings, and just as Fukuyama claimed that there was no getting outside of Western capitalism after the fall of the Berlin Wall, now there is (practically speaking) no getting outside of the attention economy and its seductive expectation of constant frenzied engagement. I think Baudrillard would have let out a mirthless chuckle if he saw how deep the hole had become. *Media über alles.*

Last night, for the first time in a long time, I was thinking about a cool Cheap Trick song from the 1970s called "Dream Police." I wrote it as a title for something I was doing in a Google doc, then erased it ten minutes later. This morning I woke up, opened Facebook, and discovered the video for the song at the top of my queue, even though

I've never looked it up and spend relatively little time thinking about Cheap Trick. Yet there it was, waiting for me to click on it, which I did dutifully, even though I was shaking my head and thinking, *This is how people end up wearing tinfoil hats*. Do you remember the lyrics to the song?

> The dream police
> They live inside of my head
> The dream police
> They're coming to arrest me
> Oh no, Well I can't tell lies
> 'Cause they're listening to me
> And when I fall asleep

Bet they're spying on me! Sometimes they really are watching—that much is undeniable in a post-Snowden world. But much of the time, it just feels that way because the algorithm knows us better than we know ourselves. What is being harvested, processed, and consumed in the swirling new economies of the digital century? Go look in the mirror. Because it's a truism nowadays that if you're not paying for a service like Facebook or TikTok, *then you are the product*—and your most intimate data is being served up to the real customer (marketers, governments, who knows?). That is the point of Shoshana Zuboff's 2019 masterpiece, *The Age of Surveillance Capitalism: The Fight for a Human Future at the New Frontier of Power*.[4] When everything else—from coal seams to fisheries to fresh water to forests—has been exploited, corralled, drained, pumped dry, and brought to market, then one of the few remaining landscapes worth exploiting is *human interiority*. That is why in the increasingly obscene delirium of ubiquitous media, at a time when screens dominate our professional and personal lives, the ability to recognize, manipulate, and monetize our desires, dreams, identities, and obsessions is infinitely more valuable than gold.

24 Animal People

I have a very nice friend who gives most of her emotional resources to animals. She is also very good to the people in her life, which is not necessarily the case with an emphatically self-described "animal person," who sometimes deal with their fellow bipedal mammals with a disdain that one would normally reserve for wayward priests and lawyers.

My friend prioritizes the world of baby raccoons and broken birds in a way that can seem excessive to the point of theatricality. Like a self-appointed deputy to Mother Nature, a righteous Karen of the wild, she needs to intervene whenever some small creature might be in need. A deer seems lonely living in a hay-strewn pen at a rural seminary? She springs into action, visiting it for months, even if it requires an hour's drive each way. An owl is hooting mysteriously in a neighbor's tree? She laser focuses on the possibility that it's telling her something in *secret owl language*. A black-eyed possum is crawling across a rural highway? She declares she would rather cross into oncoming traffic and cause a head-on collision than kill the black-eared critter because "the world has too many selfish humans already."

Aside from assassinating a random family on the highway, which is a little difficult to condone, these are beautiful acts of interspecies empathy. They might seem exaggerated, even maudlin, but they are rooted in kindness and care for a world outside of herself and her species. I admire this (and like this person very much).

But what I never could grasp is how she eats meat. She was always a chowhound carnivore as much as anyone else in the slice of middle America where we lived in the nineties, and she just couldn't give it up. Did she know it was contradictory? Yes, but she couldn't change. It was just too hard to pass on sausage and schnitzel, and her guilt about her diet may have fueled her dramatic expressions of animal compassion in other contexts. Rather than singling her out for critique here, I really mean to suggest that she was a sign of things to come. Because we now live in the paradoxical era that is the best and worst of times if you have feathers, fur, or fins. The best is the endless celebration of animal charm and creativity that circulates on the internet in the form of YouTube videos, GIFs, and memes; the worst is the industrial animal holocaust that sustains our foodways.

The former is quite familiar. Most of us live in a bubble of animal sentimentality that dominates our distracting, restorative daydreaming about how kind, cuddly, and wonderful these creatures are. *Piglets! Manatees! Puppies! Sloths!* It seems they exist to perform cuteness that elicits a smile in our corporate cubicles or when we're trapped in some uncomfortable anxiety zone. I don't think I've ever gone down the rabbit hole (literally!) of cute creatures as much as I did during the pandemic and the years since. Some days it's the only thing I really want to do. One morning I watched a video of a child holding six yellow ducklings in a patch of mint. The whole scene looked like it had jumped out of a child's picture book, and with addition of a soft folk soundtrack, the short video made it hard not to well up. I feel my face changing as I watch: the adult face of responsibility and toil, the "game face" of work and obligation, drops for a moment, and something else that feels like joy fills my chest. Ironically, in the earlier days of the internet, I used to mock people who enjoyed silly animal videos, assuming that they were twee softies cruising for a cheap sentimental fix, but now I'm the one tearing up at the sight of a rescued fawn. I've been won over to the feathered and fluffy and make no apologies at this stage of Trump/Caligula's descent. The genuine hardness of American life invites this turn toward the softness, no matter how maudlin and cheesy. We take the relief where we can find it.

So, I don't begrudge anyone their little zones of tenderness, their need for a therapeutic oasis in an unfeeling world. Any expressions of kindness toward any creatures are a net gain in our lives.

Yet there's something unsettling about loving these telegenic critters in videos, gifs, and memes in a society blithely engaged in the unprecedented slaughter of actual animals. Of course, America is not alone in its animal hypocrisy, but it does eat more meat per person than any country except China and Australia. The U.S. statistics are staggering next to the discourse of sentimental sharing. How many pigs were killed last year versus how many videos of cute little piglets were circulated? It might be a one-to-one ratio, but who knows? PETA estimates 120 million pigs were slaughtered in 2018 in the United States, which is a small fraction of the billions of chickens, goats, lambs, cows, turkeys, bison, buffalo, deer, and fish killed for food, clothing, and other uses that we destroy each year for little reason, in most cases, other than "It tastes good" and/or "Tofu is weird."

How does someone send a GIF of Babe the wonder pig to a friend while ordering bacon at Denny's? I suppose a version of this has always allowed Westerners to eat cows and pigs while ridiculing "foreign" cultures that eat dogs or whale. To my mind, this paradox of appreciation and decimation is what characterizes an unhealthy relationship with animals. It is a kind of mass cognitive dissonance that allows for incredible cruelty beneath a veneer of love.

I haven't held a bird since 1977. He was a nervous baby-blue parakeet that I called "The Great Waldo Pepper," which might seem overly grand but made perfect sense in my eleven-year-old brain: that same year I had written *Randolph the Great* in a mess of glue and glitter on my Christmas stocking, which was a little peculiar next to the ones simply marked Dad, Mom, and Erik.

Because I hadn't been allowed to have pets, the parakeet was a big event when he came home from the mall. I thought he was beautiful but impossibly delicate. I remember being anxious to touch him, and he vibrated with panic whenever I held him (or maybe we both did). No one showed me what to do, how to care for him, and so he would escape his cage and careen around the room, smashing into the windows and making me feel inept and freaked out. My mother would come in the room to help, but it wasn't much use. I had to wait until he was exhausted behind the couch and then reach in to pull him out with shaking hands, like a civilian delivering a baby.

I don't remember how he died. It wasn't long after he came to our little house. But I remember what came next.

Birds disappeared for forty years. Somehow I was disconnected from a lot of things I had known early on while I tried to survive a tricky childhood, a chaotic marriage, professional setbacks, and the duties of a parent. Once I turned fifty, I rebooted my life, and the old things started to come back, bit by bit.

Now I have a bird feeder to watch over coffee, and I marvel at videos of cockatiels, parrots, and parakeets on YouTube. I love the intelligence of crows solving problems; I love stories of ravens, like one in which a rescued bird yanked its owner's hair to wake him, opened the fridge and threw its contents on the floor, and allegedly flirted with its owner's girlfriend, so much so that the owner called the bird "a dick" (he was kidding because he liked the bird as a visitor, even if he was a bit much as a roommate). I'm not a birder per se, but I'm never more relaxed than when watching the tenderness of people toward birds, and birds toward people.

In the summer of 2024, burned-out and bleary-eyed from ill health and overwork, I took a leave of absence from my job to remember how to be a person rather than a jittery flesh monkey. Using a technique known as EMDR, a therapist guided me through a free flow of mental images to help me process trauma. Something strange happened in the first session: every time I imagined something upsetting, a large black bird appeared in my mind and guided me to safety in the mountains. This happened three times in one hour. Not being the kind of person who has mystical visions, I wondered: *Why were birds saving me? And why was it a big black crow or raven, birds often associated with death and loss?* Other than watching bird videos that made me dream about having a crow friend who would walk beside me and my dog, I only had one other rational explanation. During a visit to an animal sanctuary a few years earlier, I had a raven land on my arm, and I felt the heft in its four-pound frame along with its considerable intelligence. I guess my subconscious remembered that injured raven.

The following week I left Austin and went to the West Texas desert for some dusty quiet. It settled me somewhat, but when I came home a few days later, I was ragged beyond belief. I had gotten through six fractious years running my department and endured the worst period of bad health in my life. Desperate to experience a different kind of life, I decided I was leaving Texas and not coming back until someone forced me. I was lucky to have a research leave—I could carve out almost seven months away, giving me my first semester far from campus in twenty years. Three days later I was alone on a plane to Chicago, a place where I know no one, to see if I would feel better in a town where I could walk between brownstones and funky mom-and-pops without melting from the heat. I walked all over Logan Square, Wicker Park, Ukrainian Village, and other neighborhoods that were as exciting as anything I had seen in London or Berlin, two cities I fetishize. I loved the walkability of Chicago; I loved being in a blue state; I loved its diversity. I loved the novelty because I didn't know anything about the neighborhoods, as opposed to its downtown. I left Texas under a heat dome with a "feel like" temperature of 115; I arrived where the evenings slipped into the 50s while the highs stayed under 80. And then I took a train from the city and went to the water an hour away, in Union Pier, Michigan. Walking down a narrow dirt road on my way to a surprisingly beautiful white sand beach, a few minutes after I had talked to a college friend about our respective burnout and general lifelessness, I heard a raven in the forest. It was talking to me from some branches twenty feet off the ground. Birders will point out that ravens prefer the land somewhat north of Union Pier, but I'm pretty sure a big fat raven delivered some important metaphysical updates before it flew through the clearing and disappeared. Weirdly, it was just as I had envisioned in therapy. I really didn't know what to do with this mystical corvid encounter, but I liked it. A lot. The next day I returned to Chicago and found a small tattoo shop beneath the L. Working with an artist whose eyes were glazed with THC, I got three black ravens inked onto my shoulder to represent liberation, nature, and self-compassion. It was an impulsive gesture of the sort I never regret, but rarely indulge, in this case because I didn't want to seem like a cliché (weary middle-aged pilgrim marks small moment with splash of ink, News at 11!). Maybe it was cliché, maybe it was dumb, but I was happily doubling down on the irrational instead of remaining in the old lockbox of sober rationality. My ability to endure that cage has made me pretty good at my job and extremely good at taking care of the people around me; it had also made me miserable to the point of wanting to take a permanent dirt nap.

Perhaps I'll get a real bird someday. My wife likes the idea, or more accurately, she likes the idea of me being delighted—but I'm still wary. After reading about the raven being "a dick," I read about cockatoos: "In general, cockatoos do not make good pets for a first-time bird owner because of their constant need for attention, need for large amounts of time outside of their cages, and tendency to squawk and scream." After living through the first Trump administration and hopefully surviving the second, I may not be ready for a preening creature with "a tendency to squawk and scream," but I am ready for viral videos in which parakeets hide in cowboy boots, silky ravens talk smack to their human companions, and parrots pretend to make coffee on the kitchen counter and then perform circus tricks like flinging themselves into a crazy rotation around a stick like a mad feathered pinwheel. That much I can do. If it can work for a hard case like Robert Stroud, the so-called Birdman of Alcatraz, who befriended and reared sparrows in his cell as a way of surviving the brutal conditions in California penitentiaries of the 1920s, something like aviary therapy might work for the rest of us. I know birds are not for everyone, but animals are. If we could restore animals to their rightful place in our world, as totems, guides, and friends rather than raw materials for industrial dismembering, we might have a profound realization: we need them much more than they need us.

25 Dreams Never End

I was about fifteen when Ian Curtis hanged himself. He was already well-known as the singer of the post-punk band Joy Division, whose reputation has dilated crazily in the years since his death in 1980. He was many things in his short life: a gifted poet, a mesmerizing performer, a young man who was handsome in a pale, contorted way, not to mention stylish in the grayed-out manner of Northern England in the seventies. Dark work pants, heavy long coats, short hair, thick old-man shoes, no color. A little like Brecht in East Berlin: austere and serious to look at. Behind the scenes he could goof around like any twenty-three-year-old, but in most photos Curtis is a solemn yet shining creature, like a boy at his parent's funeral. All the light lands on his face and gives him a sepulchral glow. And because he suffered from epilepsy, he held himself with a kind of stiffness, almost like he was bracing for the next seizure.

All these things I found immensely significant as a teen. Still do. But more than anything, I was riveted by the fact that he killed himself on the eve of his first American tour. I was young and didn't think it was possible to have so many gifts, so many new things unfolding, so much grace and grandeur, and still want to foreclose everything yet to come. I couldn't understand how he gave up so much.

I do now. At least in a sense. And for this morbid understanding that I never sought, I blame the haunted dreamworld where we spend almost half our lives. I've heard some people slumber happily every night, not fighting for their subconscious lives, but at least in my circles, nocturnal chaos seems more common than bliss.

When Curtis died and his bandmates bravely reconstituted themselves as New Order, quickly becoming one of the most important English groups of the 1980s, their first album featured a song called "Dreams Never End," which moves propulsively through the gloom of an LP suffused with mourning and tentative rebirth. "Dreams Never End" could be an exhortation, like something on an inspirational poster about reaching for the stars, but instead, it's more of a curse. The song churns in despair, mechanical and cold, and makes me think of the cognitive darkness where we spend so much of our lives, never quite pulling free.

Night could be restorative for a well-loved middle-aged man with a warm bed. Instead, like everyone I know, I spin into an anxious headspace where I chew my mouthguard like gum and half-sleep through vague feelings of losing things, running from people, drinking paint, and going obsessively over the same emotional terrain. It's an exhausting way to rest. Our collective fears get imported into our unconscious lives and are reworked into a mad parade of imagery (without sound, at least for me). Last night I dreamed of a huge porcelain hippo standing alone, like a sentry in the middle of an abandoned construction site, before his face cracked off for no reason and out poured some unexpected piñata innards—all I know is that it wasn't candy. At moments like this I wonder where I went wrong: "WTF brain? What did I do to you? This is what I get when I close my eyes? Why can't I just dream of puppies and rainbows and old episodes of *Cheers*?"

COVID dreaming was even worse, as if the pandemic had infected our deepest thoughts. In the early months of COVID's spread, psychologists in Finland studied more than four thousand people and discovered they were sleeping "substantially more," waking more often during the night, and experiencing 26 percent more nightmares than before the pandemic.[1] Working on a parallel path, a Harvard researcher explored pandemic dreams that she collected in great detail, suggesting that they are a continuation of our waking concerns about succumbing to COVID, often manifested as a nightmare onslaught of bugs or worms or simply being trapped in a hospital bed.[2]

After so many months of living with the threat of COVID-19, I've never had such a literal pandemic dream or even an obviously figurative one in which bugs, for instance, represent the small virus cells attacking our bodies. Instead, I get a lonely hippo with a face like a disintegrating mosaic, standing near a highway construction site. Such idiosyncratic dreams might be a source of worry in the near future: I read that Nokia Bell Labs has automated the study of dreams, making it possible to quickly analyze thousands of dream reports with a sophisticated algorithm. The researchers claim their magic tool can even determine which dreams fall into the normal range and which dreams are "outliers" that may signify "stress or potential mental health issues."[3] I certainly don't want to get in trouble for abnormal dreaming.

My upbeat partner is not so different. Horrible things that never happened were now happening in her pandemic dreams. She had been reading about the terrifying orange skies over the Bay Area in summer 2020 and was upset before bed. Like me, she fights her way out of dreams every morning, something that wasn't the case before COVID. She distracts herself with coffee and news and bustling, until she forgets. But dreams never end, do they? They lurk. They wait. They return. And I have to ask: *What do they want?* Psychologists claim that they want to prepare us for the challenges of real life: by this way of thinking, dreaming about being trapped in a COVID ward should encourage us to take precautions during the day, but I find this pretty dubious. The mental screen inside my head is not serving any daytime function that I can detect; instead, it's like Salvador Dali is the visual DJ for a zonked-out rave in some chaotic underworld of dark tunnels and dead ends where the images are changing faster than I can count, each one vividly drawn, exceptional in quality, and seemingly unrelated to real life. The broken hippo prepares me for precisely nothing in my actual life, yet there he is, disintegrating majestically, like the final shot in a Tarkovsky film.

I used to drink more than I do now, not because I'm wiser but because at age fifty-seven I'm more fragile, and so I miss the feeling of erasure that heavy drinking used to provide. It's something like the sublimely deep snuffing out you get from a general anesthetic before surgery, which you can't do too often unless you own your own hospital or hire a personal doctor like Michael Jackson (it didn't work out great for either of them). When you go to sleep so completely like that, it feels deliciously like *nothing*—and unnervingly like a dress rehearsal for oblivion. Maybe that seems bleak and gothic and somewhat Joy Division in spirit—but I don't see it that way. That blackout sleep is a gentle holiday away from the hard laboring we do in the dreamworld of REM sleep, a gift even for those like me who want to live.

26 Lowered Expectations

I get how hard it is to admit defeat, to lower our expectations. Even when things are breaking down in every part of the national machine, from public health to education to foreign policy to law enforcement, it's hard to let go of the easy triumphalism that has characterized so much of American life.

Triumphalism is a domineering mentality that took off when the United States became a superpower in the mid-twentieth century. A by-product of the old American exceptionalism—the belief that the United States is unique and even divinely blessed to lead humanity to a brighter future—triumphalism promises that the United States will always magically prevail. It may be bloodied and dazed like Rocky Balboa, perhaps, but it'll still knock out the bad guys in the final round. Such intoxicating nationalism can provide a useful survival mechanism, offering promise and comfort in the crazy time of COVID-19 that the United States deserves to wag the giant foam finger that says, "We're Number 1!"

But even in its most understandable form, American triumphalism is wishful thinking. To create a more ethical, sustainable, and humane country at home as well as moral credibility abroad, Americans need to see the consequences of our collective actions with clarity, rather than hiding behind comforting mythologies that keep us from seeing the obvious defects in our plans for Afghanistan, Iraq, or the pandemic. We need to acknowledge our national limitations, not pretend that

Fig. 11. Local business destroyed by fire: Texas French Bread, Austin, 2023. Photo by author.

they don't exist. Like a narcissist on a dating app, we need to lower our expectations.

This became vivid to me in the second pandemic summer, here in the sunny boomtown of Austin, Texas. One day I was out enjoying a swim at the beautiful Barton Springs, watching hippie yoginis and grad students reading philosophy in the sun, feeling that Austin was still a cool little blueberry in the middle of inflamed red Texas. The next day, at the Texas Capitol just a few miles away, Governor Greg Abbott signed S.B. 8, a notorious law—referred to as "the heartbeat bill"—that empowers citizen vigilantes to file lawsuits against anyone helping someone get an abortion after six weeks, even in cases of rape or incest, even if their only "crime" is providing a ride to a clinic.

It shook me. Everywhere I looked around Texas in the following weeks, I saw democracy being smothered under a pillow of meanness, privilege, and the narrow self-interest of a slim conservative majority. Throughout the summer Governor Abbott rolled out new voting restrictions targeting the poor, Black, and brown in ways that can only be called Jim Crow Redux. The state adopted a "permitless carry policy" that lets anyone walk around with an unregulated handgun in full view, even though police chiefs lobbied against this one, which could make things messy for them during the active shooter incidents that are almost as regular here as Friday night football.[1] And the state began blocking teachers from engaging students in discussions of white privilege and other political subjects that offend right-wing sensibilities. Conservatives have been shilling these kinds of exclusionary and retrograde policies for decades, hiding behind the flag—and an imagined, monolithic, triumphalist America—as they chip away at Americans' actual rights, one by one. It's a stance that convinces too many Americans that, simply because they *are* American, they possess a kind of inherent virtue. Donald Trump, the purveyor of endless bogus sales pitches (Trump Steaks, Trump Air, Trump Vodka, *Trump Magazine*, Trump University), is just the latest face of it, though he did brag about being "more humble than you would understand."[2] When it comes to being humble, he is the best!

The influential Christian philosopher Reinhold Niebuhr thought a lot about dynamics like the ones playing out in America today. A believer in the "ineluctable tragedy" of the human condition and a complex vision of Christianity that has nothing in common with the huckster megachurch "prosperity gospel" of today, Niebuhr argued for a thoughtful politics of humility and moderation, not boastful certainty—in the United States or anywhere else. He said that the United States "must slough off many illusions which were derived both from the experiences and the ideologies of its childhood innocence," warning that "otherwise either America will seek escape from responsibilities which involve unavoidable guilt, or it will be plunged into avoidable guilt by too great confidence in its own virtue."[3] Dr. Martin Luther King Jr. extended this critique of American victory culture in the 1960s, rejecting U.S. imperialism and capitalism with a fury that has often been whitewashed out of popular memory. A decade later Jimmy Carter asked Americans to lower their thermostats a few degrees and wear sweaters to save energy. The right wing mocked him as a wimp and a clown—how dare he imagine life with any limits, in God's special garden of privilege and power?

People who assume America is always the champ (and always *should* be the champ) cannot understand our real history of oppression, exclusion, and failure to secure a prosperous and secure life for many of our own citizens—let alone for the people in countries where we intervene as a global hegemon, promising to bring freedom to the masses but delivering a much more brutal outcome.

Recognizing our shortcomings is neither nihilistic nor anti-American. To the contrary: if America has the capacity for collective goodness and greatness as a country, we must earn it through the hard work of self-honesty, not simply by declaring victory while stumbling forward into the next quagmire at home or abroad. In red states like Texas, it means challenging the obscene war on historical truth, reproductive rights, and racial justice that mythmakers on the right are waging for their own self-interest. As a country, it means we must reject the empty promises of MAGA victory culture in favor of real American virtues that rest on evidence, nuance, clarity, compassion, and an acceptance of our own limitations. It's the only way to debunk the narcissistic nationalism that Trump has ridden to political dominance.

27 Electric Kool-Aid Acid Reflux

Something cracked in the national facade in 2020. For those who hadn't slurped the MAGA Kool-Aid, the old blue-chip illusions of American exceptionalism and sublime democratic vistas started to seem like penny stocks from a boiler room in Queens, the borough where the spray-tanned con artist in the White House had learned his tricks. The government's inept response to the pandemic ensured that fear was everywhere, and death was just an unmasked cough away for most of the population.

Meanwhile, around the world, allies and enemies alike shook their heads in astonishment, often with no shortage of schadenfreude, wondering how a cocky nuclear superpower with crazy deep pockets could be undone so quickly by bumbling venality and general stupidity, both of which dictated Trump's response to the pandemic as well as the election he lost. No doubt it was a long time coming, but *the great unraveling* felt sudden and terrifying. Whatever forces had brought the seditious orange menace known as Donald J. Trump to the citadel of power had also blown a fuse somewhere in the national basement, and in the weeks after the November election, the machinery of democracy began throwing off an unprecedented shower of smoke and sparks, culminating in the made-for-TV spectacle of a psycho-dada white riot comprised of the cast of *Idiocracy* smearing feces and taking selfies in the U.S. Capitol.

Finally, on January 20, 2021, after failing to steal an election he had previously failed to rig properly, the flabby incubus-in-chief finally rolled off the body politic like Jabba the Hutt with erectile dysfunction, retreating angrily to his natural habitat of suntanned gargoyles and beachfront scammers along the Florida coast. Decent people everywhere, at least the ones who weren't stacked in trailers converted into temporary morgues for the COVID dead, let out a sigh of relief that was four years in the making. We had survived—sort of, maybe?

Maybe not. I suspect that something cracked inside many of the survivors of this political trauma, something that shifted how they saw the country and how they regarded their fellow Americans. We all got additional confirmation (unneeded, unsought) of what was wrong in the deep structure of a nation locked in "permacrisis" (2022's "word of the year"). By the end of 2020 anxiety and depression rates had quadrupled from where they were a year earlier, while the United States slipped below Slovakia and Chile on the democracy scale for its lowest ranking ever.[1] By the time Trump's campaign manager was texting in dismay about his former boss stoking *a real civil war* while the top U.S. general was lamenting that the United States had reached its "Reichstag moment," imperial squalor and institutional dysfunction had become the new normal. America had gone, as the kids say, totally bong-cloud.

If the scale of the awfulness was almost impossible to comprehend, anyone with any sense knew something terrible was in the air and it wasn't just a killer virus that was out of control and mismanaged with blithe indifference to the worst suffering imaginable (dying on a ventilator, alone, gasping and afraid). If a skywriting plane scrawled "WTF?" in giant letters visible from Maine to California, it still wouldn't be enough to capture the enormity of the shock, confusion, fear, and anguish in the country. An illiterate regime of buffoon fascism had taken control of the United States for four years and then in 2020, despite overwhelming evidence of incompetence, ideological toxicity, vacuous nepotism, and political thuggery, was *barely* defeated at the polls (well, it wasn't *that close*, but for a contest between a human man and a grifter troll, it was a nailbiter). One thing was very clear: it wasn't an inspiring story for a high school civics class. (Wait until they hear about 2024!).

Sigh. If the poignancy of living through a pandemic and an all-out assault on democratic norms hasn't been overwhelming enough for Americans, we were then pummeled by images of the latest war zones to break our hearts. I've made small donations to kids in Gaza, but it's a pittance compared to the billions my own government pours into the destruction of their homes, families, and futures. Likewise, I've given a little money to the Ukrainian cause, but it's nothing in comparison to the personal welcome of the Poles and Berliners who met Ukrainian refugees at the train stations with flowers and baby carriages and places to stay.

This European war has shaken Americans in an unusual way, at least in its first year. More than the ugly racialization of empathy at work that partially accounts for our collective fascination with Ukrainian heroism while ignoring other conflicts, such as in Africa, Western support for the underdog in the war against Putin seems based on something else—my hunch is that Ukrainians are demonstrating what *a living citizen* might look like in a country that desperately wants to survive. To a land of ghosts, this is an astonishing sight.

28 Sweatshop Barbie

I guess even the worst brand associations can be overcome if there is a loyal customer base willing to stick with a shoddy product. I mean, somebody flies on United after the engines fall off. Somebody orders seeds from Monsanto despite its environmental record. Somebody uses Facebook despite its privacy violations, tax avoidance, and willingness to experiment on users without permission.[1] And so it is with political brands, as I first discovered when I was living and working in a city in eastern Sicily in the early 2000s.

At certain times of year, the chaotic streets of Catania are home to trucks whose drivers are shouting the name of candidates through old-fashioned loudspeakers straight out of a Fellini movie. On a few occasions, while I sat on the seventh-floor balcony of an otherwise unspectacular apartment that enabled me to gawk at Mount Etna like Goethe's slack-jawed cousin, I heard an unusual name echoing up the urban canyon from the streets below, and by the time it reached me, it was almost like an aural ghost was haunting my ears. At first I assumed I was getting it wrong because *surely not,* but eventually I found myself on the street when the truck went past, and I heard it plainly: *Mussolini* was being shouted through speakers with an enthusiasm to match the bold lettering on the sides of the truck. Yes, Il Duce's granddaughter Alessandra Mussolini was on her way to a successful bid for a seat in the EU Parliament, another step in a long career in Italian politics that continues into the 2020s.

I had half-forgotten about Alessandra until recently, when she took on a new relevance in my mind. Now when I think about the surprising, unsettling renaissance of the most notorious fascist family in Italy, I think about Alessandra not as a relic of the past but a worrisome sign of the future. After all, she is the prototype for another blonde heiress with right-wing politics and a curvy, flirty Playboy aesthetic. I'm talking about Ivanka Trump, who said she could be "the first female president" in the early years of Daddy's reign (after her father's convictions in civil and criminal cases in 2024, she may have lowered her sights to a frumpy old congressional seat).[2] Ivanka's connections to *Playboy* are not merely stylistic. Just as Alessandra posed for *Playboy* covers in the 1980s, Ivanka not only dressed as a (visibly pregnant!) Playboy bunny for a photo shoot in *Harper's Bazaar*; she went to the Playboy Mansion with her father and posed between his mistress and her stepmom. *Check please!*

I suspect these two would get along famously if they didn't start fighting for attention. Indeed, if Ivanka ever stopped looking in her golden mirror of self-absorption for a moment, she might wonder if the Mussolini family offers some useful lessons for her fun-loving German American political dynasty in the making. Filled with the excitement of meeting a fellow household name, the future presidential hopeful would probably rush up to Alessandra, blaze her megawatt smile, and exclaim: "A modern career woman balancing work, family, and fascism? You go, girl! It's time to 'lean in' and claim our seat at the authoritarian table."

So much in common! Ivanka would learn that they both have three children, that they both worked as actresses (it's now well established that reality TV is just another acting job), and that both are married to controversial men. On the Italian side, we find a husband who was charged with child prostitution, while on the Trump side, we have the nepo baby Jared Kushner, whose tragicomic White House portfolio included everything that you could possibly imagine, even conflicts of interest and secret Russian meetings, all in the hands of an empty suit who probably couldn't manage a Starbucks.

Here's a thought: *Jared and Ivanka are just as bad as Donald.* While he's an old crazy racist grandpa wannabe dictator who doesn't even understand why his views are noxious, Ivanka and Jared should know better—which makes them *preternaturally awful.*

While it goes without saying that professional politicians are the most vainglorious twerps in American society, I never would have thought that the literal worst people would run the White House. But here we are, and if you start from the very bottom of American humanity and count upward, the list now goes: Freddy Krueger, J. Edgar Hoover, Tucker Carlson, the "Dating Game Killer," the ghost of Ted Bundy, Charles Manson, Ivanka Trump, O. J. Simpson, Rush Limbaugh, Jared Kushner, Stephen Miller, Jared from Subway, Harvey Weinstein, Dick Cheney, Elon Musk, Richard Nixon, and the various Trump boys, especially big pappy Trump and his over-long tie and ill-fitting suit, who, based on the suffering he inflicted, will always be in the running for *worst president ever* (even if George Bush and LBJ had much higher death counts abroad, Donald can always boast about having killed hundreds of thousands of his own countrymen through indifference, ignorance, and malfeasance during the pandemic).

Understandably, Donald gets 98 percent of the scorn from anyone who doesn't drop the phrases *anchor babies* or *fake news* in casual conversation, but we really should save some anger for his creepy-phony daughter and creepy-phony son-in-law, both of whom have only started their long careers of grift and entitlement and are always scheming for another bite at the political apple. Don't think the bad press or private wealth is going to dissuade them from "public service"! Nor will her declarations of being done with politics (by 2024 her friends said she was reconsidering her political options, and sure enough, she was back at her father's side in the victory photos on election night).[3] Nor will their lack of positive human attributes give them pause in their quest for power. Let's just think about them as human beings: I mean *really* . . . would anyone willingly befriend Jared, who looks like the internet phantasm known as "the slenderman" if he wore nothing but the Brooks Brothers version of skinny pants?

Add to that the bottomless ego of the trust fund scion who apparently thinks he *earned* his spot in the 1 percent, and you have someone who would take credit for the shining of the sun.

And who would want to collaborate with his, uh, "better half," the equally plastic creature who was long mocked as "Sweatshop Barbie" for manufacturing her company's shoes in a factory in Ganzhou, China, where the workers were beaten bloody? Well, at least we can say this for her: Ivanka's presence on my semi-facetious list of *worst Americans* is a special tribute to the working women of the world because she has broken through the glass ceiling and opened up a formerly male enclave of luxury grifters to go-getter gals such as herself. Just like Virginia Slims used to say in the 1970s to women in ads that co-opted the language of feminism in a way that is *oh so Ivanka*, "You've come a long way, baby!"

But really, what is so bad about her? Well . . . any catalog of Ivanka's sins would exhaust the devil's hard drive. This posable doll of a person has feigned compassion and undermined progress in so many contexts that it's dizzying to contemplate them all. But for starters, I blame her for: interfering with statements by the Centers for Disease Control that she had no qualification to edit during an epic public health crisis, thereby undermining confidence in one of the most reliable medical institutions in the world during a time of near panic. Pretending that she opposed separating kids from their parents, when she only made a tepid pseudo-dissent after the policy was authorized, despite having ample opportunity to lobby her father not to approve it in the first place. Letting her father claim she created fourteen million jobs, double the number that had been created at all, when she had created zero jobs except her own sinecure at Daddy's office. Uttering chirpy platitudes in a self-consciously sexy voice with a sexy baby name (Ivanka is Czech for "baby Ivana," her birth name) that makes her seem like a perfect blend of a faux feminist dating app CEO and one of the former beauty queens who now serve up lib-owning quips on Fox News. I also object to her being the kind of creepy gal who publicly calls her father "Daddy" at age forty, while he calls her the equally inappropriate "honey" and leers at her surgically sculpted torso.[4] Moreover, she loses major points for propping up the lie that is her empty suit husband, whose galling lack of expertise, compassion, and decency made him the worst person to be in charge of getting pandemic supplies and who, despite being very tall, was *always* over his head in every endeavor he pretended to lead at the White House.[5] Worst of all, Ivanka gets karmic demerits for aiding and defending the master of the "big lie" himself, the least qualified and competent president ever, the worst businessman (the numbers don't lie) of the past half-century, the skeeviest perv this side of Ron Jeremy's venereal wang, big daddy Donald himself. As he got worse and worse, she went right with him, doubling down on his carnage-inducing agenda, teaming up with her husband to undermine good science and clear communication about COVID.[6] Ivanka stood by when Jared compared COVID to the flu and argued that lockdowns were not "grounded in science."[7] He failed to use her favorite-child status to save desperate people, thereby exploding the much-peddled myth that she was somehow a moderating force on his savagery. Only long after the damage was done, well after the scandals, the elections, and the insurrection, did she cynically begin to distance herself from Daddy's fallen star—for a few years at least.

Oh Sweatshop Barbie and Plastic Slenderman of Death? How do we undo thy damage? You've given nepotism a bad name, and then you went prancing scot-free to the next scene of your white-collar crimes. Just weeks after the bitter end of the first Trump administration, you were already jogging in Miami, not far from your $30 million property, like a couple of regular folks with nothing to answer for. A couple of years later, and you were yachting around the world, with you, glorious Ivanka, posing with a surfboard under your arm in one photo, while in another you grace the Temple of Apollo with your goddess visage, along with a humblebrag caption that says you "reread" the Odyssey while on your fancy-schmancy sojourn. How do we balance the scales in favor of the people who died, the kids in the cages, and the scientists whose expertise you "trumped"? Especially when Biden-era social media suggests that *Ivanka and Jared have never been happier!* As Greg Olear put it in *Slate* in early 2024,

"Ivanka's Instagram feed is an alternate reality. It's what her life would have been like if her loutish old man had never been president, had lost in 2016, had never gone into politics, had never sold himself to the Russian mob, had dropped dead of a massive coronary on the set of *Home Alone 2*."[8] Does this mean she's gone from politics? Don't bet on it. I think she's a little coy possum hoping we'll give her a second chance if she plays politically dead for a few years and keeps her distance from Daddy. Once she noticed the furious backlash against Trump's election chicanery and January 6 thuggery, she muted the succession narrative that she had nurtured throughout Daddy's term and went into a well-coiffed reputation rehabilitation mode, like an exiled queen who was awfully, awfully sorry for all the beheadings. But once Daddy's brand was ascendant once again, she came back and "made a dazzling return to the political arena on election night when she stood by father Donald Trump's side in Florida as he surged to victory in the 2024 presidential election."[9]

In China, when Deng Xiaoping took power in 1978, he sentenced his predecessor's wife to death in a trial that was broadcast on television for multiple nights. The beautiful, cruel, and defiant Jiang Qing, also known as Madame Mao, had been a successful actress who used seduction as a path to power, which she wielded brutally during the Cultural Revolution of the sixties. "Sex is engaging in the first rounds," she explained. "What sustains interest in the long run is political power." The worse Mao became, the more she dug in. "I was Chairman Mao's dog," she said. "Whomever he told me to bite, I bit."[10]

I cannot suggest that the president's daughter should suffer the fate that befell Jiang Qing, who refused to recant her views and hanged herself in her cell before her death sentence could be fulfilled. Nothing in the U.S. Constitution allows for show trials to punish political figures who have fallen into disfavor, no matter how much they deserve public censure. Yet Ivanka and Jiang have something in common, even if it's not intelligence. After beginning as a seemingly apolitical figure, Ivanka followed her father into the darkness, functioning as his true political wife, enabling his deceptions, putting a glamour-puss face on his cruelty and vindictiveness. With zero thoughts of her own, something that was not true of Jiang, Ivanka has always been a decadent nepo baby on the make, enriching herself and her hubby to the tune of half a billion dollars while working in the White House, not to mention repeatedly violating the Hatch Act that prevents federal employees from making partisan statements (she violated it eight times in forty-eight hours, according to one report).[11]

I don't scorn her for using her plastic Barbie looks to her advantage or for running a rip-off fashion brand or even for having political ambitions that were the worst-kept secret in Washington. I scorn her because her political sins were consequential, and a society has a right to expect some sort of compensation. Maybe we don't do gulags and reeducation camps in the United States (we call them "internment camps," "detention camps," or "federal prisons"), but neither should we let the wicked prosper and prance off with book deals and softball interviews as if nothing happened. At the very least her name should be mud: unmarketable for purses, shoes, perfume, and most of all, political offices yet to come. Instead, she spent the Biden years wakeboarding near her secluded paradise on the Miami island called "Billionaire Bunker," posting Instagram shots of herself in deep but glamorous prayer at the Western Wall in Jerusalem, and responding to her father's first indictment by saying, "I am grateful to have had the honor of serving the American people, and I will always be proud of many of our administration's accomplishments." By summer 2024 she was reconsidering the possibility that she might serve in the White House once again.[12]

Really?

In 1876 Ulysses S. Grant, who was a brutal general, mediocre president, and terrific drunk, which may account for the fact that he was one of the best writers ever to stumble across the Oval Office, said, "If we are to have another contest in the near future of our national existence, I predict that the dividing line will not be Mason's and Dixon's, but between patriotism and intelligence on one side, and superstition, ambition, and ignorance on the other."[13] I love the association of patriotism with intelligence, which is rare in an era when cynical con artists wrap themselves in the flag for nihilistic purposes.

To defeat this new brand of "superstition, ambition, and ignorance," we must be able to name it. To rid the nation of the moral stench that the Trump regime and its enablers left behind like a flatulent corpse on a coroner's table, we must be able to shame it. People are tired of tiptoeing around the obvious: like a COVID patient injecting bleach, American democracy is being poisoned by craven opportunists like Ivanka and Jared. If people without character, insight, or expertise are allowed to run the country, the democratic process will not survive as anything other than an empty spectacle during election cycles, when it will provide a superficial pageant of egalitarian, meritocratic values meant to distract us from the creeping authoritarianism and civic dysfunction obvious to everyone except the self-interested and dim.

To my mind, every good cultural critic in the United States feels like a footnote to Frederick Douglass, who saw the original sins of the republic and called them out with righteous fury. "At a time like this, scorching irony, not convincing argument, is needed," he said in his justly famous and utterly blistering speech on July 4, 1852, in Rochester, New York. What he said next bears repeating: "Oh! had I the ability, and could I reach the nation's ear, I would today pour out a fiery stream of biting ridicule, blasting reproach, withering sarcasm, and stern rebuke. For it is not light that is needed, but fire; it is not the gentle shower, but thunder."[14]

29 Stress Test

The inauguration of Joe Biden and Kamala Harris seemed like demonstrable proof that the great American system, despite being stress-tested to levels not experienced since the Civil War, actually worked. *Phew!* We could all breathe a deep sigh and marvel that the bulwarks of our democracy held against the racist assault of political figures like Marjorie Taylor Greene, Josh Hawley, Matt Gaetz, Kristi Noem, Ron DeSantis, Paul Gosar, the QAnon shaman brigade, white supremacists, and Christian Nationalists and media fabulists like Ben Shapiro, Sean Hannity, and Tucker Carlson—but most of all, the original "Diaper Don" himself, Donald "Von ShitzInPants" Trump, as the Lincoln Project dubbed him, had left the building.[1] The "fascist, loofa-faced, shit-gibbon," as a Pennsylvania state senator mockingly called him, was gone.[2] *So glad that's over!*

Sort of. Between the "shit-gibbon's" first term and Kamala Harris's painful defeat in 2024, we entered the phase of U.S. history that might be known to future historians as "The Biden Band-Aid," in which the bleeding wounds of the past four years were lightly dressed but never quite healed. At first Biden's victory allowed a continent-wide sigh of relief among progressives, who were grateful for the return to semi-normalcy after the degenerate influence of the forty-fifth president. But I didn't think we were under blue skies—the early 2020s felt more like the eye of the storm. Biden could have pushed substantive action, deep structural reforms, and a long overdue racial accounting, but I never banked on getting more than a return to the old status quo from the centrist Democrat. "Don't fool yourself into thinking that the end of the Trump Administration marks the dawn of a new era," Julia Craven predicted in January 2021 in *Slate*. "The same whiteness that uplifted Trump's egregious policy agenda existed before him and will be around after he's gone. . . . If history serves as an accurate predictor, the desire to speak plainly and directly about racism will wane, and the idea that we have moved beyond this ugly moment in history will prevail. And so will whiteness, yet again."[3] In hindsight Biden's economic accomplishments often seemed more impressive to liberals than they did during his term, but what he offered wasn't enough.

Agreeing with Craven is depressing but apt. White people often want to externalize the evil, cordon off the threat, and imagine that the problem of white supremacy in the United States has been addressed, rather than facing their own complicity. I am as guilty of this as most whites. Last fall my dental tech told me that people coming *from* the small towns outside of Austin were refusing to put on masks even during COVID spikes, so her general rule was "If they have a drawl, they're not gonna wear it." But when I blame "rednecks" for spreading COVID or for attacking the U.S. Capitol or for spreading toxic ideas, it is a form of scapegoating that implicitly exonerates me, even though I'm the problem too. "The quieter phenomena of white complacency, downplaying, and silence are what gave whiteness the guts to violently storm government buildings wearing preprinted paraphernalia celebrating the attack," Craven wrote in *Slate*. "This is what empowered whiteness to attempt to rewrite history, disenfranchise Black voters, build pipelines through Native American reservations, and construct an entire conspiracy theory upholding Trump as a savior."[4]

The bar is set so low nowadays. When a former special forces officer, Christopher Miller, took the post of acting U.S. defense secretary in late 2020, his stated goals were "no military coup, no major war and no troops in the street," which, as *The Guardian* put it, were pretty "bleak aims for a country which considers itself a beacon of democracy worldwide."[5] We have cleared that bar (barely), and I'm glad for it, but I'm preternaturally nervous about what comes next. Like anyone else, I would prefer to have hope for the United States, but too often, hope feels like it's been evacuated of its real potential and what's left is just a truism for inspirational posters. *Hang in there, kitty!*

It's hard when I look at what is in front of us in the years ahead. The great scavenger hunt to stave off the next variant. The right-wing attack on democratic norms. Cruel deportations. Scrounging for health care. Flat tires. Bad smells. Broken systems. Colorful websites that don't work. Robocalls and spam texts. People who can't work because Jeff Bezos knows it's cheaper to program an AI to simulate "customer service," despite the fact that it's surreal, humiliating, and deeply ineffective on the customer side of the arrangement. I see the spaced-out and listless teens, my students among them, and know they struggle with unprecedented levels of anxiety, depression, and self-harm. I get it.

Looking for help with the yard, I hire two teenage boys through social media—their mom claims they are looking to make some pandemic money. I hope they don't represent the youth of America because my conclusion is this: *you'll never work harder than on the day you hired teen boys to help you with yard work.* The halting speech. The slouch. The perverse mix of total ignorance and weird *teensplaining*. Instead of working, they're talking about how octopuses are immortal and can reincarnate themselves forever, and as far as they're concerned, it's God's truth because they saw it on YouTube. I stare at them with a mixture of empathy and irritation, noting the black Walmart hoodie that is the universal signifier of the white working-class teenager as well as the black knit hat, even when it's seventy degrees, with long dark hair streaming out the sides. They're harmless, fundamentally decent, but ineffective—I don't know what to do with them because they don't know how to do very much. After twenty minutes they start whining that their back hurts or "there's dust in my eye"; you go around the corner and come back, and they're both sitting down drinking Mountain Dew and staring into an ant hill like it's a television set.

Don't they understand? America is unrelenting in its severity for everyone but the very rich. It's not a videogame you get to play on your sofa while poleaxed on edibles. And they were looking for work.

It's not like I captured them behind the Sonic and made them do this. But then I realized that maybe *they do understand,* at least at some unconscious level, and that's why they are the way they are. I'm sorry they had to grow up in such a fraught moment. I'm sorry we couldn't give them a better inheritance than a country teetering on the edge of civil war.

30 Walmart Salvation 2021

All through the second COVID winter, the *can't-find-a-vaccination* blues were echoing in my head, combined with too much work and not enough hope. Everyone was worn down. Nothing was available on the vaccine sites, and people under sixty-five who found a shot often did so by luck or lying. The whole dysfunctional landscape was depressing AF, as the whippersnappers say, and for the first time since the opening salvo of the great COVID war, of which my brain was starting to feel like a casualty, I was getting into the wretched mindset in which you're utterly convinced that *life is what happens when you're waiting for the drugs to kick in.*

One night I had too much of a substance called Delta 8, and the next day I woke up feeling like a used condom in the sand. It's a legal hemp derivative that is supposed to be somewhere between CBD and THC, but based on the experience of my middle-aged friends and me, all looking for something to help us sleep or relax, it has more in common with a very large horse tranquilizer. Maybe we overdid it, but we were all incapacitated by this utterly legal, totally unregulated substance, with the unluckiest one finding himself immobilized in a torpid panic of sweats, fever, and nausea. I was only slightly better off: I went to sleep feeling existentially adrift like a puppet without a puppeteer and woke up feeling hollow and cold and devoid of any discernible human emotions. I skipped breakfast, let the water run on me in the bath, and waited for the drug to wash out of my system.

So dumb but human. Every once in a while, as the pandemic wore on, I thought I needed to up the medication levels and would dip into opiates, benzos, weed, alcohol, and would have huffed a bottle of Febreze fabric spray if it had street cred as an ontological analgesic. Dreaming of pharmaceutical relief is such a dead end because nothing really knocks out the psychic horror of pandemic downtime like a good old-fashioned bucket of wine. Seriously, wine takes me closer to the promised land than anything other than watching *Adventure Time* or running blindly on the elliptical. But like Las Vegas, which I revisit every ten years and then immediately realize why it's a manic kind of suffering that should be avoided at all costs, I have to learn this pharmaceutical lesson in painful cycles repeated throughout my life, which probably means that I'm not learning it at all.

Today is going to be better though. In the middle of spring break, I wake up and realize that it's the last day of pandemic for me. Sadly, it will go on for many people, and for those with "long COVID" or anyone who can't or won't get a vaccination, it may never end. But at least symbolically, in the sense that I could lower my guard a few inches, my pandemic ends on a beautiful, breezy day in March 2021, a year after we went into lockdown in Austin. It was often grueling and disorienting, but of course, I was on a luxury yacht of velvety good fortune compared to most people. And even if the pandemic is going to continue for me in the form of masking and worrying about my parents not being able to get a vaccination in rural Texas, for psychological and ritualistic reasons, I'm going to mark a line on the ground, a geographical boundary on the map of my life, and say that's it, *finit, bastante*, enough. I want to have some control even if it's an epidemiological daydream. I have to mark some kind of milestone—like the horizontal black marker lines on the door jamb that document the growing height of a child, I want a black line that says: "Randy survived until this tall."

But getting to my make-believe last day of pandemic wasn't easy. Because America is a place ruled by luck, decentralized chaos, and privilege, even someone as well-off as I am (employed, able-bodied, insured) must wait for random good fortune to descend upon my computer screen with the news that a vaccination is available somewhere, anywhere, in the giant state of Texas. For weeks I was unable to even log onto my university's health portal, which we were told to use for vaccination appointments. Neither the broken portal nor my employer offered a helpline or anything else that could solve the problem. So, I was stuck in COVID limbo, deprived of my best chance at a vaccination, and I was not alone. At the biggest, richest, STEM-heaviest institution in the state, its proud flagship university, many employees had given up on its promises and were scrounging off campus for any signs of a vaccine. An anthropologist told me that everyone he knows is driving three hours to little Texas farm towns to get a jab. A Spanish professor told me that his wife got an out-of-town shot through a tip from a neighbor. And eventually, that's how it was with me. After months of looking on dozens of websites and shared Google Docs with all the links that one could check, I finally got lucky through a friend of my wife, who told us about a website that might work, and it did. I got an appointment not in a hospital or a clinic but in a Walmart supercenter in a town south of Austin named Buda, which looks like it should be pronounced like *Buddha* but is more like *byoo-da*. Which means I'll be the Buddha with the bubbas in Buda, seeking vaccine Nirvana and post-pandemic enlightenment as soon as they can get me on the schedule.

That's fine with me. I am grateful to get the vaccine at all, and especially grateful to the scientists who produced it in record time, often in the face of political and public hostility. But when you live in a big city filled with hospitals and medical researchers, it seems peculiar and maybe a little pitiful to get vaccinated with a lifesaving serum in a small-town Walmart after a long, chaotic, and mysterious search. It's as if I'm shopping for sweatpants and laundry detergent and motor oil and Greek yogurt and bran flakes and cat litter and then look down at my list and realize that one item has not been x-ed out—"miracle cure for death plague." As if I'm going to get home with the groceries and hear a voice from the kitchen: "Honey, did you remember to get the eggs? And what about that lifesaving injection?" It's ridiculous in an emblematic way.

But truly, I am thankful. The state of Texas couldn't help me, my employer was incommunicado for months, but the much-maligned Walmart came through. Of course it did: it's totally appropriate in the libertarian free-fire zone of Texas that big ugly corporations would be our only real chance, not the state government, not even the big public university where I work. The right-wing activist Grover Norquist once said that the goal of modern conservatism was to shrink government until it was small enough to drown in a bathtub, and boy howdy, have they succeeded—so much so that we have little choice but to pray that Walmart, CVS, Walgreens, and other generally unlovable corporations will save us with a vaccine produced by Big Pharma, which is already itching to raise the price at a time when only 20 percent of Texans have received a shot. It's a strange system, and at a different superstore, run by a different corporation, my wife waited for her shot in a gigantic line next to a woman who yakked so much in every direction that her nose kept popping out of its mask. Even in the crowded queue for a vaccine, some Texans *still do not know how to wear a mask*. It makes you wonder if these people know how to put on socks or if someone does it for them. The comedian Tom Segura has a similar question for people who seem in the gray area of functionality: "Hey man, do you drive to work or . . . *did somebody drop you off*?"

I'm hoping Walmart won't be like that. As we drive almost an hour south in the middle of one of the prettiest afternoons in recent memory, I realize I know very little about the neighboring town of Buda. A real estate website says, "Living in Buda offers residents a *sparse suburban feel*."[1] I learn that residents of Buda are known as "Budans," not Buddhists or Buddettes, and that the town's name is an adaptation of the Spanish word *viuda*, meaning "widow." It was a tiny nothing of a place until Austin started to sprawl into it over the last few decades: "Buda was incorporated in 1948," says one website. "By the mid-1980s it had attracted a cement plant and some craft industry."[2] Reading on, I learn that the town gets "national attention for its lighthearted wiener dog races, organized every April by the Buda Lions Club." Now all that sounds pretty charming, like I'm going to Mayberry and might find Don Knotts and Andy Griffith strolling around with Opie and Otis, but the reality is the typical "geography of nowhere" strip mall hardscape that constitutes 77.3 percent of all Sunbelt settlement (I made up that number, which is probably higher).

And so here we are. With a huge fading sign announcing an ocean of asphalt, the Walmart Superstore is exactly the same as every other version of its kind. I'm expecting the worst when I walk in: long lines, chaotic mismanagement, hostile people, short shorts, and long mullets. But it's not like that at all. There is no line, just on-time efficiency, and the two young women in white coats who check me into the system are relaxed and friendly (one is even reading a novel on her worktable). Right away I'm able walk behind a small screen, where a slender, elegant man with an Indian name prepares the shot, but not before swabbing my arm with alcohol and then fanning it with tender theatricality that is a delight to watch (so often Texas is not what you think, for good and ill).

I'm pretty moved by the experience, even as I marvel at the ragged scene around me. A lot of poor people are here, whispering to kids sitting on the floor. On the wall next to the vaccination area, the sheetrock has caved in and the linoleum is dirty. A twenty-two-inch tabletop griddle is jammed on a weird angle into a cart, like somebody got mad and stopped talking to it. Bags of Purina Cat Chow, boxes of baby toys, and inexpensive cruiser bikes seem abandoned in every corner—suddenly I realize I'm in the windowless "return room," which has been converted into a makeshift vaccination center.

I get the shot without sensation, just some surprise when the man drops the syringe and it clatters on the floor—"Don't worry," he says sweetly, "it went in." Almost immediately, I have what my partner dubs the *post vax glow*. I've been somber all week as I think about the freedom that the vaccine will provide, virally and psychologically. It's not natural, or at least it's not humane, to live with an unusual threat of extinction (on top of the usual ones) and to feel stuck in the endless routines of COVID safety. And now I'm able to feel slightly *unstuck* for the first time since 2019. My emotions are way ahead of the scientific reality—I know I'm not safe, especially not until the vaccine has a few weeks to work its magic, but I'm confident and joyous that I'm *safer*.

Perhaps we won't forget to address the collective trauma and individual wounds. Perhaps we will remain attuned to the desperate need to reinvent ourselves as a country that traps wonderful people (and a good many miscreants) in some pretty dire situations. Perhaps we will consider the need to repair the broken infrastructure at so many levels of American life, including what you might call our emotional infrastructure, that very frayed and fragile web of feeling that barely holds us together as a people but could form stronger bonds of community and belonging. But we also need to improve the regular kind of human infrastructure, the kind that could roll out a vaccination during a pandemic in an orderly, equitable manner, rather than forcing people to look for clues on social media, ask their friends if they've heard any hot tips, and refresh their screens for hours while they look for a chance to breathe without fear. That would be real freedom.

Such optimism will certainly be confronted by some deep cultural deficiencies. For one, America is a glutton's paradise. Too many things here are pitched to some level of desperation that reaches for cheap, fatty, and oversized (à la Walmart in its less heroic moments). It provides the illusion of abundance for this mythical "people of plenty," as a historian described us in the 1950s. I remember taking a language class in my thirties from an Italian woman who wore a beautiful black sweater on the first day of class. It looked like it cost three hundred dollars, and I glanced down, a little embarrassed by my cheap sweatshirt. But then she wore the sweater on the second day of class and the third day and the fourth day. She wore the sweater every day for three weeks before a different outfit appeared. And I realized it was because this suave woman from Palermo would rather have one extraordinary object than ten fast fashion sweaters that would quickly dissolve into skeins of junk in the wash.

I just want to have *one good sweater*, instead of a closet full of junk that is always almost ready for Goodwill. But somehow, with our Big Gulp extra-large Texas-tough mindset, which applies throughout most of the Lower 48 and Alaska too, we've never understood that quality matters more than quantity and that the worst feeling in the world is when you're full of something you despise—and how could you not unconsciously hate your poorly made shoes, soulless subdivisions, and beverages composed largely of corn syrup and bubbles? It's a superficial kind of satisfaction that clogs up too many lives. Stuffed to the gills, you can't eat anymore, but you remain hungry.

With its fluorescent acres of fast fashion, particleboard furniture, and junk food, Walmart is a massive part of that problem, but today it is my unlikely hero. I just wanted a little bit of closure—not the kind when the coffin lid comes down—and I found it here in Buda, Texas, in a glorified dollar store on the hot ugly interstate.

Of course, I'm lucky to have even the illusion of closure because there is no official end to the pandemic, no armistice, no parade. Like other friends who got the vaccine in late spring 2021, we were silly with possibility for a few weeks: we could visit one another without masking, we could touch a doorknob with a little less fear that we would rub our eyes and put a toxic droplet in our system; we could feel a little bit more confident about sitting in a restaurant. At times it felt like seventh grade had just finished and we were running down the streets at 3:15 p.m., untucking our shirts and screaming for candy.

This was amazing while it lasted, but mostly, we just went back to work, back to school, back to the movie theaters and bars, where sitting with strangers still seemed a little uneasy. Implicitly, we made some kind of agreement to move forward, to walk into rooms filled with strangers, to make our listening faces, to make human contact of a vague sort but nothing too heavy, too deep, too real—simply because the wrong sort of facial expression, the wrong sort of glance, maybe one filled with the chaos and sorrow of a species under serious duress, would trigger the release of something uncontainable in each of us—some disorienting surge of memories, feelings, and anxieties about the Trump years, the pandemic, the Biden response—something that can't be bottled or channeled, that would just run everywhere all at once, an emotional tsunami, submerging the flimsy structures of the modest little beach town called "me" under the waves of "it." And that's probably why we pantomime this thing called normalcy. Because we can't bear the surge.

31 Norway/Uvalde

It's hard to be somewhere so beautiful and feel so sad. These are the first words I type on the longest fjord in Norway at the end of May 2022.

All spring I had once again dreamed about getting out of Texas, and not just because the heat and humidity arrived much earlier than usual. The dumb viciousness of Texas politics is exhausting, even for someone like me who doesn't have a trans child being bullied, who didn't freeze to death in the killer grid failure of February 2021, or who isn't a migrant parent grieving a child in a detention cage. I'm luckier than most, and I still wanted to flee. To settle some frayed nerves. To imagine another way forward. Or maybe just to hide from the awfulness of it all.

Even in late May, it is still very cold in Norway, which is a welcome change for a couple of temporary Texans who hate the heat. Two hours north of beautiful Oslo, in a mountain valley blanketed with deep snow, my wife and I tried not to skitter off the narrow road in a rented Suzuki SUV. The vast lake to our right was still frozen all the way across but probably not thick enough to keep us from a Norwegian cold plunge.

You've probably never seen anything as stunning as the Norwegian countryside. I haven't. It's just like the YouTube travel videos that sustained me through pandemic loneliness and Sunbelt emptiness—the short videos always promised something better than home, some distant country with astonishing natural beauty, a pleasant built environment, and a sane way of living. My partner and I went through endless cycles of geo-fantasy in front of our devices. One week it was Portugal, then it was Ecuador, and finally it was Norway.

And that's how discount airfares brought us here, to the Sognefjorden, the largest fjord in the world, more than four thousand feet deep in spots, lined by snowcapped mountains even in summer, and filled with an abundance of wildlife that sometimes includes orcas on the hunt more than one hundred miles from the coast. Even though we are almost in the middle of the country, the ocean is still here in a literal sense, with its tides churning seawater deep inside the Norse heartland. It's a sublime thing to witness.

But being here offers no quick cure, not when the news from Texas follows us everywhere. The shooting in Uvalde on May 24, 2022, feels unbearable to add to the list of similar tragedies, past and future, in a political climate that favors the sale of weapons over the safety of children. I don't have ties to the anguished town, but I had spent the night there about six weeks earlier. I went to their Walmart, which is what you do when you're in a Texas town and you need something. Because places are like people and first impressions count for something, I got a small sense of the precarity and decency of this quiet Mexican American community in the weeks before the shooting.

The news makes me queasy. After the shooting, I read that Americans have purchased twenty million firearms in the past year and that we've endured thirty-five hundred mass shootings since Sandy Hook. But we have made ourselves unfixable, at least in the short term. A few politicians will talk about reform, but they will be drowned out by the Republican noise machine that is waging an equally devastating war on racial justice, historical understanding, and scientific truth. The same politicians who were in charge of Texas during the Uvalde tragedy were easily reelected later that year, leaving the charismatic challenger Beto O'Rourke in the dust, never to be anything more than the would-be Bobby Kennedy of El Paso (and I'm talking about the father of the raspy anti-vaxxer working with Trump).

America has a political sickness that follows you everywhere. Even overlooking the grandeur of the fjords, I feel a depth of sorrow about my country and its self-inflicted wounds. When an English reporter presses Senator Ted Cruz about America's unique problems with gun violence, he dismisses the question as propaganda and then counters with his own snake oil—how could America have such problems when everyone in the world is dreaming of coming to its shores? It's a crazy statement, a patriotic sales pitch on acid, and it rings false on every level. The senator doesn't mention the fact that he has received more money from the National Rifle Association than any other member of Congress, which might tend to color his perspective on gun safety.

I'm now walking up a hill overlooking the fjord where the townspeople have engraved large flat stones with various phrases alongside the path. As I'm typing the words about Senator Cruz on my phone, I stop short. In a strange coincidence, the next one is in Spanish, an uncanny sight along the fjords. "Qué huella estás dejando en el mundo?" *What footprints are you going to leave in the world?* In a country that has become a danger to itself and others, and I'm certainly not talking about Norway, it's a clichéd question that deserves an answer.

Everything went wrong that day in Uvalde, and pretty much everything went wrong in its aftermath. Despite the NRA's rhetoric about the proverbial good guy with a gun being able to stop evil in its tracks, almost four hundred armed officers responded to Robb Elementary School but failed miserably, refusing to breach the classroom and engage the shooter until it was much too late. To a casual observer of the American scene, this horror might seem like an obvious turning point. Of all the mass shootings in recent Texas history, Uvalde might be the most chilling—not just the slaughter of innocents in a church or Walmart that we saw in Sutherland Springs or El Paso but an entire classroom of kids murdered while law enforcement looked at their phones and waited for instructions. If the inaction at Uvalde didn't galvanize political reform, what could?

Over the following year, Uvalde families became a potent force for gun reform in Austin. Some stood in front of the governor's mansion at 5:00 a.m. with bullhorns, yelling, "If we can't sleep, how can you?" One Uvalde mother sat for thirteen hours to testify before a legislative committee that rudely kept her waiting. These grieving families were powerful advocates for some practical reforms, nothing extreme, but were no match for old white men with a favorite special interest. Once again, Republicans chose to embrace their Second Amendment pieties, essential red meat in their primaries, at the expense of all other competing values, including human life. For over a year, people in power didn't even let the public see the embarrassing police records from that horrific day, until a judge forced them to in summer 2023. Not that it made a difference.

Ultimately, Texas Republicans offered window dressing that would allow them to boldly announce that they had fixed the problem without actually doing much. They agreed to require security guards (without funding the mandate), some stronger doors, and more frequent meetings to discuss school safety, all of which are fine but ultimately immaterial when it comes to the root cause of the shootings—the easy access to military-grade weaponry among damaged young men. The Uvalde families couldn't even get the state to raise the required age for purchasing an AR15 assault rifle, a gun that would be banned altogether in a sane country (indeed, the United States had done just that with the Assault Weapon Ban from 1994 to 2004, which only lapsed when Republicans took back control of Congress). No one in a position of authority in Texas was willing to say, "Maybe these young men should wait a few years before acquiring a weapon designed for killing human beings," which is an apt description of the AR15 despite the claims of hunters, who insist it is the ideal gun for shooting mountain goats and jackrabbits (seriously).[1] But the AR15 won out.

A certain kind of a red state dude isn't kidding when he emblazons his pickup with the NRA bumper sticker that warns, "I'll give you my gun when you pry it from my cold, dead hands." They don't understand that this phrase could also be a suicide note.

In March 2024 I returned to Uvalde for several days. My timing was a little surreal: Meghan Markle, the former Duchess of Sussex, had been in Uvalde the day before to reconnect with victims' families she had met in 2022. I don't know if her appearance was more than moral grandstanding designed to augment her lifestyle brand: *Look how much I care! The healing power of the celebrity is on display!* I'm going to assume the best and hope that her visit provided some comfort to the locals—though her appearance got much less publicity than I would have thought. While ordering breakfast in a Main Street diner, I asked the waitress if she had seen Meghan. She wasn't sure who or what I was talking about. "The once-future Queen of England was here . . . yesterday!" I explained in the voice reserved for Bigfoot sightings. The waitress shrugged, smiled, and walked away.

I guess my story sounded a little sus because Uvalde doesn't seem like a place to bump into well-coifed royals. Eighty miles west of San Antonio and forty miles from the Mexican border, Uvalde is a modest city of fifteen thousand that is 78 percent Latino and 21 percent white, which means there are fewer than fifty Black people.[2] The town sprawls along a standard Texas "stroad" (a highway for cars masquerading as a street for pedestrians and shops) with the usual corporate carbuncles attached to both sides: Walmart, Dollar General, EZ Pawn, Subway, Hobby Lobby, Dairy Queen, Whataburger. Quirky local joints fill in the gaps: Billy Bob's Hamburgers, La Charreada Mexican Restaurant, Joe's Gun Shop, El Amigo Bail Bonds, the Blackbelt Academy of Uvalde, a few trailer parks, and a thrift store called Cowboys N Lollipops. As of November 2023, the town also included twenty-one new large murals dedicated to each of the victims.

I headed to the old town square to look for the murals scattered throughout the historic district, but first I experience a different kind of mourning. Walmart and its ilk have hollowed out places like Uvalde. With the real commercial action on the highway leading out of the city, downtown Uvalde feels like it's sleepwalking: its standing but not quite awake. It's a shame because the heart of the town was once a lovely place. Although I find a few pockets of prosperity, many of the buildings are either abandoned or underutilized. These old Texas towns were harsh places in many ways in 1880 or 1920, but they weren't ugly to look at. With their mix of Victorian hotels, Mission Revival stores, Greek Revival churches, and eccentric flourishes, these places used to have charm. Instead of beautiful nineteenth-century buff brick buildings, the free market has given us a row of giant ugly boxes, built without style or substance, selling cheap foreign goods instead of local products for local owners.

I walked past the M-16 Gym, a fitness center "where every round counts" and whose symbol is a large military machine gun painted on the wall. I watched old ranchers driving past in their battered pickups, pulling flatbed trailers stacked with bales of hay. I paused in front of a smoothie store, a modest concession to fitness in the land of the fried. Nearby I found the first of the twenty-one murals, billboard-sized testaments to familial love and loss, each one developed in partnership between artists and family members. A community project dreamed up by a local art teacher, who relied primarily on donations, the murals were painted in fall 2023, six months before my visit, making them an unusually organic expression of grief and loss. Children appear smiling with favorite toys or sports gear; some murals have allusions to the child's career aspirations. Rojelio stands with his Pokémon friends, wearing a T-shirt that says "Difference Maker." Nevaeh is depicted with a school photo smile under a ribbon that says, "I Love You!" Jackie poses in front of the Eiffel Tower and says, "I love you to the moon and back." Maranda holds a flower in her outstretched hands. Makenna poses with a dog and horse that nuzzles her. Xavier stands next to words that say, "Honor Roll." Layla smiles over the words *Sweet Child O' Mine*. Jose holds his baseball bat with a confident smile and looks like he's ready for the big leagues. "I can't . . . I have softball," says the speech bubble next to a girl in glasses on a twenty-by-thirty-foot mural.

Next I drove to the soon-to-be demolished Robb Elementary—schoolkids will never again set foot inside the buildings. Right now it looks like every other elementary school, except it's partially fenced off to preserve the crime scene; it has a lawn filled with homemade memorials to the victims; and it has a single Texas trooper stationed out front, 24-7, for reasons I'm curious to discover.

I parked on the street and walked toward the empty school, quiet except for the trooper and a few families gathering around a homemade memorial on the lawn. There was no way I was going to disturb

Fig. 12. Large public mural in honor of the victims of the Uvalde shooting, Uvalde, Texas, March 2024. Photo by author.

them in their grief, so I approached the trooper on duty to find out why he was guarding an empty school. A jowly country boy in a tan Stetson, he explained that some idiots had broken into the school and sawed-off bullet-ridden sheetrock as souvenirs. He mentioned that he was based in the part of East Texas where my family lives, some six hours away. When I asked why he was way out here, he admitted that the Texas Highway Patrol didn't want local troopers on the scene, presumably because they would be subject to ridicule and derision, so they rotated troopers from distant counties for two-week assignments. The Highway Patrol takes care of its own.

I wandered out of the parking lot and move toward the front lawn, stopping in front of a low brick wall emblazoned with the words WEL-

Fig. 13. Stuffed elephant on a playground never to be used again. Robb Elementary School, March 2024. Photo by author.

COME/BIENVENIDOS ROBB ELEMENTARY SCHOOL. At its base were stuffed animals, a prayer candle, a baseball, and a little green Matchbox car. Nearby were twenty-one white crosses, each one with a name and photo of a victim. Dozens of rosary beads were dangling from a wooden cross with a homemade sign at its base: "Don't Offend the Students . . . Do Something!" Hand-painted rocks were piled at the base of a tree. One said, "Grief only exists where love lived first." Another said, "Love Wins." With two exceptions, the names were all Latino.

I sighed and hoped I was doing something more than rubbernecking here, before wandering to the backside of the school, where I found a stuffed elephant tied to the chain-link fence around the playground. I leaned on the cold metal and watched the swings dangle in the wind.

After a few more minutes, I trudged to the car and drove back to the historic district to see the murals again. I didn't know what else to do. There is no silver lining to a school shooting, but at least these murals made me feel something other than horror and sadness. As I walked from brightly colored wall to brightly colored wall, I imagined the emotional resilience that went into this project, which represents a beautiful response to the worst kind of violence. These are extraordinary cultural artifacts—especially extraordinary as folk art that memorializes a loss that should never have happened. The murals in Uvalde are the most profound expression of collective morning that I've ever seen from a community working with limited funds. They're not on the scale of the 9/11 Memorial, but they are brilliant expressions of love and mourning whose homemade qualities make them even more poignant, at least to me. I'm in awe that Uvalde came up with such a humane and generous response to the violence.

I wish I could end with the murals. But as you drive north from Uvalde, you encounter a very different relationship to gun culture than what you can deduce from Robb Elementary and the twenty-one murals. Noticing something the global media seemed to overlook in its coverage of the shooting, I am pop-eyed with disbelief: Uvalde is home to "THE WORLD'S ONLY LIVE FIRE TANK ADVENTURE," where you can fire live rounds from a Sherman tank or its Soviet equivalent. Or for five hundred dollars you can grab a machine gun and discover that, as the advertisement explains, "firing 3000 rounds per min this weapon allows for maximum destruction and is the ultimate machine gun!" Or you can wield a Vietnam-era flamethrower that shoots 260 feet. "That's almost as long as a football field," the website promises with gusto, before adding: "It is a man handheld inferno!"[3] Or if you prefer the weapons of the Third Reich, well, they have lots of Nazi stuff in the mix, along with Russian and American gear, and you can rent Nazi submachine guns that fire 550 rounds per minute.

This machine gun amusement park is the American obsession with guns in extremis—an obsession that the Uvalde shooter shared. On his eighteenth birthday, he ordered a military assault rifle known as an AR15 from an online vendor that, if we can judge from their mar-

Fig. 14. Murals in honor of fourth grade teacher Eva Mireles. Uvalde, Texas, March 2024. Photo by author.

keting materials, aims their wares at young men hoping to feel macho, powerful, or cool. The shooter had the AR15 delivered to a local gun shop in Uvalde. You can watch security footage that shows him getting the gun for the first time. You can watch him pick the gun off the glass counter and pretend to fire it. He then ordered two thousand rounds for the weapon and bought several other weapons, including a second AR15. He used it to shoot his grandmother in the face before driving to Robb Elementary to kill nineteen small children and two teachers while dozens and eventually *hundreds* of police hid outside, fretting about the power of the shooter's AR15. Almost four hundred cops were ultimately on the scene, talking about how powerful the AR15 was, while kids were being killed and maimed a few feet away.

"Its bullets flew toward the officers at three times the speed of sound and could have pierced their body armor like a hole punch through paper," the *Texas Tribune* explained in its brilliant reporting. "They grazed two officers in the head, and the group retreated." Yet as we know already, nothing happened after Uvalde to make kids or anyone else feel safer in Texas, and hyper-manly gun culture keeps chugging down a darkly obscene road.[4]

32 Vegas Loopy

Most American cities have rolled their eyes at Elon Musk's proposal to tunnel under their streets for the benefit of a small fleet of Tesla taxis. Even the few that have expressed interest in the Austin-based Boring Company bringing their magic tunnels to town have been sorely disappointed. According to the *Wall Street Journal*, the Boring Company "ghosted" them whenever legal or engineering obstacles popped up. Only Las Vegas, quite characteristically, has been willing to bet on Musk's strange tunnel vision.

Barely a glimmer in the billionaire's eye a few years earlier, born of a moment he was stuck in LA traffic and tweeted in annoyance about the need for a radical solution, the Vegas Loop opened its first tunnels in 2021. When a massive expansion of the tunnel network was announced in early 2023, potentially increasing the number of stations from four to more than sixty, I flew to Vegas to look at what the Boring Company had accomplished.

So far, so *meh*. You can't drive yourself even if you have your own Tesla, which is the only kind of car allowed in the proprietary tunnels. Instead, you wait to get in a chauffeured electric car, ride underground for a few minutes, and emerge a few blocks away, not much faster than a person can walk. Limited to only four small stops along a very short route, the Loop is not much more than a curiosity in its present form. But even in its expanded form, with dozens of possible stations, it smells like a boondoggle. When the expansion of the Loop was up for a vote in 2023, Mayor Carolyn Goodman lamented: "I think it's impractical. It is not proven yet. We don't have any raw, real data that's confirmed . . . . I find it unsafe and inaccessible. It is operator driven, therefore, it's not on a rail and cannot move us all safely." But because casinos were sold on the idea, she voted yes to the expansion.[1]

Its defenders might say, *What does Vegas have to lose?* It costs the city almost nothing to build or run this private tunnel network restricted to Teslas with professional drivers, ferrying two or three people at a time between "stations." "It's a very interesting project where a developer comes to us and says, we want to build a private transportation system. . . . And we want to do it all with our own money," Mike Jannsen, the executive director of infrastructure for Las Vegas, told the local news.[2]

Instead of addressing water scarcity or affordable housing, Musk is creating a weird amusement park ride that lets a few people zip through a brightly lit tunnel, one Tesla at a time. It's inferior to an articulated bus network or a well-designed subway system for moving large numbers of people safely, reliably, and sustainably. Compared to either of those options, the Loop moves people more slowly (one driver means only three passengers per car), more unpredictably (closed for two weeks without warning?), and more dangerously (if a car catches on fire in the tunnel, there is barely enough space for the doors to open, let alone for rescuers to reach the fire). These tiny Tesla tunnels are a joke.

But that doesn't mean the Loop is insignificant, either to Vegas or Musk. More than a whimsical response to Vegas's transportation woes, the Loop is emblematic of something deep in the billionaire's worldview. Although I am interested in the project as someone who cares about sustainable cities, I am also worried about a broader phenomenon I call "Muskism," a virulent new strain of charismatic techno-capitalism that is reshaping the places where the billionaire operates: massive Tesla "Gigafactories" in Germany, China, Texas, Nevada, New York, and (possibly) Monterrey, Mexico; fiery SpaceX launches from a fragile ecosystem in Boca Chica, Texas; and a new Tesla lithium processing plant near Corpus Christi, Texas. Now managing these projects from his corporate headquarters in central Texas,

Musk has become a key figure in the American West (not to mention his willingness to use his money to sway the election for Trump and then to bully his way into a position of extraordinary influence over the federal bureaucracy). He wasn't wearing that accidentally backward ten-gallon cowboy hat at a Tesla launch for nothing.

His westward expansion is troubling because Muskism is a neurotic mode of celebrity entrepreneurship that revolves around one man's erratic personality, his childishly sci-fi-infused futurism, his willingness to mock and bully vulnerable people, and his narcissistic vision of himself as a solitary genius who will save our species (tickets to Mars anyone?). He claims he bought Twitter to preserve "free speech," that "woke" AI could "end civilization," and that he has "done more for the environment than . . . any single human on Earth." No doubt, he has a bold vision of IRL action that includes cars, rockets, batteries, and tunnels that he claims will remake human existence. His critics might wince at his overblown rhetoric as much as his unsavory antics, but it is undeniable his companies are building things that few companies have succeeded in creating at a similar scale.

That does not make them a social good. Taking a page from the political playbook of Republicans in the United States, where he has increasingly found his closest allies, Musk expects the public to believe that a private tunnel network under a major U.S. city is necessary, beneficial, and inevitable because local or state governments are incapable of providing for our collective needs. This exclusionary framework is what the theorist Mark Fisher famously called "capitalist realism," which is "a pervasive atmosphere" that shapes "not only the production of culture but also the regulation of work and education, and [acts] as a kind of invisible barrier constraining thought and action, resulting in a 'business ontology' in which it is simply obvious that everything in society, including healthcare and education, should be run as a business."[3] With the civic "disruption" of the Loop, Musk is privatizing an important part of the urban fabric, namely its mass transit, thereby killing the accountability that public ownership can provide. Mass transit can take us on a very strange ride when it's a private business driven by a single individual, especially one who is not very familiar with the cities in question—and most especially one with authoritarian compulsions. But first let me explain something about Vegas, which might be America's weirdest and most wasteful city.

In 1976 I was a sneaky ten-year-old kid trying to play a slot machine in the old Dunes casino on the Vegas strip, only to have my arm grabbed by a security guy who gave me a "Hell no" frown and sent me back to my parents' table. In the decades since, I've been coming back to this beautiful but exploited Mojave basin on a regular basis—not every year, for sure, because my uncorrupted soul could not withstand that much of its arid decadence (kidding!), but often enough to know that Vegas is a very weird place that makes very strange choices about its development. Whatever moral chaos Hunter S. Thompson famously detected there during the Nixon years has only gotten weirder, more spectacular, and far more lucrative.

No matter what its local defenders might say, and those have included interesting figures such as the art critic Dave Hickey, waking up in Vegas often feels dirty, at least for anyone who cares about healthy, well-designed cities. Even if you can greet the morning with a clean conscience about the previous night, free from the usual Sin City transgressions that could precipitate the loss of a marriage or a home, you might feel a twinge of guilt by association. You might wonder, *Should this massive city even be here, growing at a record pace, in an ecologically sensitive valley devoid of water?* And more specifically, you might ask, *Is there anything in the realm of urban planning that is as absurd, wasteful, and dumb as the Vegas strip?* With its endless orgy of spectacular consumption, it functions like a four-mile-long middle finger to urban sustainability and good taste—which is emblematic of a city where turbocharged development, ominous expanses of asphalt and concrete, severe congestion, grave water scarcity, serious air pollution, and five billion pounds of trash per year conspire to create the most unsustainable city in America—and not surprisingly, the fastest-warming city as well.[4] When viewed through this lens, Vegas is a monstrous thing.

But that's not how the strip is generally understood or experienced. Close to forty million visitors each year make it one of the top travel destinations in the world, and Vegas is at the top of the list for population growth for reasons other than low taxes and cheap buffets. The city has attracted thousands of talented chefs and performers who make the meals and put on the shows that are genuinely impressive. It offers thousands of good jobs and relatively low housing costs. And the beauty of the surrounding natural landscape is undeniable—especially where it remains undeveloped. The low humidity means the weather is wonderful in the mornings and evenings even on the hottest days. What I'm suggesting is that other stories could be told here, and better futures could emerge. With proper limits on its environmental impact and population growth and a greater attention to mass transit and other urban necessities, Vegas could become a promising place to live or visit for something other than the cheap thrills of the casino floor.

For now, however, its urban woes are unmistakable. Thanks to its laser focus on sex, food, and money, the Strip's infrastructure of desire has little room for other human needs. Mass transit is woefully inadequate, and walkability is a joke. There's not enough shade from the brutal heat. It's hard to find healthy food. And the harsh sounds of the traffic-clogged Strip are a stark contrast to the silence of the desert just a few miles away. Pedestrians appear tipsy, amped up, beat down, scheming, hustling, and dreaming as they move between structures the size of the pyramids—literally in the case of the Egyptian-themed Luxor casino. The dull thud of bass and auto-tuned arias rarely lets up—the dumbest brand of dance music is grimly omnipresent. If you ever wonder who listens to, say, anything by Vanilla Ice, the answer is sunburned people wandering the Strip with a giant daiquiri. To be fair, they didn't ask to hear this kind of music, which seems at odds with either their young age, gnarly Metallica tattoos, or senior citizen status, but they seem to endure it uncomplainingly because *the Strip is officially fun, and we are officially having fun whether we like it or not!* It's an impressive mental feat, perhaps related to the absence of open container laws that allow alcohol to flow more abundantly than water—or the recent legalization of marijuana in Nevada. The constant smell of weed is a new feature of the Strip, although I'm surprised it wasn't legal all along in a state where sex work has long been celebrated like it was missionary work, which I suppose it often was. All this combines to make the heart of Las Vegas into a pedestrian nightmare—it's like walking inside a pinball machine filled with flashing lights and revving engines. Even brief spells of strolling on the Strip are ill advised—this is an urban planning free-fire zone, a flesh, steel, and concrete jumble where cars press too close to vulnerable crowds that swell drunkenly over the curbs until the traffic cops blow whistles and wave their flashlights in dismay.

Relief won't be coming from the city or state leaders who bow to the gambling industry, local developers, and conservative retirees who demand low taxes. And it won't be coming from the sixty casinos that are doing just fine with the lucrative status quo. These places have prospered for decades by repeating a simple pattern that doesn't pay much attention to transportation or mobility. Instead, they start with a theme that could have been conjured by a dim child: *Paris! Italy! NYC! Egypt! Circus! Rock music! Pink flamingos! Mussolini!* (well, not yet). Then they erect a hyperbolic structure that eliminates any semblance of nuance to maximize its visual impact. At the front there is always a showy entrance that pulls you into a seductive zone of internal spectacle—a shark tank, a hot-air balloon made of flowers, a simulated French street, or a chocolate fountain that splatters viscous brown goo on a glass tray in a manner that is distinctly fecal (thanks Bellagio!). But streaming turd fountains are not the only treat for guests on the Strip. Even if gambling is the main event for many people, high-end restaurants, spas, theaters, and shops provide a lot of competition on a casino floor that often feels like a super-upscale mall filled with tipsy weekenders and beleaguered cocktail waitresses.

It's no revelation that the Strip is one of the most decadent, superficial, and wasteful spots in a country that invests heavily in those three things. Yet this is where Elon Musk chose to focus the energies and resources of his tunneling company—an elaborate urban bullshit zone for a network of tunnels that he calls "the Loop" even though it only runs in a straight line.

Granted, Musk's project will get loopier in the years ahead. It has approval for sixty-five miles of new tunnels with sixty-nine stations, a number surely chosen to titillate the billionaire's adolescent sense of humor, but so far it has only completed an initial tunnel that runs a short distance from the luxury retail and gambling mecca called Resort World to three parts of the vast Convention Center.[5] We could generously call it the pilot stage of the Loop, which has not been a resounding success. When I arrived for a research trip in May 2023, the whole system was "out of order" for two weeks with no reason given, like a restaurant that closes because no one has dined there for ages. A single Tesla was parked at the above-ground station, with no cars or people in sight. I could barely peek into the tunnel to wonder what was going on. Many locals seem equally mystified—even in 2023, the Loop was surprisingly unknown to the residents I met. When I talked to Vegas locals, including a dozen Uber drivers who might be expected to know about their subterranean competition, they seemed either dismissive or unaware of it.

The location does the Loop no favors either. On its east end, we find the ultra-high-end shopping of the Resort World Casino but also the ramshackle stores across the street: massage parlors, grubby marijuana dispensaries, and a small office that rents out Lamborghinis to tourists looking to make an impression on Instagram. The Loop could have connected North Vegas to benefit the impoverished neighborhoods there, but no, that doesn't conform to Musk's juvenile sense of "cool," and city officials seemed fine with whatever he wanted to do, as long as they weren't footing the bill. More comedically, he could have offered routes to the world's biggest sex bike at the Erotic Heritage Museum or the amazing jam room in the new punk rock museum or the world's largest weed store, Planet 13, all in less touristy parts of town where normal people live and work. But no. Even in its expanded form (yet to be built), it's all about casinos and conventions.

Looking at this initial route as well as the plans for a massive expansion begs a question. Why not build a subway? Why not build a monorail, even if *The Simpsons* hilariously warned us against monorail hucksterism? Instead, a supposedly visionary billionaire, looking for his first big urban project, chose to create a transportation system that might (maybe!) somewhat shorten the time between casinos in the most environmentally destructive and aesthetically infantile city in America.

I stayed just off the Strip in the Virgin Hotel and Casino, which is the former Hard Rock Casino. Six months prior, while reporting on an event in Austin, Texas, where Elon-obsessed crypto companies handed out swag, I got a free shirt depicting Elon Musk on a gleaming rocket. I only wear it at home, and even there, quite ironically. However, on this morning in Vegas, I wore it on the elevator to go downstairs and get coffee. When I stepped onto the elevator, I was suddenly self-conscious about the racist billionaire's face on my chest because there were two older Black people on the elevator. And I turned to them and said: "I'm sorry. It was a free shirt. Uh . . . I don't like him." They peered at my shirt, chuckled, and said earnestly, "Who is that guy?"

The truth is that he's a ketamine-fueled mystery, and his ambitions in Vegas remain unclear. But a few things are clear to me after a week in the desert. I don't like to gamble. I don't want to see David Copperfield. And I certainly don't want to ride in the Tesla taxi tunnels.

Of course, Musk and his rabid admirers will not admit defeat. For his fans, the expensive urban chaos of Vegas is a perfect place for him to show up like electric Superman: *Elon ex machina! Gloria in Excelsius Deo! For he is risen from the woke mob to redeem us*—or something like that. But more neutral observers might ask some pointed questions about the Loop and its owner. What is the long-term impact of Musk's projects on the places across the American West where SpaceX, Tesla, and the Boring Company are operating? Of those who celebrate his EVs but wish to distance themselves from his unsavory politics and bullying personality, we should ask how it's possible to admire his companies but reject its domineering CEO. Can a city reap the imagined benefits of his companies without Musk's toxic sediment seeping into the water table, figuratively and literally? Is it even possible to see clearly what Musk is offering, or is he moving too fast, on a scale that defies public comprehension? Just as his detractors allege he's gotten liposuction and cheek implants, the billionaire is performing

Fig. 15. Vegas Loop station, out of order, May 2023. Photo by author.

a kind of plastic surgery on capitalism that makes it appear smoother, greener, and more attractive while still being the same old industrial exploitation with a techno-messianic twist.

I had a theory about where all this was heading that was interesting in 2022 but obvious by 2025. If you ride the Vegas Loop from the

Convention Center to the Resort World casino at its eastern terminus, you can walk outside and see the real destination of all things Musk. From the street corner just south of Resort World, you can look east from the Strip and get a clear view of the tallest residential condo in Nevada, a gleaming golden brown slab with a former president's name on top: the Trump International Hotel, which includes hotel rooms, condos, and timeshares. All hype, all vanity, no substance, no sustainability—Musk's Vegas experiment reveals his MO as little more than a tech-heavy version of Trump's narcissistic grifter capitalism. And more than another example of Vegas's failing, the Loop is a potent metaphor for where Musk is headed with his Trump-style braggadocio, hype, and tolerance of risk (as in highly leveraged firms that often run dangerously close to the red in their early days). He is Trumpy in his extreme bullying of dissenters and critics. He has a similar skeleton in his closet when it comes to sexual harassment. He has the same grandiose rhetoric of salvation with a Manichaean spin (Elon good, critics bad!) and shares Trump's disdain for journalists, who are all out to get him (allegedly). Also, like Trump, Musk puts an extreme concentration of value in himself as CEO. Ultimately celebrity Elon is the brand, just as Trump is his brand, and in both cases their narcissistic self-regard has curdled into authoritarian arrogance, which is the last thing Vegas, or any other democratic polity, should tolerate.

33 Exile

Trump is getting arraigned yet again in the summer of 2023, but I'm winding through the old colonial streets of Querétaro, a city of a million that is one of the safest places in Latin America. Three months ago I had barely heard of it. Now I'm walking along its cobblestone lanes and wondering if I could start a new life in the mountains of Central Mexico. If you drive fast, it's maybe twelve hours from the blistering heat of the Lone Star state, with its smug reactionary politicians, cookie-cutter suburbs, and median property taxes that would rival an annual salary here in Mexico—but the city of Querétaro feels so different it might as well be on the moon.

Today the air is perfect. Instead of gasping while I run from the air-conditioned car to air-conditioned house, cursing our oil-rich, climate-denying state, I'm strolling in a colorful city with mild temperatures and low humidity, not to mention delicious food that includes, quite gloriously, green enchiladas for breakfast on every corner. For my wife and me, a couple of potential climate and political refugees looking for a fresh start, Querétaro is dazzling because it's half the cost and twice the charm we have back home. There is an unusual beauty in its old narrow streets as well as the undulating mountains that encircle the city from a distance.

What could be better than a safe, colorful, walkable city awash in great scenery and delicious food? Such places are the apex of the collective human experience that we used to call civilization (nowadays we just call it "privilege"). Flush with an unfamiliar calmness, I gaze at the outline of the Sierra Gordas on the far horizon. I'm amazed I can see the mountains from the heart of the city—we're exploring the historic *centro*, where Spanish colonial architecture reigns supreme, which means there are no McDonalds or Walmarts, just small *tiendas*, makeshift taco stands, funky little repair shops, elegant plazas shaded by square-cut trees, and chic little boutique hotels that offer a glimpse of how the 1 percent lives for a fraction of the price. We are living large for middle-class Americans: for eighty dollars a night, we are staying in a hotel with a swank library and an idyllic pool that could be in *Architectural Digest*. It's stunning what a little imagination and effort can create in a country, even a poor country, where aesthetics matter. People know what is beautiful here; as my Spanish professor friend Jason says, Mexico is a land of visual sophistication that often exceeds anything we have back home.

Not everything is perfect in my half-price paradise. Outside of a few central neighborhoods, Querétaro is becoming a little bit like everywhere else, succumbing to a turbocharged form of gringo modernity, with Costcos, Home Depots, skyscraper condos, and traffic jams, the same mess we have back home in Austin, Dallas, Houston, Atlanta, Phoenix, Las Vegas, and so on. But its heart still feels pure—the locals light up when they talk about their city, and I understand why. So much of their built environment seems handmade and human scale: doors, decor, tables, buildings, even the old VW bugs still sputtering around the city with flared fenders and luminescent paint, all feel like someone crafted them with their hands, not like they rolled out of a factory. The food feels the same way. Back in Austin, the old hippie restaurants are disappearing, casualties of rising rents in the archetypical Sunbelt technopolis of the twenty-first century, but we find them here, like little time machines that remind us of the utopian corners of Austin before speculators took control and squeezed out the weird. At least for now, Querétaro's counterculture is still vibrant, weird, and filled with sustainable dreams of sharing a killer veggie burger and a delicious coconut *licuado*.

At a scenic overlook called Mirador de los Arcos, we gawk at an eighteenth-century aqueduct, a three-hundred-year-old marvel that extends for a mile through the heart of the city. Almost totally intact, it is gorgeous and mysterious, a tribute to Spanish engineers who worked with hand tools, ropes, donkeys, and massive sandstone blocks to create something that still elicits a sense of awe. I can hear my academic friends wincing when I talk admiringly about colonial architecture, but what can I say? The aqueduct was a beautiful exercise in symmetry, texture, and light, even if the conditions of its making were brutal and wrong. (It was probably not much different than working on a construction site in modern Texas, where water breaks are no longer required, heatstrokes be damned, thanks to our "business-friendly" governor.)

Young Mexican couples are giggling through selfies along the fence line, and we join them, posing with the booming city in the background and imagining ourselves in this unfamiliar landscape, a couple of hopeful gringos eager to seem like not-so-ugly Americans. *Could this be the place?* I don't want to participate in some kind of slacker imperialism, I don't want to displace or irritate anyone, but I want to be part of this kind of warm and interwoven world where people seem more alive, connected, and real. After kicking around Central Mexico for five weeks while our plants die at home, we are feeling won over by something indescribable, something we've been missing as the sky slowly darkens over the United States. Certainly, the great white lie of Texas—that the Rio Grande River separates heaven from hell, safety from danger, democracy from degradation—seems more preposterous than ever. Of course, white Texas has thrived on its contempt for Mexico for two hundred years—it's a foundational mythology that props up the political careers of its know-nothing politicians even today.

A better way of describing this myth is a cheap lie that quickly falls apart when you explore the more fortunate parts of Mexico (and there are many). No one could deny that Mexico is often in grave distress: the cartels kill journalists who ask too many questions, thousands of women end up in mass graves in the deserts of northern Mexico for crossing paths with gangs and sex traffickers, and ecological despoliation goes unchecked around the maquiladoras of the border. But

Texas has little room to talk smack about anyone. It has its own mass graves, though they are a bit older: in 2018 the remains of ninety-five African Americans were discovered in an unmarked grave in Sugarland, Texas. Nowadays, Texas border agents throw migrant children back into the Rio Grande, where they encounter razor-bladed buoys to cut their hands when they try not to drown; there are regular mass shootings in churches and schools; and small towns ban books for mentioning gay marriage—not to mention the everyday violence of Texas's big cities or the fact that Texas was ranked the worst place to live and work in the United States in 2023.[1] When white Texans complain about the violence in Mexico, they often forget that Houston had four hundred murders in 2022, and the odds of being the victim of a violent crime there was one in seventy-eight. Other statistics reveal the surprising truth that Texans are more likely to get killed at home than in Mexico's tourist destinations.

Mexico is broken but beautiful—that much is clear to even the most casual traveler. And part of that beauty is in its candor: it's honest about its shortcomings and sins, something I haven't felt in a country since I lived in Sicily twenty years ago while it was still wriggling free from Mafia control. These are rough places from the perspective of a sterile American suburb, but they are astonishingly real, attractive, and seductive for someone who craves a deeper kind of human engagement and solidarity, not to mention architectural and cultural solidity. They are not delusional about who and what they are; they are not pretending to be God's favorite nation or the all-seeing arbiter of global ethics; they are not supplying weapons that kill random civilians on the other side of the planet. There is a humility and a sense of limitation that is compelling in Mexico. And philosophically, Mexicans often embrace a tragic view of life that Americans, with their mythology of new beginnings and blinkered optimism, can rarely fathom. Maybe it sounds peculiar, but their tragic outlook is comforting because it lines up more accurately with the reality we are experiencing. With its chirpy exceptionalism and "can-do" rhetoric spewing out of the mouth of every intern-seducing politician, America often remains in denial about its tragic origins in slavery and genocide in ways that breed

Fig. 16. Mineral de Pozos, a small town not far from Querétaro, Mexico, July 2023. Photo by author.

hypocrisy and delusion, not to mention the uber-rancid nationalism of Trump and his supporters. Mexico has its agonies, but self-delusion is not one of them.

We don't get to stay in Querétaro nearly long enough, and on our last day, a local realtor hands us her business card, which we squirrel away like a password that we are going to need in a few years. We are contemplating a life in exile, a life in a new country because the old one just isn't working out. Querétaro, my imagined paradise, is only one of several options we are exploring in Mexico, Costa Rica, Columbia, Ecuador, and Chile (we're too late for Portugal, where expats blew up their real estate market, causing locals to spend up to 90 percent of their salary to rent an apartment). We know that Mexico is a flawed place: it's a country where you can get scammed and disappear for good (it happened to a grad student and his wife in my department while I was living in Mexico City in 2024), where sewer smells reach the rooftop pizzeria because "that's normal for our neighborhood," where you can get the anti-gringo, anti-imperialist pushback in ways that make it depressing even to move around a city eager for tourist cash, and where there is far too much grinding poverty that gnaws at your soul. Yet there is also more kindness, beauty, warmth, texture, style, here than anywhere I've ever been, especially if you judge the country from its best attributes, which is how Americans judge themselves. (Six months in Mexico the following year only confirmed my sense that Mexico has a creative and communal appeal that the United States has mostly lost.)

I'm not sure if we can pull off the grand exodus from the air-conditioned nightmare. We need to go someplace where we are accepted, not just tolerated, and certainly not resented. We want to go somewhere we can become a contributing part of the local scene, not interlopers going to garden parties with other expats who never learn the local language. I don't want to be mocked as a *rico gringo* in tragicomic stories like the one I overheard between women in the Querétaro airport. I want to bring something to Mexico, rather than simply taking from it.

On that last day in Querétaro in summer 2023, I posted online about enjoying my summer in Mexico, honing my Spanish, and meeting amazing new people, but my happiness was short-lived. A pious former graduate student publicly lectured me about the nature of privilege, claiming that the only reason I was happy in Latin America was that I was, as she put it, "tall, white, and male." *Okay* . . . Like any semi-decent person working in academia, I can recognize those privileges without prompting from moralizing acquaintances, but more important, I know it's something more, something atmospheric, that draws me here, hoping to find a way to negotiate the tripwires of privilege that are inherent to expat living.

For now Austin is still home: my daughter is in the local community college, doesn't know how to drive, and often needs a ride to work;

and more pressingly, I need the income and insurance that my job provides. But it's sobering to realize why I'm not moving today—*simply because I can't.* As it was for a surprising number of nineteenth-century immigrants who returned to the old country after earning money in the United States, America might once again become a place where you go for work, not for the good life that happens elsewhere in another place, another time.[2] I've been waiting for the country to change for decades, but it feels stuck in something bad, like an addict who doesn't see the harm in "a little fentanyl" on the weekend. Not surprisingly, everyone I know is dreaming about some sort of exile, whether to the untamed mountains of Colorado, the coast of British Columbia, or the affordable beach towns of Spain. Young people want to live in Berlin, old people want to live somewhere warm, and everyone wants to live in Portugal. More and more Americans, from twenty-something digital nomads to sixty-something wannabe retirees, are trying to flee to places with better climates, more affordable healthcare, less toxic politics, and a lower cost of living. Exact numbers are elusive, but the number of people receiving Social Security benefits outside of the United States increased from 307,000 in 2008 to 450,000 in 2021, and the pandemic further fueled the rise in "digital nomadism."[3] Looking ahead at what I can expect in the United States as an aging American, I wince. Super-hyped American cities like Austin are already too expensive for fixed-income living. Besides, like most Sunbelt cities, it was designed for cars, not the mass transit or walkability that older people often need—although no one wants to walk very far in a city with a five-month-long summer in which the weather is Dubai-hot and Manilla-humid (I looked it up to confirm these comparisons) and so miserable that life becomes a sprint between the AC of the house and the AC of the car from 8:00 a.m. to 10:00 p.m.

Meanwhile, in Querétaro I look again at the shadow of the Sierra Gorda extending across the horizon and smile with the knowledge, or even just the hope, that I wouldn't grow tired of this view. But before I can really enjoy my exile fantasy, I hear the voice of that former grad student and imagine what she would say. Is my dream of exile just another neocolonial imposition on a country that has suffered too many gringo delusions? Am I succumbing to a romantic daydream about a place that's ultimately the same as anywhere else? Would buying an apartment here drive up prices in a way that would hurt ordinary Mexicans? Is it unethical to take my American wealth, limited though it is, and use it to upgrade my lifestyle in a suffering economy? And besides, could I ever be free of the American miasma, all the crazy cultural baggage that I've accumulated in five decades here, no matter how far I move away from the insanity and bitterness of Trumpland? I don't know.

Back home in Austin, I flip through real estate listings for Mexican houses the way a fourteen-year-old boy looks at pornography and mutter, *There has to be a way out*. For me right now, as I'm languishing through waves of bad health and bad vibes in the turbulent 2020s, my American dream is somewhere else than my native shores. Leaving feels like freedom to me—which, ironically, might be the most American impulse there is.

I sometimes think about Malcolm Cowley's brilliant 1934 book, *Exile's Return*, which artfully chronicles the exodus of Hemingway, Stein, Fitzgerald, and the rest of the so-called Lost Generation from the United States to Paris, Zurich, Berlin, and Vienna in the 1920s. Cowley shows them leaving for the exact same reasons I'm itching to go: cheaper living in a more cosmopolitan place without the small-mindedness of home. His book explains exactly why they left, what they experienced in exile, and why those foreign experiences changed the way they wrote, composed, or sculpted. It used to be taught regularly in seminars about twentieth-century U.S. literary culture but not so much anymore: Cowley seems to have gone out of fashion, which makes sense because it's one of my favorite books—in part because it ends with a surprise.[4]

After spending three hundred pages blasting the provincialism of the United States in favor of European-based modernism, Cowley added a radical appendix that is often overlooked in which he explains why the "exiles" came home. Yes, the stock market crashed, writers ran out of money, friends committed suicide, middle age was approaching, and suddenly getting a job back in Chicago or Oakland didn't sound so bad. But something deeper propels the appendix: a kind of leftism that is earnest and straightforward and explains that these writers and artists came back to fight, using the tools of art and intellect, against fascists of all forms. Maybe it was too naked in its politics, too sloganeering as a way to end a subtle, smart book, but his appendix was also right. *Sometimes you have to go home and fight.* At least someone does. I'm just not sure if that someone is me.

34 Sway

A tornado of cultural madness tore across the beleaguered soil of North America in the late 2010s and early 2020s, and it could take decades to rebuild the emotional infrastructure that allows us to feel safe, connected, and hopeful about our collective prospects. The first step lies in surveying the damage. The gallows humor and blunt assessment in this book are coping strategies for anyone working to enshrine empathy, community, human dignity, and a general softening of American life as national goals. And eventually, probably years from now, maybe after the second reign of Donald Trump, life might feel safer, freer, more sustainable, but only if we resist the madness of the present and work together—as activists, dreamers, friends, and neighbors—to create something decidedly less awful. As the Canadian psychiatrist, trauma expert, and Holocaust survivor Gabor Maté has put it, we must "bend the future in a humane and loving direction." We must dismantle the sick systems that make living in Bummerland such a slog.

Looking back on the Biden years, we have done little to repair the deeper damage of the past decade: civic bile, judicial corruption, police violence, uneven health care, uncertain jobs, unaffordable higher education, unsustainable cities, cruel foodways—the list can seem endless. Of course, *fixing all that* was beyond the capacity of an octogenarian Democratic president and his establishment liberalism. Even if he was someone who, unlike his rival for the White House, was not an abject menace to the public good, even if he was a better steward of the economy than his predecessor, he couldn't persuade a sufficient number of voters that his approach was going to improve their lives.

As we roll into the middle of the 2020s, being an American feels bad in new ways, which are layered on top of the old ways of feeling bad in America (being Black, Latino, queer, trans, Asian, migrant, poor, incarcerated, or "white trash"). Living here has become an exercise in decadence for the few, exhausting precarity for the rest, and too often pockmarked with ugliness and danger. We don't often have the sense of belonging to something that should endure, something that is getting better, something that is fundamentally good and worth saving—unless we are hiding in the alternate reality of religious piety or reactionary politics. Instead of having something to cherish for the next generation, almost everything—the presidency, the courts, the Congress, the workplace, the mediascape, the schools—feels mangled by corruption, greed, prejudice, or violence. Too often, the best solution that our fellow citizens can conjure is a desperate *ex machina*: "Maybe Elon Musk can fix it?" It's an understandable, if delusional, response to the heat wave of trouble that we've experienced, at least until he mangled the federal government in the name of DOGE cost cutting.

It's hard, but we can still grab moments of joy when we can find them. Right now I'm giddy with helium delight that a particularly rough season is coming to an end and I am still standing. I played a lot of music to get through months of enervating work and sandpapered nerves, but lately I've been gifted with the zipper-endowed original 1971 pressing of the Rolling Stones' *Sticky Fingers* LP, which has given me a reason to obsess over lesser-known tracks like "Moonlight Mile" and most especially "Sway." The latter is a raucous American blues track fused with louche Byronic Romanticism. It also features the most dexterous guitarist in the band's long history (Mick Taylor, with his amp positioned in the fireplace at Jagger's country house for the recording session). From the opening chords, the song pulls you into its mournful, broken, weary "sway" but does so with a boldly defiant strut (thank you, Charlie Watts) that seems to fit the present moment, so much so that I've been entertaining the notion of getting the chorus tattooed on my arm: "It's just that demon life's got you in its sway." Besides, is there a more gorgeous and evocative word in the English language than *sway*? And was there a more seductive rock band circa 1970 than the Stones, who would soon begin their descent into commercial grubbery as if they were nothing more than the Great Rock and Roll Costco? It's only odd that the great survivor, Keith Richards, did not play on the track. I followed him on Instagram during the pandemic like a talismanic figure. Almost thirty-five years my senior, he's always been there in the background of my life, floating high in the ether of pop culture somewhere, outlasting the scandals and dissipation and self-destruction in a way that boggles the brain. He is the "soul survivor," to quote another of their song titles from almost fifty years ago, and a model of decadent determination and the perseverance of the imperfect. Anyhow, I found solace in all that and hope others find some kind of "Sway" to propel them through these uneasy times, whether it's a comfort food track from Taylor Swift, A Tribe Called Quest, Fugazi, Charley Crockett, Lucy Dacus, E.S.G., Meat Puppets, or even the weather-beaten, Boomer-bait Stones who are, admittedly, easy to write off as mere fossils. Whatever playlist you turn to at the end of a long day, we need *something* danceable to get us through the long American night, even if it's just an old rock song from some charmingly raffish sell-outs. Never underestimate the jolt of possibility that a good song provides.

35 Unobtanium

I can hear the former Fox News host Tucker Carlson and his cynical army already. Any criticism of the United States is tantamount to celebrating the evil overlords of China, North Korea, and France while dancing on white Santa's grave. *Hey college boy, how come you hate 'Murica? Why come you want to destroy kindergarten nap time and backyard Bible studies?* Well, only an idiot or an ideologue would read my words and come to that conclusion, but the present moment is well stocked with both. To be clear, I'm aware that Americans are not living in Vladimir Putin's Russia or Xi Jinping's China, which are a bit farther down the authoritarian regime spectrum. But one of my central points is that we're not living in "America" either—which is something Henry David Thoreau could have told you before the Civil War in his brilliant rejection of American norms (same goes for Grace Lee Boggs, Frederick Douglass, Thorstein Veblen, Elizabeth Cady Stanton, James Baldwin, Allen Ginsburg, Ken Kesey, Molly Ivins, Angela Davis, Gil Scott-Heron, Jello Biafra, Yolanda Lopez, or Robert Frank). We have *rarely* been that mythic place of noble democracy and equality under the law no matter how much FOX News's Sean Hannity stamps his little cloven feet in mock outrage. For too many profoundly burdened and exhausted people, America exists primarily as a tarnished brand, like an old corporation running on fumes, a bit like JCPenney in the 1990s—well known, omnipresent, but shoddy and dysfunctional. (Oddly, Trump makes a funhouse mirror version of this argument with his MAGA crusade.)

According to most polls in summer 2024, Biden was not a popular president, even though he had replaced the most bilious creature to ever throw food at the walls of 1600 Pennsylvania Avenue. Perhaps few mainstream politicians could have repaired the damage of Trump's first term, especially when his unindicted coconspirators were mostly unbowed and unshamed—and most especially when he was able to reclaim the White House. Through the Biden years, too many things continued to spiral around the drain of disappointment for most Americans, and it seemed that recent years have taken us ever closer to the grim satire of the film *Idiocracy*. Some days I wake in a torpor and wonder: *What the hell happened? Is my American dream made of unobtainium?* Which is an unsettling thought when so many people have it worse than me.

In a recent book on American decline, the literary scholar Jed Etsy argues that the United States needs to jettison its "superpower nostalgia" and other exceptionalist illusions about "making America great again." Instead, it needs to focus on achieving a basic goodness that has often eluded a nation built on white supremacy and other forms of violence. It's a pragmatic and even hopeful argument about the power of lowering the bar and working toward a fairer, more inclusive, and more humane country—and a far more reasonable and necessary goal than continuing the masquerade of inherent "greatness" in a nation that is often pitiless toward its own citizens and downright barbarous to migrants.[1]

If big, cheap, loud, and fast is the essence of contemporary unsustainability, we need to reorient ourselves to a human scale and a slower pace. As I said at the beginning of this book, we need a nonviolent "soft revolution" in which we can become gentler, warmer, more trusting, more self-aware, more communal, more sustainable, with a full acceptance of limits to growth and profit, with a new dedication to intimate scale, interwoven neighborliness, and meaningful community, all under the banner of compassion, beauty, equity, and joy. If we can't do it as a society of 350 million, we need to break away from the mainstream and create experiments in living as Americans did in the nineteenth century everywhere from Brook Farm, Massachusetts,

Fig. 17. Weed shop along the interstate, central Oklahoma, December 2024. Photo by author.

to New Harmony, Indiana, to their 1960s counterparts like the Sea Ranch community in Northern California or Arcosanti in Arizona. If we can't even do that much in the United States in the 2020s, then we need to grab our passports and leave. We will have to try somewhere else where liberty and possibility are nurtured instead of policed and contained.

You might say this book is pessimistic, but that's not the real story. Underneath its black comedy and sociological anguish, there is a kind of utopian hope. I know we could pivot off the despair; I know we could find the seeds of restoration within the ruins of the present. Despite the dangers of finding ourselves stuck in a labyrinth of dysfunction, I know we could survive if we can get a good look at the beast that's stalking us, and that's something I've tried to provide. I believe in possibility even if the moment has not quite arrived. I believe in the politics of lucidity. And I believe in the micro even as I'm wary of the macro because the big revolutions of the twentieth century were unmitigated disasters for humanity. I have faith in what the media studies scholar Carolyn Pedwell calls "revolutionary routines," the small shifts in behavior and attitude that add up to something meaningful over time.[2]

If the punk rocker Joe Strummer is right that the future is unwritten, it's the footnotes that will make the difference, not the bold strokes that get the most attention. An accretion of miniscule improvements, thoughtful attunements, worthwhile pauses—that is what is needed to turn this dirty barge around.

An adjustment of expectations. A revolution in sensitivity. A transformation of affect. That's the future I'm betting on.

Epilogue

On November 5, 2024, the day of the American presidential election, I was sick in Mexico City. For six months I had been living all over Mexico, moving between Mérida, Querétaro, San Miguel de Allende, Oaxaca, Guanajuato, and of course the immense capital city. In each of these places, I was captivated by the energetic street culture that infuses strolling with delight, the creative ambition that gives Mexican art and architecture its swagger and charm, the culinary depth that enriches even the simplest street taco, the DIY genius that allows mechanics to fix things that would be headed to the scrapheap in Texas, and especially the beautiful rush of solidarity between strangers that I've rarely experienced anywhere else—a quality I discovered the hard way when I wiped out on a cobblestone street in San Miguel. With my feet stuck in orthopedic nerd shoes that make Frankenstein's boots seem like Chinese slippers, I had tripped hard, sprained my ankle, and bloodied my knees under the summer sun. Right away, a crowd gathered around me, invisible hands lifted me vertical, and a woman reached into her purse for a tube of antibiotic cream. A minute later, my wife flagged down a taxi driven by a sturdy grandfather in *Top Gun* shades. He sped us across town to a doctor he knew from weekend soccer matches, and when I couldn't manage the stairs, he insisted I grab his shoulders and half-piggy-backed me to the second floor. Then, without removing his Ray-Bans, he stayed through the appointment to make sure I understood the doctor's instructions. Later, when I tried to pay him for his kindness, he brushed it off with a cool "De nada," which is a Mexican way of saying, "I'm only doing what any decent person would do."

During the bitter election season, sprained ankles were the least of my troubles. For months I had been fighting *E. coli*, headaches, and fever, all of which had worn me down. By election day I was seeking out yet another doctor in the heart of Mexico City. Paying in advance, I was astonished that the fee was only three dollars, though my friends would later say, "Well, you got what you paid for." That wasn't quite fair. I was grateful that I could get medical care without a wait. I was grateful that the doctor had a clean little space, even if I was in the hands of a young hipster with pink old-lady glasses and a concert T-shirt that didn't conceal a belly that made him look like the Mexican Jack Black. After asking the usual questions, he reached into a mug crowded with scuffed-up pencils and pulled out an old plastic thermometer. When I popped it into my mouth, his eyes widened in alarm. Apparently, the thermometer was for somewhere else. I didn't know if it had been in dozens of armpits or if it had taken a few trips farther down south, but I was too loopy-queasy to inquire.

It was a revolting surprise, which, of course, was election day in a nutshell.

For the first time ever, I had voted in advance. Three weeks earlier, at the bunker-like U.S. embassy on Avenida Reforma in Mexico City, I had cast my vote against the P. Diddification of American politics. Nothing about the process inspired confidence in our democracy. Despite watching explanatory YouTube videos, I was stumped by the Ikea-like instructions on the overseas ballot and hoped I could get some guidance from the embassy staff. That's how I ended up taking an Uber to a part of town where sex workers and tipsy tourists turn La Zona Rosa into a cross between Bourbon Street and Bangkok. Positioned next to a Starbucks, barely outside of Mexico City's hyperactive erogenous zone, the U.S. embassy sits in a JFK-era building, presenting a grim, militarized face to the tree-lined boulevard out front. I shuffled through several layers of TSA-style security before being sent upstairs to Room 101, which Orwell fans will remember as the ultimate torture chamber in *1984*. Although I didn't notice any face-mounted rat cages, the embassy did offer its own small tortures. In both bureaucratic spirit and brutalist form, it's a bit like the fluorescent-lit DMV where Patty and Selma chain-smoke and belittle the public on *The Simpsons.*

Here it was—my tax dollars at work. I counted a dozen State Department employees behind the glass in a midsized room, each of them studiously avoiding my eyes. Eventually, a weedy fellow in a cardigan approached the counter and winced at my ballot. I asked my simple questions, but he didn't know if I needed to sign the ballot, if I should fold it up or keep it flat, if I should stick it in an envelope and, if so, where I would get one. I made a sad, confused face until he finally slid a kindergarten glue stick under the glass and told me to fabricate an envelope out of a stray piece of printer paper. *Okay*. I start making a Mr. Bean–style mess with the glue, but after an awkward minute, I gave up and rapped on the glass. Cardigan man returned and stared at me with a despairing gaze. "Let's try something else," he said.

He then handed me a manilla envelop somewhat larger than the ballot box, which wasn't a steel lockbox emblazoned with a proud American eagle or a smiling Joe Biden but simply a taped-up shoebox with U.S. BALLOTS scrawled on top. Somehow, in a year in which democracy itself is at stake, this little fourth grade craft project is the only place to drop an absentee ballot in Central Mexico. It's all slightly dysfunctional, and I feel a rush of relief when I stuff everything into the shoebox, zip downstairs past the guards, and clear the metal gate to freedom. Outside, life feels normal. I tell the street vendors that I voted against *el idiota monstruo naranja* (the orange idiot monster). They seem pleased but also wary about talking politics with a random gringo.

Darting across the crowded Avenida for the long walk back home, I tried to manifest some happy(ish) thoughts to help me remember what hope feels like. I told myself that Trump can't win because his ideas don't make sense to any semi-independent, semi-rational observer. Or because he's clearly exhausted and increasingly incoherent. Or because his rallies have lost their old zing, so much so that the MAGA faithful are sneaking out early like bored teenagers ditching Sunday school. Or because J. D. Vance, his fauxbilly running mate, has all the stage presence of a farm stand turnip. Or simply because Kamala Harris, for whatever her flaws, shines like a diamond next to a spite-ridden authoritarian and his mephitic cult of personality. How could voters forget that Trump lethally mismanaged the pandemic and fomented an insurrection? How could they believe that American elections are stolen only when a Democrat wins or that Haitian immigrants in Ohio are cooking their neighbors' pets for supper or that we should deport twenty million Latinos who form the backbone of the hospitality, agriculture, and construction industries? In other words, how could *anyone* double down on Trump and his cronies once so much was known about their venal, lawless incompetence, not to mention their general vibe of existential uncoolness (aka "evil")? Walking through Colonia Juarez while I rapid-fire texted my friends, mostly academics in the United States, I created a little bubble of progressive hope in which it seemed possible that an outspoken Black woman had a chance at the Oval Office in a racist, sexist country.

When election night arrived a few weeks later, my wife and I headed to an expat watch party in the heart of the Mexican capital. At the north end of a posh area known as Polanco, we entered a cavernous BBQ joint called "Pinche Gringo's"—it roughly translates as "Fucking Americans," which is an interesting choice for an event hosted by the local chapter of the Democrats Abroad. Maybe two hundred people were positioned around the room on little islands of coleslaw and beer, mostly staring at phones and picking at their food. Each table had a little blue sign to help you find your electoral homies. The Utah table had a few guys working on brisket, New Jersey featured a boisterous group of well-lubricated souls, while two fellows with combovers were holding down the Texas fort. Because my wife grew up in Wichita, we moseyed toward Kansas with a Hummer-sized slice of cheesecake half-dipped in fudge. The moment we sat down, a young fellow in a red-white-and-blue hat hopped onstage and started playing a trombone for unknown reasons. Next, a low-charisma emcee shared some CNN coverage on a big screen. It was bad news, really bad, especially for early in the evening. As if to distract us from the distinct possibility that our democracy was going into the intensive care unit, the emcee launched into a civics trivia game. What state has twenty-eight electors? When was the Constitution written? Name one of the two longest rivers in the United States? *Uh . . . who cares when the country is imploding?* Bad news. Bad food. Bad noise. The sound system was so deafening that we asked them to turn it down, but they said they couldn't during the trivia: "It has to be loud." Meanwhile, awful news kept appearing on the big screen.

A few minutes later we gave up. We left, feeling alienated and lost as we wandered into the traffic outside. Another emblematic failure—we had been hungry for some kind of expat solidarity and hopeful mingling, but instead we got a little taste of what sucks back home. Disconnection. Disappointment. Corporate simulations. With its wood picnic benches, oversized U.S. flags, and drippy brisket slopped on butcher paper, the venue offered the same generic, focus grouped Americana that you find wherever a multi-brand restaurant investment group manufactures a "gen-yine" downhome experience to tickle customers right in the old cracker barrel. This was where the loyal opposition had convened for its historic defeat at the hands of Trump, Vance, and Musk.

Welcome to the oligarchy of despair.

What a night. Trump singled out the most vulnerable groups (trans, migrant, poor) for anti-woke ridicule and abuse, and his supporters cheered like sadists at a cage match. Just barely outnumbering the Democratic opposition, seventy-seven million Republican voters returned a rage-fueled felon to the White House along with the prospect of a cabinet that would soon contain every huckster and bozo this side of Carrot Top. Powered by Elon Musk's deep reserves of wealth and bile, not to mention the self-serving cowardice of Jeff Bezos and Mark Zuckerberg, Trump won with a message that pondered what Lincoln called "the better angels of our nature" but then took an explosive rage dump—much in the style of January 6 rioter Francis Connor, who texted his friends, "I was in the Capitol . . . and I pooped in Pelosis *[sic]* desk."[1] He added, "Come lock me up there's nothing to live for if Trump isn't in office." While the old Republican

Party of Ronald Reagan had celebrated the idea of "personal responsibility" and the importance of character, Trump and his cronies come from another planet, one where cruelty reigns and immoral conduct goes unpunished, even for consequential sins such as fomenting an insurrection and undermining the peaceful transfer of power. No doubt, in his second term Trump will exonerate and enrich himself with the reckless gusto of the mature Elvis devouring a fried peanut butter banana bacon sandwich, all while returning the nation to the orange-hued mayhem that almost incinerated us the first time. Another bold step toward *Idiocracy* achieved.

It hurts to say it, but we're living in cruel and shallow times. In 2023 the writer Cory Doctorow coined the term *enshittification,* which was lauded as the "word of the year" even before the sewage fest of 2024.[2] Spoofing the concept of the Anthropocene, Doctorow claimed, "We're all living through the *enshittocene,* a great *enshittening,* in which the services that matter to us, that we rely on, are turning into giant piles of shit."[3] While I like the Anglo-Saxon vigor in the word, I would prefer to live in an epoch characterized by something other than its defecatory prowess. It's not exactly the Age of Aquarius.

The news is all so depressing, and I tell my friends *I can't take it.* They tell me, *I can't take it either.* I tell them, *I feel like a disgruntled circus clown in goblin mode.* They don't know what to say to that, but clearly, I wasn't taking the election in stride. Not too long ago, at the start of the pandemic, I had the dark hair and smooth face of a much younger man; now I look like Joe Biden on Ambien. Like most of my friends, I'm internalizing the political news in a way that feels toxic. I have an acid tongue, but there's not much else about me that is particularly tough. I'm terrified of poverty, illness, pain, loneliness, and humiliation (and snakes). I'm a jittery cat in general, but the election has added something darker to the mix, some kind of syrupy historical melancholy about being stuck in the wrong place at the wrong time. It's agonizing to look out the window and think, *It's beginning to look a lot like fascism.*

Everyone I know is scared and disappointed, other than some gloating Republicans and positivity-manifesting New Agers. In the days after the election, the queer Black journalist Lydia Polgreen wrote that the election created a "new, excruciating sense of vulnerability" in many Americans.[4] Another pained response came from the influential writer Rebecca Solnit. After surveying the electoral wreckage, Solnit gave her verdict: "Our mistake was to think we lived in a better country than we do. . . . Our mistake was to think we could row this boat across the acid lake before the acid dissolved it."[5]

Of course, a few well-paid pundits responded to the election with lazy mythologies, often along the lines of "Well, despite everything we saw and heard during this election season, we're still the greatest country in the world." I don't think so. To my mind, that's like saying, "Yes, it's true that Grandpa got my sister pregnant in the porta-potty at the church softball game while he was on parole for that drug smuggling thing, but we're still the greatest family in the world." It's a blinkered form of batty.

Instead of hiding behind soothing illusions, we need to face the darkness of Bummerland and acknowledge that an authoritarian cancer grew out of a thousand preexisting conditions that went untreated for decades. In this sense what's happening is shocking but not surprising. The new American oligarchy of Trump, Musk, Bezos, Zuckerberg, and Murdoch represents a grotesque intensification of a very old problem: immoral elites running an immoral system with a "friends and family" discount. What's new, at least in the American context, is the lack of restraint. What institution or cultural norm will keep them from punishing workers, migrants, women, or anyone else who stands outside their circle of wealth? Unlike previous generations of conservatives, Trump and his admirers have shown an astonishing disregard for precedent. What will prevent ecocide, labor abuses, the suppression of free speech, religious bigotry, and a thousand other sins of power? What will prevent the spread of "brain rot" authoritarianism? (*Brain rot* is another depressing "word of the year," in this case Oxford's from 2024, because it describes the mental and cultural dementia that results from extreme social media consumption.)

This is a pessimistic book but not a tale of resignation or surrender. As always, people of goodwill will need to band together and fight to make a better world rather than accommodating themselves to the rancorous lot they've inherited. I'm not keen on giving advice in a culture that is not keen on listening, but if I have to put a Hoka on the soapbox, I would say: *Witnessing is essential. Confrontation is inevitable. Irreverence is crucial. Cohere with your brothers and sisters. Make political art. Make noise. Make jokes. Make education free. Love thy neighbor. Respect facts. Honor truth. Heal up. Turn off the digital spigot. Disconnect from disinformation. De-commercialize health care. Support independent media. Reign in the oligarchs. Crush white supremacy. Debunk the zealots. Demilitarize the police. House the unhoused. Pivot from despair to action. Avoid violence but otherwise forget the high road. Put your queer shoulder to the wheel, as the beat poet Allen Ginsburg once said. Defy the oligarchs. Do something even if you can't do everything. Blast Fugazi and Pussy Riot and Public Enemy and* M.I.A. *and the eternal genius of A Tribe Called Quest. Know your rights and fight like hell. Don't go quietly into the dark authoritarian night. Political depressives of the world unite—you have nothing to lose but your meds!* I would say all that inspirational jazz with sincerity and passion, even if it feels maudlin and obvious and vaguely cringe in a scarred, cynical age in which a few billionaires decide what it means to be an American and even what information we can access—especially galling in the case of foreign-born plutocrats like Elon Musk and Rupert Murdoch, whose media outlets are corroding the American soul with a toxic blend of fearmongering, anti-factual nonsense, and cruelty.

Sigh. There's no easy way to wrap up a book about our weird national descent into a neo-gilded age that serves no one outside the 1 percent. Ideally, I would box up some nifty wisdom nuggets for the reader to take home from what might seem like a pessimist's banquet, but it's harder than it looks. Trying to offer quick and easy lessons can veer into boring sloganeering (More activism!) or useless nihilism (We're screwed!). But the list of ways to proceed, like the rest of the book, might be a starting point toward reimagining this complicated thing we call America. We can't let our cultural dreams and our political expectations be forever narrowed and "deflated," to borrow a term that the English writer Mark Fisher used near the end of his life in

2017 ("The slow cancellation of the future has been accompanied by a deflation of expectations").[6] Perhaps America is starting to feel like Germany in the 1930s but with Instagram and Botox and ChatGPT and Hawk Tuah, but we can demand a different outcome from our national story, one that doesn't ravage the world in kleptocracy's dark carnival. To do so, we need to inflate our expectations and expand our sense of the possible. We need to say, *This is not working—and we demand better*. And yes, we need hope, especially when optimism is untenable.

If you're anything like me, you just want to be a part of something you can believe in. If you're anything like me, you just want out of the cultural dysfunction and political decadence that I've sketched in the previous chapters. What we need, quite desperately, is a gentler country with a gentler way of life, one devoted to humility, well-being, creativity, equity, sustainability, and solidarity, rather than angry ideologies of exclusion, accumulation, and domination. I know I'm not alone in my dismay about where we've ended up. "I don't like this ride, and I want to get off," someone complained on Reddit after the election, and I suspect that's the closest thing we have to a universal feeling among the kind and gentle people trying to make their way through the queasy, scary American 2020s.

ACKNOWLEDGMENTS

I needed to write this book, but it wasn't easy. My first thank-you goes to my editor Matt Bokovoy, who responded to an early version of the manuscript with fifteen single-spaced pages of structural suggestions and historical insights. A passionate historian as well as a buzzsaw punk guitarist, Matt has both the academic knowledge and editorial heart to dig deep into a manuscript. Working with him has been a great experience, and this book would not exist without his guidance. In addition to providing a humane, literate kind of support that went above and beyond the editorial norm, Matt also lined up an outstanding manuscript reviewer in Russell Cobb, a sharp writer whose suggestions were very helpful.

I'm equally grateful to my close friends and family, starting with my wife, Monti, who lived through everything in this book and never lost her nerve or heart. She's tough, creative, and amazing, and not just because she shared these tragic-gonzo adventures, stayed in the room with me during four MRIs, and kept me together during severe bouts of chronic pain and a nervous system that pretty much gave out in the middle of the Biden years. She's the funniest, kindest, coolest person I know, and I love everything about her. Likewise, my soulful musician daughter, Miranda, and the country she will inherit, was always on my mind as I was writing. And so was my younger brother, Erik, who texts with me multiple times a day, sharing thoughtful missives about indie music, art cinema, and political frustration. I dedicate this book to him, a supremely kind soul who tracks the implosions of our time from our parents' house in rural East Texas. As a good-hearted progressive and a former social worker stationed deep behind the pine curtain, listening to Bauhaus and Björk and Rachel Maddow like a POW in the culture wars, he deserves some special recognition for surviving in a tricky state with something like Zen fortitude. He was an advocate for this project at every step, and I'm lucky to have his brotherly support for more than a half-century and counting, even if typing that sentence makes me feel older than Yoda.

As for friends and colleagues both on and off campus, I've been lucky to have many conversations with Steve Hoelscher, Jason Borge, Joe Thompson, David Delgado Shorter, Karen Engle, Karl Offen, Ralph Beliveau, Yoke-Sum Wong, Erika Bsumek, Robert Devens, Jonathan Silverman, Steve Marshall, Carrie Andersen, Stephanie Kaufman, and my longtime fellow traveler in creative strangeness, Christian Pitt. Getting to know her husband, the photographer Geoff Winningham, during the final stages of this project was an inspiration—and Geoff's reading of the manuscript was a gift when I was at a low moment. The poet Kyle Schlesinger also offered encouragement along the way as well as a chance to stay with his two black labs on his Vermont farm when I was burned-out from Texas heat and politics in summer 2024. My friend and colleague Chad Seales offered some crucial, well-timed advice as well. Two professional editors, Kat Catmull and Larry O'Connor, offered superb advice on the macro and micro levels of the text, as did the sociologist Lindsey Freeman, one of the most gifted writers in academia. A few years back, Lindsey offered a wonderful intervention into the life of this project with a careful reading of a much in-flux manuscript. A cool Arizona skateboarder turned photography professor, Bucky Miller, was another plucky reader. Likewise, my Berlin buddy Florian Grundmüller gave the manuscript a last-minute reading and even suggested a joke that I happily accepted (an Austin subdivision named "Rhinoplasty Grove" is his Bavarian wit in action). Finally, Epoch Coffeehouse on North Loop in Austin was the punk-infused site for much of the writing—what a great blast from the *Slacker* past it is.

I must also thank my students in the Department of American Studies at the University of Texas at Austin. At a time when I could barely sit in a chair without electric nerve pain, I squirmed for three hours to discuss the manuscript with a wonderful group of graduate students in fall 2023. Colleen Small and Alec Ainsworth were especially generous with their feedback.

In the past decade I've been in a small writing group with Katie Stewart, Lauren Berlant, Lindsey Freeman, Ann Cvetkovich, Marina Peterson, and Craig Campbell, all amazingly creative scholars who color outside the lines of expectation. Some of these pieces grew out of our monthly meetings. The anthropologist Katie Stewart has always been a model for finding a path of deep originality within academia, and I could say the same thing about Craig Campbell. In the fifteen years since we met at a sleepy faculty orientation, Craig has offered extraordinary kindness, low-key weirdness, gentle radicalism, and creative support in ways that will always make him my favorite Canadian hippie and a superb friend. Ann was an amazing organizing force in every sense of the word, while Marina offered wonderfully cerebral feedback. Finally, I should say something about Lauren. In the pandemic days in which this project began, I took special inspiration from Lauren's faith in what she called the "world-making power of writing" even in the midst of profound suffering: that she brought her blazing intelligence into our conversations despite chemo and ten-hour surgeries and titanium spinal implants and shooting nerve pain was both staggering and humbling to behold. I knew her the least of a Zoom gang we called "the pandemic silver linings writing group," but her oracular commentary and encouraging words had a big impact on me.

In the unsettled present moment in Texas, you're poking a rabid bear if you scrawl anything other than celebratory odes to the state (one small example: the lieutenant governor blocked an event with the authors of *Forget the Alamo: The Rise and Fall of an American Myth* because it challenged the third grade version of the state's origin story). Although I tried to bring the funny along with the critique, I know some people will get a bee in their little red, white, and blue bonnet. If you feel hyper-defensive about Lone Star living because you're wedded to the idea that it's the greatest thing since John Wayne sashayed through the Alamo in the name of hot wings Jesus, well, I'm sure you stopped reading a long time ago—and I mean books in general, not just this one. The undeniable truth is that Texas is a crazy ugly beautiful place with ridiculous extremes of wealth and suffering. It certainly has some of the most colorful, creative, and hilarious people you'll ever meet—and these folks, including my extended family, deserve better than the stagnant, poisoned water that has flooded the state along with the rest of Bummerland.

Bringing these pieces into the world was a mysterious and sometimes maddening task akin to birthing some kind of psychogeographical baby without anesthetic. Even though I've been writing books and making documentary films for a quarter-century, I often felt like *Bummerland* was bleeding me dry. Not only was I writing through the heaviness of everything I've described in the previous chapters, but I was also attempting something I hadn't tried before: to distill three decades of academic experience into a collection of personal essays. I didn't want to write a book that only scholars would read or craft some heavily footnoted articles that would be marooned behind a paywall. Instead, I wanted to write in a way that might have more kick than a standard-issue "thought product" in the neoliberal knowledge economy and could connect with anyone willing to laugh their way through the darkness.

Speaking of which, I should thank the readers whose attention span has endured to this point. I know you could just as easily be scrolling dank meme subreddits, playing Candy Crush, sleeping one off in a damp alley beyond a bowling alley—or even engaging in some rare and noble pursuit (air hockey?). I'm glad you're here. If I'm lucky, maybe *Bummerland* will endure a little longer than the average book, somehow finding an audience of creative malcontents and jazzy free-thinkers until 2032, when newly sworn-in President-for-Life Ivanka Trump bans any book, photo, or Tweet that isn't about her family or her white "Pomsky" (a Pomeranian and Husky hybrid). By then, I'll either be scrubbing floors in a patriotic reeducation camp in Alabama or slurping horchatas in blissful Mexican exile.

NOTES

Introduction

1. Christina Cauterucci, "Americans Just Voted to Burn It All to the Ground," *Slate*, November 6, 2024, https://slate.com/news-and-politics/2024/11/trump-wins-2024-election-president-harris-loss.html.
2. Aimee Picchi, "Retirement Savings: How Much Americans Need," *CBS News*, April 18, 2024, https://www.cbsnews.com/news/retirement-savings-how-much-americans-need-1-46-million.
3. Frank Jacobs, "These Maps Provide Graphic Evidence of How Parking Lots 'Eat' U.S. Cities," *Big Think*, March 26, 2023, https://bigthink.com/strange-maps/parking-lots-eat-american-cities.
4. "Why America Is Going to Look More like Texas," *The Economist*, March 16, 2023, https://www.economist.com/leaders/2023/03/16/why-america-is-going-to-look-more-like-texas.
5. Ella Lee, "'Trump Train' Drivers Who Tried to Run Biden Bus Off Road Sued under KKK Act," *USA Today*, June 25, 2021, https://www.usatoday.com/story/news/politics/2021/06/25/trump-train-drivers-almost-ran-biden-bus-off-road-sued/5348859001.
6. In autumn 2023 a CNN headline claimed that "Americans Have Never Been Wealthier," a misleading way of talking about a country with wealth increasingly concentrated at the top. Matt Egan, CNN, September 11, 2023, https://www.cnn.com/2023/09/11/economy/household-wealth-economy-stocks/index.html.
7. Russell Cobb, *The Great Oklahoma Swindle: Race, Religion, and Lies in America's Weirdest State* (University of Nebraska Press, 2020). This book is one of the most insightful commentaries on the Sooner State since Angie Debo's *And Still the Waters Run: The Betrayal of the Five Civilized Tribes* (Princeton University Press, 1940).

1. The Technopolis of Despair

1. Jay Peters, "Apple Is Now the World's Most Valuable Publicly Traded Company," *The Verge*, July 31, 2020, https://www.theverge.com/2020/7/31/21350154/apple-worlds-most-valuable-company-saudi-aramco.
2. Heather Long, Andrew Van Dam, Alyssa Fowers, and Leslie Shapiro, "The COVID-19 Recession Is the Most Unequal in Modern U.S. History," *Washington Post*, September 30, 2020, https://www.washingtonpost.com/graphics/2020/business/coronavirus-recession-equality; Dominic Rushe, "Coronavirus Has Widened America's Vast Racial Wealth Gap, Study Finds," *The Guardian*, June 19, 2020, https://www.theguardian.com/us-news/2020/jun/19/coronavirus-pandemic-billioinaires-racial-wealth-gap; Alicia Adamczyk, "Inequality Has Been Building for Decades in the U.S., but Experts Say the Pandemic 'Ripped It Open,'" CNBC, October 23, 2020, https://www.cnbc.com/2020/10/23/coronavirus-is-exacerbating-economic-inequality-in-the-us.html.
3. The estimate of forty-five hundred comes from ECHO (Ending Community Homelessness Coalition) in 2023 and can be found in Grace Reader, "Why an Article You May Have Seen on Austin Homelessness Is 'Not Based in Fact,'" KXAN, June 29, 2023, https://www.kxan.com/news/local/austin/why-an-article-you-may-have-seen-on-austin-homelessness-is-not-based-in-fact.
4. A KUT public radio post about the Texas Housers study also showed 23 percent of renters spending a whopping 50 percent of their monthly income on rent in Austin. Audrey McClinchy, "Nearly Half of Austin-Area Renters Live in Housing They Can't Afford, Study Finds," *KUT News*, January 26, 2024, https://www.kut.org/austin/2024-01-26/nearly-half-of-austin-area-renters-live-in-housing-they-cant-afford-study-finds.
5. Mike Davis and Daniel Bertrand Monk, eds., *Evil Paradises: Dreamworlds of Neoliberalism* (New Press, 2007).
6. Vance Cariaga, "Everything's Bigger In Texas—Including Taxes, Which Are Outpacing California," *Yahoo News*, September 17, 2022, https://www.yahoo.com/video/everything-bigger-texas-including-taxes-162135063.html; Abe Asher, "Texas Roasted for Paying More in Taxes than California: 'The Joke Is on You,'" *The Independent*, September 6, 2022, https://www.independent.co.uk/news/world/americas/texas-california-higher-taxes-policy-b2161227.html.
7. Tahera Rahman and Billy Gates, "Report: Houses in Austin Selling for More Over Asking Price than Any Major U.S. City," KXAN, March 26, 2021, https://www.kxan.com/news/local/austin/report-houses-in-austin-selling-for-more-over-asking-price-than-any-major-u-s-city.
8. Anna Weiner, *Uncanny Valley* (MCD, 2020), 51.

9. See Andrew Busch's fine book, *City in a Garden: Environmental Transformations and Racial Justice in Twentieth-Century Austin, Texas* (University of North Carolina Press, 2017).
10. Emily Badger, "Study: Austin Is Most Economically Segregated Metro Area," *Texas Tribune*, February 23, 2015, https://www.texastribune.org/2015/02/23/austin-most-economically-segregated-metro-area.
11. In January 2024 the Austin City Council perversely approved a two million–dollar contract for the uber–corporate consulting firm McKinsey and Company to study homelessness in the city. The contract was canceled a month later. Chad Swiatecki, "City Nixes $2M McKinsey Homelessness Study, Signaling Poor Cooperation among Partners," *Austin Monitor*, February 23, 2024, https://www.austinmonitor.com/stories/2024/02/city-nixes-2m-mckinsey-homelessness-study-signaling-poor-cooperation-among-partners.
12. Although the number of unhoused Austinites continues to rise, some slow improvements have been made in terms of housing systems. See Antoinette Odom, "Homelessness in Austin Steadily Rising, but Housing System Improves," *Spectrum Local News*, May 26, 2023, https://spectrumlocalnews.com/tx/austin/news/2023/05/26/homelessness-in-austin-steadily-rises-but-housing-system-improves.
13. Roshan Abraham, "A Palantir Co-Founder Is Pushing Laws to Criminalize Homeless Encampments Nationwide," *Vice*, March 15, 2023, https://www.vice.com/en/article/qjvdmq/a-palantir-co-founder-is-pushing-laws-to-criminalize-homeless-encampments-nationwide. See also Eliza Relman, "A Think Tank Created by a Palantir Co-Founder Is behind a Slew of Bills Criminalizing Homeless Encampments," *Business Insider*, March 15, 2023, https://www.businessinsider.com/palantir-cofounder-joe-lonsdale-cicero-institute-criminalizing-homeless-encampments-2023-3.
14. The official House Research Organization's bill analysis is the source of the quotations. Capriglione et al., "HOUSE RESEARCH ORGANIZATION Bill Analysis, (2nd reading), HB 1925," Texas House Research Organization, May 5, 20221, https://hro.house.texas.gov/pdf/ba87r/hb1925.pdf.
15. Joe Robison, "Outside Austin City Limits: The moveBuddha 2022–2023 Austin Migration Report," moveBuddha, September 20, 2023, https://www.movebuddha.com/blog/moving-to-austin-migration-report.
16. Christine Sanchez, "Austin Bumped Down to No. 40 Spot on U.S. News & World Report's Best Cities to Live 2023–4 Ranking," *Spectrum News 1*, May 18, 2023, https://spectrumlocalnews.com/tx/south-texas-el-paso/news/2023/05/18/austin-drops-to-no--40-on-best-cities-to-live-from-u-s--news---world-report-2023-2024-ranking.

17. After local backlash, SXSW quietly discontinued its partnerships in 2025. Andrew Weber, "SXSW Says It Won't Partner with the U.S. Army—Or Weapons Manufacturers—in 2025," *KUT News*, June 26, 2024, https://www.kut.org/austin/2024-06-26/sxsw-wont-partner-with-u-s-army-weapons-manufacturers-2025.
18. "Bum Steer of the Year Award: Austin," *Texas Monthly*, January 2023, https://www.texasmonthly.com/news-politics/2023-bum-steer-of-year-austin.

2. Into the Wasteland

1. For an excellent short history of California City, see Diana Budds, "California City: A Utopian Dream Turned Ghost Town," *Curbed*, May 31, 2019, https://archive.curbed.com/2019/5/31/18639098/california-city-failed-utopia-ghost-town. For more on California's history as a location for utopian dreams, in particular Joan Didion's influential "understanding of the fictional(ized) West-as-myth in the canonized fashion of promise, redemption and rebirth, of being the 'last good place,' the 'golden land' and the 'fresh start for the Americans,'" see Eva-Sabine Zehelein, "'A Good Deal about California Does Not, on Its Own Preferred Terms, Add Up': Joan Didion between Dawning Apocalypse and Retrogressive Utopia," *European Journal of American Studies* 6, no. 3 (2011). See also Ronnie D. Lipschutz, "Eco-Utopia or Eco-Catastrophe? Imagining California as an Ecological Utopia," *Elementa* 6, no. 1 (2018). For a more general treatment of California in the western imagination, see David J. Weber, *The Spanish Frontier in North America: The Brief Edition* (Yale University Press, 2009), https://doi-org.ezproxy.lib.utexas.edu/10.12987/9780300156218.
2. A version of this question has been attributed to various theorists, including Fredric Jameson, Mark Fisher, and Slavoj Žižek. It's usually rendered as "It's easier to imagine the end of the world than the end of capitalism."
3. Andrew Russell and Lee Vinsel, "Hail the Maintainers," *Aeon*, April 7, 2016, https://aeon.co/essays/innovation-is-overvalued-maintenance-often-matters-more; *broken world thinking* appears in Majd Al-Shihabi, "Broken World Thinking and Maintaining the Commons," *Society and Space*, December 12, 2022, https://www.societyandspace.org/articles/broken-world-thinking-and-maintaining-the-commons.
4. For more on the socialist colony's fate in Southern California, see Dolores Hayden, *Seven American Utopias: The Architecture of Communitarian Socialism, 1790–1975* (MIT Press, 1976). The quotation from the colony's founder appears in Paul Greenstein, Nigey Lennon, and Lionel Rolfe, *Bread & Hyacinths: The Rise and Fall of Utopian Los Angeles* (California Classic Books, 1992).
5. The Huxley quotation appears in Hadley Meares's excellent article about the colony, "Llano del Rio: The Ruins of LA's Socialist Colony," *Curbed*, May 1,

2017, https://la.curbed.com/2017/5/1/15465616/utopia-socialist-los-angeles-llano-del-rio.

4. Plastic Passion

1. Dainis Graveris, "Sex with Robot Stats," *Sexual Alpha*, December 2020, https://sexualalpha.com/sex-with-robot-stats; "Sex Robot Industry," Bedbible Research Center, May 1, 2024, https://bedbible.com/sex-robot-industry-market-size-technology-ai-user-sentiment-statistics.
2. All reviews appeared in August 2023 on the Real Love Sex Dolls website, https://reallovesexdolls.com.
3. Hoang Nguyen, "In 2020, Both Men and Women Are More Likely to Consider Having Sex with a Robot," YouGov, March 19, 2020, https://today.yougov.com/topics/politics/articles-reports/2020/03/19/2020-both-men-and-women-are-more-likely-consider-h.

5. Healing Inc.

1. Rebekah Levine Coley and Christopher F. Baum, "Trends in Mental Health Symptoms, Service Use, and Unmet Need for Services Among U.S. Adults through the First 9 Months of the COVID-19 Pandemic," *Translational Behavioral Medicine* 11, no. 10 (October 2021): 1947–56.

8. Jewel Thieves

1. Ciarra Hastings Blow, "How Life during a Pandemic May Have Contributed to Homicide in Houston, Texas," *Journal of Family Strengths* 21, no. 2, article 5 (2022).
2. Data on the pandemic-fueled rise in violent crime in Texas comes from Jack Highberger, "National Report Finds Startling Rise in Violent Crime during Pandemic," *NBCDFW*, February 3, 2021, https://www.nbcdfw.com/news/coronavirus/national-report-finds-startling-rise-in-violent-crime-during-pandemic/2541238. The sharp increase in unemployment during the pandemic was another important factor: "During the pandemic, the percentage of the adult population who were unemployed was 8.1 percentage points higher than expected, on average. Increases in unemployment were associated with increases in firearm violence and homicide." J. P. Schleimer et al., "Unemployment and Crime in U.S. Cities during the Coronavirus Pandemic," *Journal of Urban Health* 99 (2022): 82–91.

10. The Aging Process

1. Michael Sainato, "'At 75, I Still Have to Work': Millions of Americans Can't Afford to Retire," *The Guardian*, December 13, 2021, https://www

.theguardian.com/money/2021/dec/13/americans-retire-work-social-security.

11. Subdivision

1. The downtown is mostly valued as an upscale entertainment zone in many Sunbelt cities. For an insightful Southern California parallel, see Matt Bokovoy's essay "Ghosts of the San Diego Rialta," January 8, 2017, https://mattbokovoy.com/2017/01/08/ghosts-of-the-san-diego-rialto, in which he explains that "downtown San Diego today has become the faux historical stage set for the city's nouveau-riche and young members of Idiot Nation."
2. Eric Tang and Bisola Falola, "THOSE WHO STAYED: The Impact of Gentrification on Longstanding Residents of East Austin," Institute for Urban Policy Research and Analysis, University of Texas at Austin, March 2018, https://communitynotcommodity.com/wp-content/uploads/THOSE-WHO-STAYED-The-Impact-of-Gentrifcation-on-Longstanding-Residents-of-East-Austin.pdf.
3. Marco d'Eramo, "Bunkering in Paradise (Or, Do Oldsters Dream of Electric Golf Carts?)," in *Evil Paradises: Dreamworlds of Neoliberalism*, edited by Mike Davis and Daniel Bertand Monk (New Press, 2007), 180.
4. The concept of spatial justice comes from an interview with Edward Soja by Frédéric Dufaux, Philippe Gervais-Lambony, Chloe Buiré, and Henri Desbois, "Spatial Justice and the Right to the City: an Interview with Edward Soja," *Justice Spatiale* (March 2011), https://www.researchgate.net/publication/271135045_Spatial_Justice_and_the_Right_to_the_City. See also A. T. Sevincer, S. Kitayama, and M. E. Varnum, "Cosmopolitan Cities: The Frontier in the Twenty-First Century?" *Frontiers in Psychology* 6 (2015), www.frontiersin.org/journals/psychology/articles/10.3389/fpsyg.2015.01459.

12. Selma

1. Jonathon Keats, "For the Love of Literature," *Salon*, August 25, 2001, https://www.salon.com/2001/08/25/fitzgerald_9.
2. Chris Arnade, "Still a City of Slaves: Selma in the Words of Those Who Live There," *The Guardian*, February 4, 2016, https://www.theguardian.com/us-news/2016/feb/04/still-a-city-of-slaves-selma-in-the-words-who-those-who-live-there.

13. Pigeons

1. Animal Welfare Institute, "Texas Dairy Fire Kills 18,000 Cattle," *AWI Quarterly*, August 2023, https://awionline.org/awi-quarterly/summer-2023/texas-dairy-fire-kills-18000-cattle.

16. Behind the Pine Curtain

1. Mimi Swartz, "Vidor in Black and White," *Texas Monthly*, December 1993, https://www.texasmonthly.com/being-texan/vidor-in-black-and-white.
2. Associated Press, "Ex–Blue Bell Creameries CEO Charged in Deadly Listeria Case," *U.S. News & World Report*, October 21, 2020, https://www.usnews.com/news/us/articles/2020-10-21/ex-blue-bell-creameries-ceo-charged-in-deadly-listeria-case.
3. The Mexican general is quoted in Max Flomen's article "The Long War for Texas: Maroons, Renegades, Warriors, and Alternative Emancipations in the Southwest Borderlands, 1835–1845," *Journal of Civil War Era* 11, no. 1 (2021).
4. Southern Poverty Law Center, "Hate Map," accessed January 18, 2025, https://www.splcenter.org/hate-map.
5. See Bruce Glasrud's "Anti-Black Violence in 20th Century East Texas," *East Texas Historical Journal* 52, no.1 (March 2014). On the terrorizing of immigrant fishermen, see Dave Davies, "How White Nationalists in Texas Terrorized Refugees after the Vietnam War," NPR, August 1, 2022, https://www.npr.org/2022/08/01/1114451029/how-white-nationalists-in-texas-terrorized-refugees-after-the-vietnam-war. Finally, for some quantification of the horror, journalist Dalyah Jones wrote in the *Texas Observer* that "from 1865 to 1866, authorities issued 500 indictments statewide for 'the murder of Blacks by Anglos,' but no convictions ever resulted. In the decades that followed, the vast majority of reported lynchings of Black people in the state occurred in East Texas." "What the Black Lives Matter Protests Mean for East Texas," *Texas Observer*, June 19, 2020, https://www.texasobserver.org/east-texas-black-lives-matter.
6. Darwin Payne, "When Dallas Was the Most Racist City in America," *D Magazine*, June 2017, https://www.dmagazine.com/publications/d-magazine/2017/june/when-dallas-was-the-most-racist-city-in-america.
7. Teresa Mioli and Corynn Wilson, "Analysis Shows East Texas Has Some of the Largest Racial Disparities," *Dallas Morning News*, May 2015, http://res.dallasnews.com/graphics/2015_05/texas-racial-divide/east-texas.html.
8. "Houston: Ugliest City in the First World," *Houstonia*, November 6, 2013, https://www.houstoniamag.com/travel-and-outdoors/2013/11/houston-ugliest-city-in-the-first-world-november-2013.
9. "The Most and Least Bike-Friendly Cities," Shopify, August 2022, https://cdn.shopify.com/s/files/1/0694/7048/6848/files/most-bike-friendly-cities-4.png?v=1683249061.
10. "National Walkability Index," ArcGIS, U.S. Environmental Protection Agency, August 2023, https://epa.maps.arcgis.com/home/webmap/viewer.html.
11. Gabby Hart, "Houston Ranked Most Stressed-Out City in U.S.: ,Locals and Experts Weigh In," FOX 26 Houston, March 1, 2023, https://www

.fox26houston.com/news/houston-ranked-most-stressed-out-city-in-u-s-locals-experts-weigh-in.

12. Sukhada Tatke, "To Love Houston Is to Accept That Making Sense of It Is Futile," *Texas Monthly*, June 30, 2020, https://www.texasmonthly.com/being-texan/falling-in-love-with-houston.
13. "When People Say 'Houston Is Ugly,' What Exactly Is Ugly about the City?" Quora, August 2023, https://www.quora.com/When-people-say-Houston-is-ugly-what-exactly-is-ugly-about-the-city.
14. Fernando Ramirez, "The Weirdest Images to Come from Houston's Lack of Zoning Laws," Chron, January 8, 2020, https://www.chron.com/news/houston-texas/houston/article/Weirdest-images-from-Houston-s-lack-of-zoning-laws-9171688.php.
15. "More than Half of Houston Residents Say City Is Headed in the Wrong Direction," University of Houston Newsroom, August 1, 2023, https://uh.edu/news-events/stories/2023/august-2023/08022023-hobby-houston-issues-survey.php.
16. Maddy McCarty, "Climate Change, Flood Risk Could Pierce the Houston Housing Market Bubble," Bisnow, August 1, 2023, https://www.bisnow.com/houston/news/home/climate-change-flood-risk-could-create-a-houston-housing-market-bubble-120036.
17. Julian Gill, "Houston Distance Comparison," Chron, June 26, 2019, https://www.chron.com/news/houston-texas/houston/slideshow/Houston-distance-comparison-193926.php.

18. Big-Box Blues

1. Nathaniel Meyersohn, "Workers at TJ Maxx and Marshalls Are Wearing Police-Like Body Cameras," *CNN*, June 5, 2024, https://www.cnn.com/2024/06/05/business/tj-maxx-body-cameras-shoplifting/index.html.
2. Judge is a brilliant satirist, but Costco now seems like a surprising target for his ire. By the 2020s, it was clear that Walmart or Target had a wider reactionary streak than Costco, which managed to resist some of Trump's anti-diversity efforts. Black customers boycotted Target in 2025, not Costco.
3. Daniel Miller, *Consumption and Its Consequences* (Polity Press, 2012), 184.
4. Jus L'amore, "10 Reasons I Love Target!" *Lifehack*, January 18, 2018, https://vocal.media/lifehack/10-reasons-i-love-target.
5. "Where Are Target Clothes Made?" *Ethicaloo*, August 2020, https://www.ethicaloo.com/fashion-brands/where-are-target-clothes-made. Target imports a greater percentage of its clothing from China than Walmart. "What Percentage of Target Products Are Made in China?" *Mywebstats*, July 8, 2022, https://mywebstats.org/what-percentage-of-target-products-are-made-in-china.

6. Kim Humphery, *Excess: Anti-Consumerism in the* West (Polity Press, 2010), 122. I recommend Humphery's chapter 3, "Anti-Consumerism in Action," for an overview of consumption's critics. The Target quote appears in Lauren McGrath, "The Creepy Science behind Why You Love Target So Much," *Philadelphia*, June 23, 2016, https://www.phillymag.com/shoppist/2016/06/23/why-you-love-target.

19. Under the Violet Crown

1. Hadley Freeman, "Anne Tyler: 'Up Close You'll Always See Things to Be Optimistic About,'" *The Guardian*, April 11, 2020, https://www.theguardian.com/books/2020/apr/11/anne-tyler-up-close-youll-always-see-things-to-be-optimistic-about.

21. The F-Word

1. Richard C. Fording and Sanford F. Schram, "The Mainstreaming of Racism in American Politics," *Hard White: The Mainstreaming of Racism in American Politics* (Oxford Academic, online ed., August 20, 2020).

22. Naked Lunch 2020

1. Will Unwin, "Reggie Cannon: 'My Safety in America Was Compromised for Pointing Out Injustice,'" *The Guardian*, March 3, 20201, https://www.theguardian.com/football/2021/mar/03/reggie-cannon-soccer-usmnt-interview-boavista-fc-dallas.
2. Perry Miller, "Declension in a Bible Commonwealth," *Proceedings of the American Antiquarian Society* 51, no. 1, January 1, 1942, 67.
3. Jennifer Senior, "In Praise of Pessimism," *New York Times*, April 26, 2020, https://www.nytimes.com/2020/04/26/opinion/coronavirus-anxiety-pessimism.html.
4. "The Power of Pessimism: Science Reveals the Hidden Virtues in Negative Thinking," *Open Culture*, November 12, 2015, https://www.openculture.com/2015/11/the-power-of-pessimism-science-reveals-the-hidden-virtues-in-negative-thinking.html.
5. "Pessimism," *Psychology Today*, accessed January 18, 2025, https://www.psychologytoday.com/us/basics/pessimism.
6. Patrick Svitek, "Texas Puts Final Estimate of Winter Storm Death Toll at 246," *Texas Tribune*, January 2, 2022, https://www.texastribune.org/2022/01/02/texas-winter-storm-final-death-toll-246.

23. Obscene Delirium

1. Jean Baudrillard, *America* (Verso, 2020), 23.

2. To justify Trump being "literally" the worst businessman in the United States, I'd point to articles like this one: Walter Shapiro, "The Worst Businessman in America," *New Republic*, May 8, 2019, https://newrepublic.com/article/153855/trump-tax-returns-worst-businessman-america.
3. Jean Baudrillard, "The Ecstasy of Communication," in *The Anti-Aesthetic: Essays on Postmodern Culture*, edited by Hal Foster (Bay Press, 1983), 132.
4. Shoshana Zuboff, *The Age of Surveillance Capitalism: The Fight for a Human Future at the New Frontier of Power* (Profile Books, 2019).

25. Dreams Never End

1. Anu-Katriina Pesonen, Jari Lipsanen, and Risto Halonen et al., "Pandemic Dreams: Network Analysis of Dream Content during the COVID-19 Lockdown," *Frontiers in Psychology* 11 (2020), https://www.frontiersin.org/journals/psychology/articles/10.3389/fpsyg.2020.573961/full.
2. Colleen Walsh, "What Pandemic Dreams May Come," *Harvard Gazette*, May 14, 2020, https://news.harvard.edu/gazette/story/2020/05/harvard-researcher-says-dreams-indicative-of-virus-fears.
3. Charlotte Hartley, "This New Algorithm Can Find the Hidden Patterns in Your Dreams," *Science*, August 25, 2020, https://www.science.org/content/article/new-algorithm-can-find-hidden-patterns-your-dreams.

26. Lowered Expectations

1. Heidi Perez-Moreno, "New Texas Law Allowing People to Carry Handguns without Permits Stirs Mix of Fear, Concern among Law Enforcement," *Texas Tribune*, August 16, 2021, https://www.texastribune.org/2021/08/16/texas-permitless-carry-gun-law.
2. Chris Cillizza, "Donald Trump's Interview with '60 Minutes' Was Eye-Opening. Also, Mike Pence Was There," *Washington Post*, July 18, 2016, https://www.washingtonpost.com/news/the-fix/wp/2016/07/18/donald-trump-is-way-more-humble-than-you-could-possibly-understand.
3. Reinhold Niebuhr, "The Irony of American History," Read Something Interesting, accessed January 18, 2025, https://readsomethinginteresting.com/acx/96.

27. Electric Kool-Aid Acid Reflux

1. Alyssa Fowers, "A Third of Americans Now Show Signs of Clinical Anxiety or Depression, Census Bureau Finds amid Coronavirus Pandemic," *Washington Post*, May 26, 2020, https://www.washingtonpost.com/health/2020/05/26/americans-with-depression-anxiety-pandemic; Sam Levine, "U.S. Sinks to New Low in Rankings of World's Democracies," *The Guardian*, March

24, 2021, https://www.theguardian.com/us-news/2021/mar/24/us-world-democracy-rankings-freedom-house-new-low.

28. Sweatshop Barbie

1. Kate Bullen and John Oates, "Facebook's 'Experiment' Was Socially Irresponsible," *The Guardian*, July 1, 2014, https://www.theguardian.com/technology/2014/jul/01/facebook-socially-irresponsible.
2. Sarah Spellings, "Ivanka Trump Reportedly Had a Deal with Jared That She'd Run for President," The Cut, *New York Magazine*, January 4, 2018, https://www.thecut.com/2018/01/ivanka-trump-reportedly-planned-to-become-president.html.
3. Katherine Tangalakis-Lippert and Erin Snodgrass, "Donald Trump's Political Maelstrom Could Be Close to Sucking Ivanka Back In," *Business Insider*, May 2024, https://www.businessinsider.com/ivanka-trump-eyeing-return-to-politics-donald-trump-friends-say-2024-5.
4. Martha Ross, "Ivanka Trump Joined Family's 'Casual Cruelty' toward Tiffany, Michael Cohen Writes," *Mercury News*, September 9, 2020, https://www.mercurynews.com/2020/09/09/ivanka-trump-joined-familys-casual-cruelty-of-tiffany-michael-cohen-writes.
5. Kathryn Watson, "What Is Project Airbridge?" CBS *News*, March 30, 2020, https://www.cbsnews.com/news/coronavirus-what-is-project-airbridge.
6. See former Trump staffer Stephanie Grisham's article "How Jared and Ivanka Hijacked the White House's Covid Response," *Politico*, October 1, 2021, https://www.politico.com/news/magazine/2021/10/01/jared-ivanka-trump-covid-response-514852.
7. Mary Papenfuss, "Former FDA Chief Calls Out Jared Kushner for Comparing COVID-19 to Common Flu," *Huffington Post*, August 16, 2020, https://www.huffpost.com/entry/jared-kushner-coronavirus-schools-fda-gottlieb_n_5f39c357c5b6959911e61d0b.
8. Greg Olear, "The Rose-Colored Alternate Reality of Ivanka Trump," *Slate*, January 31, 2024, https://slate.com/news-and-politics/2024/01/ivanka-trump-instagram-slunk-back.html.
9. Charlie Lankston, "Ivanka Trump Has Been Living the High Life in Her $24 Million Miami Megamansion since She Left Politics," *Marketwatch*, November 13, 2024, https://www.marketwatch.com/story/ivanka-trump-has-been-living-the-high-life-in-her-24-million-miami-megamansion-since-she-left-politics-fd63871a.
10. Nicholas D. Kristof, "Suicide of Jiang Qing, Mao's Widow, Is Reported," *New York Times*, June 5, 1991, https://www.nytimes.com/1991/06/05/obituaries/suicide-of-jiang-qing-mao-s-widow-is-reported.html.

11. Linnaea Honl-Stuenkel, "Ivanka Trump Violated the Hatch Act Eight Times in Just over 48 Hours," *Citizens for Responsibility and Ethics in Washington*, October 13, 2020, https://www.citizensforethics.org/reports-investigations/crew-investigations/ivanka-trump-violated-the-hatch-act-eight-times-in-just-over-48-hours.
12. Tara Palmeri, "Ivanka, Interrupted," *Puck*, accessed January 18, 2025, https://puck.news/ivanka-trump-reconsiders-a-return-to-west-wing.
13. Ulysses S. Grant, "Remarks at the Ninth Annual Meeting of the Army of the Tennessee in Des Moines, Iowa," American Presidency Project, accessed January 18, 2025, https://www.presidency.ucsb.edu/documents/remarks-the-ninth-annual-meeting-the-army-the-tennessee-des-moines-iowa.
14. Frederick Douglass, "The Hypocrisy of American Slavery, July 4, 1852," *Fordham University Internet Modern History Sourcebook*, accessed January 18, 2025, https://origin-rh.web.fordham.edu/Halsall/mod/douglass-hypo.asp.

29. Stress Test

1. A. G. Gancarski, "Lincoln Project Dumps on Donald Trump Diaper' in New Ad," *Florida Politics*, May 4, 2024, https://floridapolitics.com/archives/672628-trump-diaper.
2. Ben Zimmer, "A New Breakthrough in the History of the 'S——gibbon': The Insult's Originator Steps Forward," *Slate*, February 13, 2017, https://slate.com/culture/2017/02/the-origin-of-the-trump-insult-shitgibbon-revealed.html.
3. Julia Craven, "What the Trump Era Showed White Americans about Whiteness," *Slate*, January 24, 2021, https://slate.com/news-and-politics/2021/01/trump-era-white-americans-whiteness.html.
4. Craven, "What the Trump Era Showed White Americans about Whiteness."
5. Martin Pengelly, "Chaos of Trump's Last Days in Office Reverberates with Fresh 'Plot' Report," *The Guardian*, January 23, 2021, https://www.theguardian.com/us-news/2021/jan/23/trump-florida-white-house-washington-plot-report.

30. Walmart Salvation 2021

1. Niche, "Buda," Niche.com, accessed January 18, 2025, https://www.niche.com/places-to-live/buda-hays-tx.
2. City of Buda, "History of Buda," BudaTx.gov, accessed January 18, 2025, https://www.budatx.gov/213/History-of-Buda.

31. Norway/Uvalde

1. Will Drabold, "Here Are 7 Animals Hunters Kill Using an AR-15," *Time*, July 6, 2016, https://time.com/4390506/gun-control-ar-15-semiautomatic-rifles.

2. U.S. Census Bureau, "Uvalde City, Texas," accessed January 18, 2025, https://data.census.gov/table/DECENNIALPL2020.P2?g=160XX00US4874588&tid=DECENNIALPL2020.P2.
3. Promotional quotations from the company website for Drive Tanks: https://www.drivetanks.com.
4. Zach Despart, "'He Has a Battle Rifle': Police Feared Uvalde Gunman's AR-15," *Texas Tribune*, March 20, 2023, https://www.texastribune.org/2023/03/20/uvalde-shooting-police-ar-15.

32. Vegas Loopy

1. Brett Forrest, "'Unsafe' and 'Impractical,' Mayor Goodman Blasts Vegas Loop, but Votes Yes on Expansion," *News3LV*, July 19, 2023, https://news3lv.com/news/local/unsafe-and-impractical-mayor-goodman-blasts-vegas-loop-but-votes-yes-on-expansion.
2. Kyle Wilcox and Brett Forrest, "City Council Approves Agreement for Vegas Loop Project," *News3LV*, June 15, 2022, https://news3lv.com/news/local/city-council-approves-agreement-for-vegas-loop-project.
3. Mark Fisher, *Capitalist Realism: Is There No Alternative?* (Zero Books, 2009), 17.
4. John Domol, "Heat Islands: Reversing the Irreversible," UNLV *News Center*, August 11, 2023, https://www.unlv.edu/news/article/heat-islands-reversing-irreversible.
5. Andrew J. Hawkins, "Elon Musk's Boring Company Plan for a 69-Station 'Vegas Loop' Is Anything but Nice," *The Verge*, July 4, 2023, https://www.theverge.com/2023/5/4/23711032/elon-musk-boring-company-vegas-loop-expansion-tunnel.

33. Exile

1. George Petras and Stephen J. Beard, "Buoys, Razor Wire Raise Risks for Migrants along Texas Border. Two Bodies Have Been Found," *USA Today*, July 27, 2023, https://www.usatoday.com/story/graphics/2023/07/27/texas-border-rio-grande-buoys-visual/70458101007; Kennedy Sessions, "Texas Ranked No. 1 Worst State to Live and Work In, New Study Says," Chron, July 17, 2023, https://www.chron.com/news/houston-texas/article/texas-worst-state-work-18204395.phprun.
2. Tara Tahra, "America, the Not So Promised Land," *New York Times*, November 15, 2011, https://www.nytimes.com/2015/11/15/opinion/sunday/america-the-not-so-promised-land.html.
3. Anne Tergesen and Veronica Dagher, "Here's What It Looks Like When Americans Retire Overseas," *Wall Street Journal*, May 21, 2023, https://www

.wsj.com/articles/heres-what-retirement-looks-like-for-americans-abroad-e2ee4294.

4. Malcolm Cowley, *Exile's Return: A Literary Odyssey of the 1920s* (Viking Press, 1951).

35. Unobtanium

1. John Gramlich and Alissa Scheller, "What's Happening at the U.S.-Mexico Border in 7 Charts," *Pew Research Center*, November 9, 2021, https://www.pewresearch.org/short-reads/2021/11/09/whats-happening-at-the-u-s-mexico-border-in-7-charts.
2. Carolyn Pedwell, *Revolutionary Routines: The Habits of Social Transformation* (McGill-Queen's University Press, 2021).

Epilogue

1. U.S. Department of Justice, "IN THE UNITED STATES DISTRICT COURT FOR THE DISTRICT OF COLUMBIA: UNITED STATES OF AMERICA: Case No.: 21-CR-410 (RC): FRANCIS CONNOR, Defendant," accessed January 18, 2025, https://www.justice.gov/usao-dc/case-multi-defendant/file/1498626/dl.
2. *American Dialect Society*, "2023 Word of the Year Is 'Enshittification,'" January 5, 2024, https://americandialect.org/2023-word-of-the-year-is-enshittification.
3. Cory Doctorow, "My McLuhan Lecture on Enshittification," *Medium*, January 30, 2024, https://doctorow.medium.com/my-mcluhan-lecture-on-enshittification-ea343342b9bc.
4. Lydia Polgreen, "I Never Panic. I'm Panicking Now," *New York Times*, November 20, 2024, https://www.nytimes.com/2024/11/20/opinion/trump-deportation-immigration.html..
5. Dan Merica, "Trump Said Hitler 'Did Some Good Things' and Wanted Generals Like the Nazis, Former Chief of Staff Kelly Claims," *PBS News Hour*, October 23, 2024, https://www.pbs.org/newshour/politics/trump-said-hitler-did-some-good-things-and-wanted-generals-like-the-nazis-former-chief-of-staff-kelly-claims.
6. Mark Fisher, *Ghosts of My Life: Writings on Depression, Hauntology and Lost Futures* (Zero Books, 2014).